Jacques Lacan

£21.99

150.19

Jacques Lacan
A feminist introduction

Elizabeth Grosz

Routledge
London and New York

Style . . . is the man to whom one is speaking

Jacques Lacan

First published 1990
by Routledge
11 New Fetter Lane, London EC4P 4EE
Simultaneously published in the USA and Canada
by Routledge
a division of Routledge, Chapman and Hall, Inc.
29 West 35th Street, New York, NY 1000 1

Printed in Great Britain by
Richard Clay Ltd, Bungay, Suffolk

British Library Cataloguing in Publication Data
Grosz, Elizabeth
    Jacques Lacan: a feminist introduction.
    1. Psychoanalysis. Lacan – Jacques, 1901–1981
    I. Title
    150.19′5′0924

Library of Congress Cataloging in Publication Data
Grosz, E. A. (Elizabeth A.)
    Jacques Lacan: a feminist introduction/Elizabeth Grosz.
        p.   cm.
    Includes bibliographical references.
    ISBN 0 415 01399 2. – ISBN 0 415 01400 X (pbk.)
    1. Psychoanalysis and feminism. 2. Lacan, Jacques, 1901–1981.
I. Title.
BF175.4.F45G76   1989
150.19′5′092–dc20   89–11005

Contents

Contents

Introduction

The last decades of the nineteenth century witnessed an intellectual revolution whose implications and effects are still being unravelled. The *fin de siècle* upheaval could be summarized by three names – Nietzsche, Marx, and Freud – whose works define the horizon of the contemporary knowledges of human subjectivity. Sharing little but a suspicion that the human subject, considered as a conscious, rational being, could no longer provide the foundation for theoretical speculation, each decentred the individual's pretension to sovereignty, self-knowledge, and self-mastery. Each opposed a prevailing Cartesianism which had infiltrated liberalism, empiricism, idealism, and humanism. Each distrusted the centrality and givenness attributed to consciousness, seeing it as an effect rather than a cause of the will to power (in Nietzsche), class relations (in Marx), or psychical agencies (in Freud).

For Nietzsche, the critique of consciousness takes the form of an inversion: consciousness is the consequence of corporeality or bodily forces, social and survival strategies that have forgotten their own history and processes of formation. Reason, for example, is not so much a quality or attribute of the mind as the result of political or coercive struggles between various competing perspectives, in which one gains a (provisional, temporary, historical) dominance. For Marx, consciousness is the consequence of a structure of class relations that constitute it as a 'false consciousness', a consciousness misled or untrustworthy, an ideological consciousness which inverts and thus misrecognizes given forms of economic and class relations. For Freud, consciousness and its self-certainty may be the end-products of unconscious psychical 'defences' – denial, disavowal, resistance. That is, consciousness is identified with a certain mode of self-deception. The subject cannot consciously know the material, linguistic, economic, or

1

unconscious structures on which it relies and over which it may have little or no effect. Even where an individual functions as an agent of these structures, in no sense can he or she be considered to control them.

These inversions of the Cartesian *cogito* pose a number of questions intolerable to liberal humanism – questions about the genesis and history of the subject which cannot even be raised if the subject or consciousness are taken as given. Until contemporary knowledge comes to terms with these questions – transforming the individual's position or status from producer to product – we remain caught within intellectual systems that justify or rationalize existing political norms instead of facilitating the exploration of other historically subordinated possibilities. If Descartes marks the threshold of the modern concept of subjectivity, then Nietzsche, Marx, and Freud can be seen to initiate a postmodern understanding. This postmodernity implies a de-naturalization and destabilization (that is, the historicization) of the subject who knows. To invert Descartes' formulation, where there is thinking, there is no I, no consciousness.

More directly or explicitly than either Nietzsche or Marx, Freud challenges Descartes' conflation of consciousness with subjectivity. His understanding of the unconscious, sexuality, psychical representations, and the processes involved in the constitution of the subject challenges the Cartesian subject's status as the foundation and source of knowledge. If the subject is necessarily incapable of knowing itself – that is, if there is an unconscious – then its claims to found knowledge of the world on the certainty of its own existence are also problematized. If the subject cannot know itself, why should we believe it can know anything else with absolute certainty? This does not entail scepticism or nihilism, whereby knowledge is impossible, but it may imply that knowledge, consciousness, and subjectivity need to be reconceptualized in different terms and assessed by new criteria not so heavily dependent on the subject as a self-transparent being.

Freud likened his work on the unconscious to a 'Copernican revolution', where the ego, or consciousness, like the earth itself, is no longer mistaken for the centre of the universe.[1] This book will explore some of the implications of this 'Copernican revolution' for theorizing human subjectivity, examining the ways in which a Freudian and Lacanian psychoanalytic perspective disrupts and challenges many assumptions about knowledge and subjectivity common to the social sciences and humanities as well as in everyday life. Freud inverts the primacy of consciousness with his postulate of the unconscious. Lacan performs his own inversion: more than any other post-Freudian, Lacan questions the taken-for-granted interpretations of Freud's texts, subverting the centrality accorded to the ego in ego-psychology by affirming the language-like operations of the unconscious.

This book will focus largely on Lacan's contributions to a psychoanalytic understanding of subjectivity. This means that inevitably, given that Lacan considers his work to be a reading of Freud's texts, Freud's own work must figure prominently. It is virtually impossible to understand Lacan's writings without a thorough familiarity with Freud, especially seeing that Lacan only rarely makes explicit references or footnotes to the texts he interrogates, preferring allusions, phrases, and metaphors instead.[2] I hope to provide some of this presumed background to Lacan's seminars and papers. Given their rich allusiveness, their humour, and complexity, I will not attempt a thorough or exhaustive analysis of his work (even if it were possible), but an introductory yet critical overview from a feminist perspective.

If Lacan remains my central concern here, his inversion of the primacy of the ego and consciousness is itself inverted by, or submitted to, its own 'Copernican' upheaval – this time, however, in terms of the centrality accorded to one sex in defining the other. In other words, while providing arguably the most sophisticated and convincing account of subjectivity, psychoanalysis itself is nevertheless phallocentric in its perspectives, methods, and assumptions. The last chapters of this book will examine some of the ways in which feminists have used and/or criticized Lacan's model of subjectivity and sexual difference. The earlier chapters are not free of feminist interests, either. Feminism provides the basic criteria by which Lacan will be assessed here. My analysis makes no claim to objectivity, to being a neutral or disinterested discussion or dispassionate commentary. On the contrary, I hope to make clear the passions invested one way or another in the relations between feminisms and Lacanian psychoanalysis. I will nevertheless attempt to develop a more or less systematic outline of Lacan's understanding of psychoanalysis (chapter 1), his conception of the ego (chapter 2), the oedipus complex (chapter 3), the unconscious structured like a language (chapter 4), the drive and sexual or amorous relations (chapter 5). Taken together, these may serve as an introduction to and summary of theories about the constitution of the (sexed) subject derived from Lacan's work. Clearly, given the breadth and scope of his labours of nearly fifty years, there is much I will leave undiscussed. But, if the uninitiated reader is given access to the key elements of his work, his other contributions also may be rendered more accessible.

Freud's work could conveniently if arbitrarily be divided into two themes, sexuality and the unconscious. Lacan can be seen to add the powerful insights of semiology to this Freudian bedrock. Lacan's understanding of the unconscious, sexuality, desire, and identification, implies these are sites for the production and transgression of meaning. The unconscious is structured 'like a language', for it is governed by the two poles of linguistic functioning, metaphor/condensation and metonymy/displacement. Sexual drives are the consequence of the absorption of the drive by systems of cultural meaning, by representations (we desire objects not to gratify our needs, but because they mean something, they have value or significance).

While his thought has undergone considerable evolution, and has become increasingly informed by models derived from topography, topology, and set theory, including the Möbius strip, torus or Klein bottle, Escher objects, Borromean knots, and other representations of 'impossible space' i.e. the space of the structure of fantasy, in this book I will focus on his best known texts in English, referring to untranslated works only where necessary. His 'classical texts' – those published in the *Écrits* (1966, some of which are translated in *Écrits. A Selection* 1977a) and *Feminine Sexuality* (Mitchell and Rose 1982) will provide my objects of analysis. These formulations summarize the ways in which semiology and psychoanalysis recast and criticize each other. This may also explain the mutual fascination between psychoanalysis and feminism.

My aim in this introduction to Lacan is to outline and assess his work without, however, compromising his subversive style and his radical impact on psychoanalysis and theories of subjectivity. The problem posed for any introduction to a thinker as difficult, ambiguous, and controversial as Lacan is to represent his position adequately and fairly, without, however, minimizing its troublesome status. This may mean that some elements of his work which could perhaps have been further simplified for the purposes of exegesis will remain difficult: simplicity should not take the place of an adequate contextualization and positioning of the material. The framework of sexual difference provides a conceptual and political position, not quite outside of psychoanalysis nor simply within its terms, from which Lacanian psychoanalysis can be critically assessed.

This book would not have been possible without the generous support of a number of institutions and individuals. I gratefully acknowledge the financial support and thinking space given to me in 1986 by the Humanities Research Centre, the Australian National University, under the aegis of its theme for that year, 'Feminism and the humanities'. Without this time and the calm but stimulating atmosphere, this book would not have been possible. Thanks here go to Professor Ian Donaldson, Professor Graeme Clarke, Dr Sue Sheridan, Dr Sneja Gunew, and Meaghan Morris. I would like to thank the Department of General Philosophy, the University of Sydney, where I am currently employed, for providing the political and neurotic energy needed for this project. Fighting for intellectual existence, as the department has, gives a raw edge to work that may make the difference between a mere rehearsal of issues and a working understanding of them. Special thanks thus must go to Dr Paul Crittenden and Associate Professor John Burnheim for their support and advice. The person to whom I owe most in the production of this book is Dr Moira Gatens. Her generous ideas, insights, comments, and criticisms were the true source of all that is worthwhile here. Dr Judith Allen's comments and critical suggestions were also most useful in the final stages of writing. I am very grateful for her insight and critical distance. Cecily Williams, Jacqueline Reid, Terry Threadgold, Carole Pateman, Gretchen Poiner, Barbara Caine, Caroline Sheaffer-Jones, Marie de Lepervanche, and Virginia Spate all provided much needed support and encouragement during the long gestation of this book. Above all, I would like to thank my students, who always expected the best, and deserve to have it (even if I cannot provide it). Finally, this book is dedicated to my parents, Eva and Imre Gross, with love.

E.A.G.
Sydney, 1988

1
Psychoanalysis and scandal

Since its inception, psychoanalysis has exerted a fascination for many women. It has relied on women's desire and willingness to articulate their fantasies, wishes, and hopes. It is formed out of the 'raw materials' of women's desire to talk and Freud's desire to listen. The relation between them has been one of mutual fascination, but one that has not always enriched both parties. Relations between psychoanalysis and women have always been, and remain today, highly ambivalent and fraught with difficulties. Psychoanalysis exerts an appeal for women which can also be seen as a lure or trap, especially for those who want to challenge the social functions and values attributed to women and femininity in our culture (actively affirmed in psychoanalytic theory). Freud's insights owe more than he can acknowledge to the loquacious brilliance of his first patients, female hysterics. His conception of psychoanalytic method remained, even to the end of his life, remarkably close to that 'talking cure' Anna O. so astutely described. And if Freud is indebted to a vocal if hysterical femininity, so too Lacan's earliest researches in psychoanalysis relied on the fascinating discourse of 'madwomen' – psychotics, paranoiacs, hysterics, mystics. 'The whole cast of characters in his early work consists of women . . . Not a single man is present. [He was a] man who never stopped talking about women' (Clément 1983: 61).

'Fascination' may well be an appropriate term to use in the context of relations between psychoanalysis and feminism, for its etymology involves two antithetical meanings: 'to attract, irresistibly enchant, charm'; or 'to deprive victim of the powers of escape or resistance by look or by presence' (OED). To fascinate is to entice *and* trap, seduce *and* contain, a relation similar to that between the snake and the snake-charmer, in which each charms, and traps, the other. Mutual fascination is always a risky business. Lacan suggests that it is the consequence of an imaginary identification in which the self strives to incorporate the other in an act as aggressive as it is loving. It is never clear who, snake or snake-charmer, is mesmerized by whom.

Women's fascination with psychoanalysis has enabled psycho-analysis to be used to help provide an explanation, or the begin-nings of one, of women's social and psychical positions within patriarchal cultures. Yet, at the same time, it has also contributed to women's increasing hystericization and their subsumption under male norms. In other words, psychoanalysis is an effect of women's narcissistic identifications with its promise of wholeness and self-knowledge. However, women are not simply passively assimilated by the theory, for, as feminists, they can actively intervene into it or utilize some of its methods and insights in order to understand women's construction in and by culture. Both a mode of analysing women, and a mode of analysis available *for women's use* in understanding patriarchal domination, psychoanalysis always exists in an uneasy, ambivalent relation to feminism. Since its earliest formulations, psychoanalysis has relied on the feminisms of its hysterical patients for its self-conceptions.

Correlatively, the role played by psychoanalysis in validating prevalent conceptions of masculinity and femininity has meant that feminists have generally remained critical about and distant from its central presuppositions. While it relies on certain conceptions of femininity and of women's social and sexual functions (even if it disavows this dependence), it is also amenable to transformations and upheavals in its operations. This involves challenging its central terms, assumptions, and, above all, its unspoken masculine per-spectives and interests. But because of this unspoken reliance on particular notions of femininity, major changes in its notions of femininity will necessarily transform psychoanalysis, which has assumed women's 'castration' and passivity as one of its fundamental principles. It is thus prone to far-reaching feminist questioning.

If we are to examine patriarchal power relations and forms of feminist resistance and tactics of struggle, it is necessary to maintain a balance between the tendency to a dangerous ensnarement and the lulling, pleasurable seductive appeal psychoanalytic theory exerts for feminists; we need to acknowledge the active engagement of many feminists in psychoanalytic theory, how women are culturally constructed by negative definitions, which psycho-analysis articulates. We must also place psychoanalysis in the context of a history of misogyny where feminists may be able to subvert and/or harness strategically what is useful without being committed to its more problematic ontological, political, and moral commitments.

Psychoanalytic enquiries into the nature of female identity, libido, sexuality, and development are of major significance to feminism. In spite of whatever problems it may exhibit, psychoanalysis is still by far the most complex, well-developed, and useful psychological theory at hand. It retains an 'honesty' or at least an openness about its attitude to women and femininity that is rarely visible in and yet is highly symptomatic of a more general patriarchal, cultural framework. For this reason alone it is difficult to abandon; without viable theoretical alternatives, psychoanalysis still remains the system which says what others simply presume or cover over. Freud has opened up a new discursive field, to borrow Michel Foucault's description.[1] Yet women must have the ability to speak about themselves – and to be heard – on questions that concern them. Only then will the tension between psychoanalytic and feminist modes of explanation remain productive. Women must be able to *use* psychoanalytic methods and insights, not merely to understand themselves personally, psychologically, or therapeutically (for this amounts, in effect, to an acceptance of its basic presuppositions) but also our social world, its forms of self-generation through the family structure, the 'socialization' or enculturation of children, and even the production and evaluation of knowledges. Psychoanalysis needs to be taken beyond its usual terms of reference in order to stretch or transgress its limits and become relevant in the construction of viable, autonomous representations of women and femininity.

Which psychoanalysis?

Before proceeding, we need to consider which version or form of psychoanalysis we will examine. This is particularly necessary, given the variability of terms, concepts, perspectives, and meanings lumped together under the general label of psychoanalysis. The psychoanalysis on which I will concentrate will in the first instance be that of Freud. We will examine the core presumptions of his understanding of sexuality, the unconscious, and their manifestations; and especially those elements of Freud's work undigested by Freudian orthodoxy. Yet to say that our object is Freudian analysis still does not help to specify which Freud we will utilize, and which of the competing models, methods, and conclusions that abound in his work will be preferred. Where, for example, the majority of analysts emphasize a concept of the ego as a rational mediator between the id and reality (the 'realist ego' Freud develops in *The Ego and the Id* 1923) Freud himself also developed an alternative account of the ego using a narcissistic model ('On

Narcissism. An Introduction' 1914a). I will attempt to develop as consistent a view of the *social production* of human/social subjectivity as Freud's texts allow, given their contradictory nature.

My more or less 'literal' reading of Freud will be at some variance with the stresses and emphases developed in the works of more mainstream contemporary Neo-Freudian or Freudian revisionists. This is the liberty we are granted with a body of writing as heterogeneous and variable as Freud's. Freud, however, will serve as a point of departure for a more intensive focus on the work of French analyst and *enfant terrible,* Jacques Lacan. Lacan's work occupies the centre of this text because his reading of Freud stresses Freud's originality and subversiveness and helps to vindicate psychoanalysis in feminist terms, enabling it to be used as an explanatory model for social and political relations. Lacan can be utilized to explain such notorious concepts as women's 'castration' or 'penis envy' in socio-historical and linguistic terms, that is, in terms more politically palatable than Freud's biologism. And, perhaps most significantly for our purposes here, Lacan has succeeded, where many before him failed, in signalling the importance of Freud's work to disciplines outside of psychology (narrowly conceived), making it relevant to all the social sciences and humanities which take subjectivity as their object of investigation (including linguistics, literary theory, philosophy, politics, semiotics, social theory, and anthropology, as well as feminism).

To understand even the rudiments of Lacan's work, it is essential to have a working knowledge of a number of Freudian texts and terms. Freud establishes the field within and across which Lacan's work must be situated. Lacan's work is far from a dutiful commentary or secondary text *on* Freud's primary texts. Lacan's work is not parasitic on Freud's, for it produces a certain Freud, a Freud perhaps more bold and threatening than the cautious Viennese analyst. Lacan succeeded in reinvigorating and re-energizing the scandalous quality of psychoanalysis that so thwarted Freud's earliest ambitions for respectability and intellectual acceptance. Lacan affirms the more notorious, unpalatable components of Freud's work – those very components purged, removed, silenced, or left unarticulated by the Neo- and revisionist Freudians. Lacan may have been more 'constitutionally' oriented to notoriety than the systematic, patient, even plodding Freud.

Lacan claims that Freud's work is in danger of itself being repressed. He encourages us to read Freud as if 'reading' a dream or symptom, that is, according to Freud's own interpretative methods, with an ear to what underlies or is implicit in his texts. In opposition to the bulk of contemporary psychoanalysts and therapists, Lacan argued that Freud knew exactly what he was doing. His work is not in need of revision or correction in the light of new psychological 'discoveries': on the contrary, Freudian psychoanalysis provides a series of techniques by which other social and intellectual norms can be examined as symptomatic of social relations. Lacan preserves the radical edge of Freud's writing by drawing out its implications for different theoretical disciplines and paradigms, its resonances with, and connections to other knowledges.

By sticking to the letter of Freud's texts, Lacan showed that they can be deciphered as radical interrogations of received conceptions of human reason and knowledge. For example, his postulation of an unconscious and infantile sexuality are not explicable as inversions, opposites, or doubles of consciousness and adult genital sexuality respectively. The unconscious is not a submerged, second order consciousness; infantile sexuality is not a premature or anticipatory version of adult, heterosexual genitality. There is a rift, an unmastered gap or discontinuity between consciousness and the unconscious, and infantile and adult sexualities. The unconscious is not a submerged consciousness, a rational system that is somehow invisible; it is an entirely *other* form of reason, logic, and pleasure, one not reducible to those available to consciousness. It undermines the subject's conscious aspirations by its symptomatic intrusions in behaviour which are uncontrolled by, and may be even unknown to, consciousness. Lacan resists attempts to neutralize and absorb Freud's 'Copernican' upheaval. He stresses the neglected, unrepresented, or undiscussed elements of Freud's work – those which generated psychical or intellectual resistances on the part of psychoanalysts themselves.

Psychoanalytic subversions

Wherever its implications were grasped, psychoanalysis has had scandalous effects. The publication of *The Interpretation of Dreams* (1900) and *The Three Essays on the Theory of Sexuality* (1905) caused major disquiet in medical circles. After a number of years of obscurity and ridicule in Vienna and throughout Europe, Freud was as alarmed as he was pleased to be invited to present a series of lectures in the United States in 1909 (Jones 1961: 265–7). While delighted to find a willing and open-minded audience at Clark University, he worried that the radical implications of his work were being disavowed or ignored, not taken seriously, or misunderstood. He felt as if only a few of his colleagues and soon-to-be-former-colleagues understood him – Fliess, Abraham, Jung, and Adler. On his journey by ship to the United States Freud exclaimed to Jung, his travelling companion, 'They don't realize we're bringing them the plague' (cited in Lacan 1977a: 116; Turkle 1978: 4; and Gallop 1985: 58).

While he was pleased with the American response to psychoanalysis, within five years he had grown wary and suspicious of too easy an acceptance. Acceptance of 'offensive' ideas was, he believed, a form of psychical negation (1925b). *Some* resistance is a sign of taking an idea or proposition seriously. It may have been for this reason that he claimed: 'the final decisive battle will be played out where the greatest resistance has been displayed' (Freud, quoted in Turkle 1978: 5; see also Roazen 1976: 720–32). Psychoanalysis provoked outrage and shock, not because Freud attributed sexual motives to apparently non-sexual behaviour, nor simply because of his supposition of an infantile origin for all adult sexual practices. What was and is most unacceptable is the hypothesis of unconscious motives, motives not accessible to the subject's waking consciousness and moral sensibility. From his earliest fascination with hysteria, awakened by his studies with Charcot in 1885, and his first reports on the topic in 1886 (Jones 1961: 151), he faced a wave of hostility from peers and colleagues that ranged from benign tolerance to ridicule and wild accusations.

He described his first ten years of analytic/therapeutic research as a period of 'splendid isolation' (Jones 1961: 239). During this period, he worked with a few sympathetic individuals – Breuer (at times) and particularly Fliess (Freud's letters to Fliess, Masson 1985: 182–5 are revealing). The 'misery' of lone exploration, as Freud saw it, ended only gradually, with the publication of some of his major works (1893–5; 1900), and from acquiring a number of converts and sympathizers who themselves risked isolation by committing themselves to psychoanalytic precepts. However, in spite of his growing circle of admirers and followers, he was to face bitter disappointments time and again. His expectations of an analytic milieu, an ongoing collectivity of analysts, while fulfilled, had turned nightmarish! His most favoured followers were those very colleagues who, one by one, would betray him or his work. Each in his own way was to refuse Freud the affirmation and recognition he so craved. Each, sooner or later, 'deviated' from his fundamental insights – whether from his understanding of the unconscious, the sexual aetiology of the neuroses, or the postulate of a perverse infantile sexuality. In other words, even for those sympathetic to or active within analysis itself, Freud's position remained intolerable. Even analysts, it seems, are victims of resistance and repression. The theory of repression is itself in constant danger of being repressed.

This hostility, in the first instance, was directed towards Freud's use of hypnosis or suggestion to induce, remove, or transform hysterical or neurotic symptoms. Hypnosis demonstrated that hysteria could be treated by psychological and verbal techniques. By means of the 'talking cure' the most painful and distressing symptoms – paralyses, migraines, choking, neurasthenia, depression, anxiety, etc. – were alleviated. Abandoning the hypnotic method in 1889, Freud developed the first of his (proto-)psychoanalytic techniques on 1 May of that year. He came to replace hypnosis and suggestion with a more loosely conceived 'cathartic method', which anticipated the techniques of 'free association' characterizing psychoanalysis proper. By applying pressure to the patient's forehead he would induce her to remember and verbalize memories and associations connected to the symptom.[2]

The unconscious implies a pleasure the subject seeks but cannot experience, a knowledge which cannot be known by it, and forms of representation which are themselves unrepresentable in consciousness. What seems intolerable in his 'discovery' of the interpretive technique of free association, and the key to reversing the synthesizing functions of dream or symptom formation, is an analytic procedure that seeks out the processes of production invisible in symptoms. His reversal of the illogical 'logic' the unconscious uses to express itself in consciousness, shows that this 'logic' nevertheless exhibits its own precise and decipherable rules. The verbal meanderings and recollections comprising the techniques of free association seem to come aimlessly out of the analysand's mouth: yet, if one listens to what is said with an 'even-handed attention', they form a tightly structured pattern or web of images, wishes, thoughts, memories, of which the analysand has no conscious awareness. The unconscious, in other words, is what is subversive in psychoanalysis.

If the contentious issues of psychoanalysis are those associated with sexuality, sexual aetiology, and interpretation, what is at issue in all of them is the idea of the unconscious. Sexuality is not in itself contentious; nor is the sexual aetiology of neuroses (if anything, these 'topics' lead to an increasing interest, for both professional and lay audiences, in psychoanalysis). The processes of deciphering or interpreting symptoms and dreams had a long history pre-dating Freud. What is unpalatable is Freud's presumption that sexuality functions unconsciously, that sexuality is the effect of the unconscious. What is troublesome about dream interpretation is the 'logic of the unconscious' it reveals.

Sexuality, on Freud's understanding is not, in spite of popular conceptions, governed by nature, instincts, or biology but by signification and meaning. Dream-interpretation is threatening, not because of the use of 'symbolism' or symbolic explanation,[3] but because there is a wish, a proposition, a discourse, at work in dreams that is not heard or understood by consciousness. What distinguishes his descriptions of libido, the death drive, ego-, and object-libido, etc. is his refusal to ascribe to them a natural or *a priori,* instinctual status, a biologically preformed and unalterable path or *telos* for sexuality. For him, sexuality is the consequence of the interaction of the material inscription of desire on and with the child's body.

Freud claims that there is a proposition that could not be said, or known, by the subject: 'The ego is no longer master of its own house' (1917b: 141–3). *Contra* Descartes, Freud posits a subject that is radically *incapable* of knowing itself. The subject, understood as consciousness, cannot understand the subject, understood as the creator of symptoms, dreams, and distorted messages.

> Freud, when he doubts, for they are *his* dreams, and it is he who, at the outset, doubts – is assured that a thought is there, which is unconscious, which means that it reveals itself as absent. As soon as he comes to deal with others, it is to this place that he summons the *I think* through which the subject will reveal himself . . . It is here that the dissymmetry between Freud and Descartes is revealed . . . (Lacan 1977b: 36)

This is a transgression and undermining of a pervasive humanism dominating the work of his psychological colleagues. His assertion of the unconscious amounts to an anti-humanism. Meaning is structured by more than human will or intent. Psychoanalysis is the first system of knowledge (in this century at least) to recognize the implications of the ambiguity and multiplicity of meaning utilized by the unconscious.

Where Freud may have been the first to develop a system or technique by which a radical alterity internal to subjectivity can be interrogated, it was Lacan who articulated the precise means by which the unconscious speaks. This is his major theoretical contribution to the continuing notoriety surrounding psychoanalysis.

Lacan shifts the grounds of Freud's hypotheses: instead of Freud's lucidity and concern to make psychoanalysis accessible and scientifically acceptable, Lacan cultivates a deliberate obscurity; where Freud attributes the powers of discourse to the unconscious, Lacan explains what its 'language' consists in, and what its effects on the discourses of consciousness are. Where Freud sought the respect and status of professional recognition, Lacan seemed to actively court controversy (see Schneiderman 1983; and Clément 1983, for their accounts of Lacan the man). Where Freud gains credibility from a systematic, rational, well-argued analysis, Lacan works largely by indirection, circularity, ellipsis, humour, ridicule, and word-play. Where Freud sought to ensure the status of psychoanalysis as a science, a therapeutic and an explanatory theory, Lacan sees it, not as a system of cure, explaining or guaranteeing knowledge, but as a series of techniques for listening to, and questioning desire – even those desires at work in the production of knowledge. Where Freud maintains a 'dignity' beyond reproach in his formal yet cordial reports of sexual matters, Lacan seems to go out of his way to flirt, mock, seduce, and insult (cf. Gallop 1982a). To Freud's role as Talmudic patriarch, Lacan plays the gigolo. This makes his work all the more fascinating, all the more luring and ensnaring for feminists, seeing he so actively courts (and baits) them.

Lacan's personal life has always had an element of drama, a flair for attracting attention and provoking controversy. He was born in Paris in 1901. He began training in psychiatry in 1927 and completed his doctorate in 1932, with a dissertation entitled 'On Paranoia and its Relationship to Personality'. Although he relies on concepts (such as 'personality') and frameworks (such as a medicalized model of psychopathology) which he later questions and/or abandons, his earliest researches anticipate his more mature works in a number of respects.

Two features of his doctorate are relevant to understand his later works: first, his understanding of the role of the image, and of social context (later termed the imaginary and the symbolic, respectively) in the formation of 'personality' or subjectivity ; and second, his analysis of paranoia and the similarities between the persecutory figures and the subject's ego-ideal (which Lacan will develop into his account of the mirror stage, infantile transitivism, and psychosis).

In 1934, he joined the small Freudian group, The Psychoanalytic Society of Paris, under the directorship of Marie Bonaparte (with whom he was repeatedly to clash over the years). His membership of this group is already a strong indication of his commitment to psychoanalytic principles, particularly given the great suspicion and hostility directed at Freud's work in France. One may speculate that the American ease of acceptance is consonant with its implicit negation of psychoanalysis, and especially the concept of the unconscious. Perhaps the open resistance to Freudianism evident in France engendered a more threatening and disconcerting reading.

Many of the ideas developed in Lacan's earliest works were refined and presented in a paper Lacan delivered to the 14th International Psychoanalytic Congress, held in Marienbad in 1936. It was entitled 'The Mirror-Phase'.[4] A later, revised, version was delivered at the 16th Congress, held in Zurich in 1949, published in *Revue française de psychanalyse* (No. 4, 1949; see 1977a, chapter 1). In it, Lacan announces the inherently divided, split subject, a subject divided between itself and its mirror reflection. By way of dating this paper, it is significant that Freud had not yet written his paper 'The Splitting of the Ego in the Process of Defence', (1938b) where he too discusses the ego as divided from itself, as internally alienated.

In 1951, he began the first of his controversial weekly seminars, which lasted until close to his death.[5] These were attended by many of the most respected French intellectuals over the last thirty years, including Sartre, de Beauvoir, Levi-Strauss, Merleau-Ponty, Barthes, Althusser, Kristeva, and Irigaray.

The lectures were notorious in their stylish eloquence and refinement, their erudition and audacity, and their shocking, intimidatory tone. He took on the sacred cows of French bourgeois culture and the then dominant intellectual tendencies – behaviourism, existentialism, rationalism, empiricism – in French theory. Scathing in his attacks on 'enemies', he was also highly charismatic, charming, and seductive in articulating his position. Many saw these seminars as a kind of intellectual/sexual tease; his indirect, elliptical, evasive, but always suggestive lecture technique remains striking for the promise of a 'knowledge' (the gratification of a desire to know) which recedes the closer it comes.

Together with a number of his colleagues, students, and trainee analysts, Lacan, Daniel Lagache, and other members of the Société psychanalytique de Paris seceded from the International Psychoanalytic Association (IPA) to form a break-away school in 1952, called the Société française de psychanalyse (The French Society of Psychoanalysis) (Schneiderman 1983: 141; Gallop 1985: 55). This occurred, it seems, over several disagreements: his conception of the short session – the session whose length is not determined in advance, unlike the more orthodox '50 minute hour'; his notion of language in analysis; the tendency of the analyst to act as the analysand's ego-ideal; and the nature of analytic 'cure' which for him, reveals unconscious desire.

In 1953, he presented what was to become, after his account of the mirror phase, his second major contribution to psychoanalytic theory, his understanding of the language of the unconscious, in a paper now known as the 'Discourse of Rome'. At the Congress of

Romance Language Psychoanalysts held in Rome, Lacan, who was to deliver a report, was officially asked to withdraw (Clément 1983: 111). But he presented the paper to his friends and supporters anyway. Its title was 'The Function and Field of Speech and Language in Psychoanalysis' (translated in Lacan 1977a, and Wilden 1981). It was an audacious challenge to psychoanalytic orthodoxy in terms of the latter's textual timidity and reverence for canonical interpretations of Freud, and for their refusal of Freud's account of the wayward, verbal logic of the unconscious. While not officially expelling him, in 1968 the IPA retaliated by refusing to recognize the qualifications of analysts he supervised and trained, thereby preventing them from practising as analysts.

When the French School of Psychoanalysis applied for affiliation with the IPA, the governing body of the time (1964) ruled that only if Lacan was dropped from the Society would it be admitted (Clément 1983: 106). This requirement split the French school into two factions, those who were prepared to comply with the IPA, and those who supported Lacan. In June 1964, together with his supporters, Lacan founded the École freudienne de Paris (The Freudian School of Paris) (which he was to dissolve equally dramatically in 1979). He compared his position within the International Association to an 'excommunication':

> my teaching . . . has been the object of censure of a body calling itself the Executive Committee of an organization calling itself the International Psycho-Analytic Association. Such censorship is of no ordinary kind, since what it amounts to is no less than a ban on this teaching – which is to be regarded as null and void as far as any qualification to the title of psychoanalyst is concerned . . . .
>
> So, what it amounts to is something strictly comparable to what is elsewhere called major excommunication – although there the term is never pronounced without any possibility of repeal. (Lacan 1977b: 3)

Under Althusser's patronage, he moved his seminars to the École Normale Superieure. In 1966, his massive text, *Écrits*, was published and the project of publishing his twenty-five annual seminars was undertaken by his son-in-law (and current (1989) director of Lacan's school), Jacques-Alain Miller. Its publication introduced a broader audience to his works and to psychoanalysis more generally, and seemed strongly to influence a number of students and radicals involved in the upheavals of May and June 1968, who were to become so important in marking the character of French intellectual and political life in the 1970s and 1980s.

Shortly after the tumultuous events of May 1968, Lacan was accused by the authorities of being a subversive, and directly influencing the events that transpired:

> The director of that august institution decided that the student uprising in May 1968 had been spawned by Lacan's seminar and that he would no longer be permitted to give it on the campus . . . Lacan responded by saying that the director reminded him of one of those chains you pull when you flush a toilet; this mobilised student outrage and the director found his office occupied by Lacanians, in confirmation of his suspicions about the subversiveness of Lacan. (Schneiderman 1983: 29; see also Turkle 1978: 170–1)

Lacan was thought to be sympathetic to the students; yet

> he did tell the students of Vincennes that they were puppets of the regime and that they were looking for a Master. He added his belief that they would find one. Several years later he said that the one they had found was him. (Schneiderman 1983: 39)

In 1979, after considerable internal dissent and disagreement within his own school, he intervened to dissolve it, claiming it had deviated too far from his teachings. After a series of bitter legal battles, it was reopened again in 1980 under Miller. Shortly after, in September 1981, Lacan died.

Lacan's notoriety is the result of several factors.

First, a 'style' which has provoked and outraged psychologists, philosophers, social scientists, and others who expected a clear, unequivocal model and terminology, and theory as a 'straightforward' statement explaining 'facts'. This component of his scandalous image is not altogether unexpected, given his announcement that:

> Every return to Freud that occasions a teaching worthy of the name will be produced by way of the path by which the most hidden truth manifests itself in the revolutions of culture. This path is the only training that we could claim to transmit to those who follow us. It is called; a style. (Lacan 1966: 458)

If 'style' is the object of psychoanalytic teaching and training, then Lacan's style is deliberately provocative, stretching terms to the limits of coherence, creating a text that is difficult to enter and ultimately impossible to master. His 'style' contains the same evasions, the same duplicit speech as the unconscious itself. Understanding is thus always incomplete: it involves an interminable analysis based more on the free associations of its parts than its

17

cohesion as a narrative or totality (see chapter 4). Vergote, in Smith and Kerrigan (1983: 217), argues that Lacan's *Écrits,* like the dream, needs to be seen as a rebus (see Freud 1900: 277–8). The rebus, a picture puzzle, cannot be understood unless one focuses only on its component parts. The relations between these parts rather than their copresence in a totality provides the rebus with its propositional content. So too, in reading Lacan's 'style', one must devote attention to the parts and their (additive) effects, rather than, as in conventional textual criticism, analysing the whole in view of its parts, and the parts in view of the totality (the so-called 'hermeneutic circle').

Second, if Freud's account is constantly in danger of being repressed and misunderstood, Lacan's relentless pursuit of the function and effects of the unconscious is even more intolerable. His scandal is associated with the celebration of what is censored and prohibited in social life: desire. Perhaps more than Freud, Lacan insists on the radical heterogeneity of the unconscious, its recalcitrance, and opacity to conscious intention. His stress on the particular scope and purpose of psychoanalysis thus dramatically distinguishes it from psychology, medicine, psychiatry, and the 'healing sciences' on the one hand, and, on the other, from philosophical, linguistic, and literary explanatory systems, the 'humanities' or, more anachronistically but appropriately, 'letters'. The psychoanalytic exploration of the unconscious and its privileged modes of expression do not aspire to the neutrality or objectivity of the natural sciences, nor to the modes of subjectivity supposedly constituting the humanities. Instead it takes the unpalatable middle path – the path of (symbolic) inter-subjectivity. In short, the analysis of the unconscious is founded on transference, the inter- and intra-subjective relation between analyst and analysand. Lacan's refusal to waver in the fundamentals of psychoanalytic theory no doubt scandalized all those disavowing Freud's notion of the unconscious, including a good many psychoanalysts!

Third, Lacan's subversion is also directed to the production and articulation of knowledge – and especially the 'subject supposed to know', the analyst as the object of transference. Lacan's personage became a kind of mass projective screen onto which a series of collective fantasies focused, surrounding him with legend, rumour, innuendo, 'family' romances, and personal mythos. In death Lacan seems to generate as much scandal as alive. His personal manner was clearly relevant to his expulsion from the IPA, as it also was in his mass following. A highly public figure, seen on French television (translated in *October,* No. 40, 1987), available everywhere in print, Lacan came to represent a source of knowledge overly revered by some and disdained by others. His disputes and disagreements with even those sympathetic to his work – Laplanche, Leclaire, Pontalis, Irigaray – and his demand for absolute support (a demand, like all demands, for love?) closely resembled Freud's, although it was more openly accepted as a kind of master-disciple relation by Lacan (see Roustang 1982). At least three texts available in English – Schneiderman (1983), Clément (1983), and Turkle (1978) – tie Lacan's pedagogical persona to the notoriety of his work. At once imperious and meticulous, making little concession to his audience, he both entices and intimidates them into (devoted?) submission. Flirtatious and preoccupied with the question of pleasure, wooing his audience, and particularly the women within it (cf. Gallop 1982a: ch.3; Clément 1983: 15 ff.), his seductive, Socratic teachings were bound to cause polarization in those who uncritically accepted his word – devotees and critics.

Psychoanalysis and feminisms

If it is not clear which psychoanalysis needs to be adressed, it is even less clear which feminisms best illuminate the merits and problems of psychoanalytic theory. Arguably, feminist theory has undergone a dramatic turn-about in attitude towards psychoanalysis. If we survey feminist literature on psychoanalysis even superficially over the last twenty years, the re-evaluation of positions – the positive affirmation of a theory previously reviled – has never been so stark. For English speakers, this 'moment' of radical rupture in feminist attitudes is marked by the publication of Juliet Mitchell's defence of Freud in *Psychoanalysis and Feminism* (1974). This text is clearly indebted to Lacan's reading of Freud, with its emphasis on social and significatory rather than instinctual and hereditary forms of explanation. Yet, Lacan's name is strikingly under-emphasized in Mitchell's text.[6] More significantly, Mitchell leaves untouched the radical centre to Lacan's project – his notion of language or signification – to reconstruct his work sociologically and anthropologically.

Mitchell's book alerted feminists to the ways in which Freud's insights have been popularized, misrepresented, and neutralized by interpretations that were (often wilfully) ignorant of his writings, or of the subversive threat his notion of psychoanalysis implies. She argued that Freud was not prescribing what women and femininity should be, but describing what patriarchal culture demands of women and femininity. She claims that psychoanalysis is essential to the understanding of the ways in which patriarchal ideology is internalized and lived by men and women:

> the Freud the feminists have inherited is often a long way off-centre. In violently rejecting a Freud who is not Freud, I would argue that the only important possibilities for understanding the psychology of women that we have to date have been lost and that in misconceiving and repudiating psychoanalysis a crucial science for understanding ideological and psychological aspects of oppression has been thrown away. (Mitchell 1974: 301–2)

Mitchell argued that Germaine Greer, Kate Millett, Betty Freidan, and Shulamith Firestone and most other feminists mistakenly presumed that Freud affirms rather than simply explains the internalization of patriarchal sex roles. He functions as scientist or observer, not advocate. Moreover, she continues, unless a theory *like* Freud's is developed, the divisions between the sexes cannot be explained as social rather than biological effects. Only if the positions men and women occupy are historical, and therefore capable of transformation, can psychoanalysis be useful in feminist accounts of subjectivity, masculinity, femininity, and oppression. Without something like Freudian analysis, sex roles and their social values cannot be seen as ideological/political effects, consequences of the reproduction of power relations. Sex-role theories must either assume a natural/biological/evolutionary explanation, an explanation in terms of the species; or see the individual as the result of 'conditioning' or 'learning', imprinting – a behavioural model which is necessarily committed to the *a priori* passivity and plasticity of social subjectivity. Both naturalist and environmentalist explanations leave subjectivity as such unexplained. It remains polarized: either purely given, or purely produced. By contrast, Mitchell claimed that psychoanalysis could provide 'an analysis of ideology' which may be 'tied closely to a logic of sexual struggle' (1974: xxiii).

Whatever problems Mitchell's text may, with hindsight, exhibit,[7] it ensured the centrality of Freud's work to a wide variety of feminist theories that might otherwise have had little use for psychologically oriented explanations. Mitchell demonstrated the political and social relevance of psychoanalysis, its usefulness as explanatory or interpretive model rather than simply as therapeutic technique. She is not, of course, without precedents; it is unlikely her text could have been possible or instrumental in the development of so many other feminist texts if not for her (usually implicit) grounding in the works of Lacan, Louis Althusser, and the Marxist-feminist group, Psychanalyse et politique. It was Althusser who, in his article, Freud and Lacan (Althusser 1971b: 177–202) vindicated psychoanalytic theory from the usual Marxist objections to its 'middle-class orientation', its 'elitism', and 'individualism'.

Partly as a consequence of Mitchell's stimulating defence of Freud, her work spawned a vast industry of psychoanalytically inspired feminist texts which, in the mid- to late 1970s, turned to Freud for an explanation of various aspects of contemporary patriarchy. Nancy Chodorow's book, *The Reproduction of Mothering* (1978) is probably the best known of these. Chodorow seems less influenced by the framework of Marxism and the theory of ideology than Mitchell in her accounts of the acquisition of masculine and feminine social roles. Her position is motivated on the one hand by empiricist and descriptive concerns (as exemplified by her use of object-relations theory) and by 'wholism' (concern for the 'integrated person', the completed subject as the goal of struggle). While clearly related to Mitchell's project in so far as she uses it to provide an account of infant social and parenting relations, Chodorow uses psychoanalysis to provide a sociological explanation, an explanation of the behavioural patterns, tendencies, and regularities of social life. She leaves unquestioned the distinctions and oppositions Freud so carefully represents as psycho-socially produced – the distinctions between subject and object, masculine and feminine, psyche and reality – undoing his subversion of the *cogito*.

Chodorow's book is committed to liberal egalitarianism and to 'equal rights'. Ironically, given her interest in the social production of gender and the transmission of sexually differentiated social roles (like mothering), Chodorow must in effect neutralize the specificity and psychosocial meaning of the *sexed* body, thus ignoring the particularities of individuals who are to be rendered socially equal. After all, whether women are considered to be 'feminine' or 'unfeminine', they are still subject to patriarchal oppression! Chodorow relies on Robert Stoller's problematic separation of sex from gender, minimalizing sex (here conceived in *purely* anatomical or biological terms)[8] and focusing on gender (understood as purely social) as if it functions somehow independently of sex.

Chodorow assumes that Freud's analysis is an empirical description, which is thus capable of clinical verification or falsification. It is on this assumption that she can describe Freud's position as 'biased' (the presumption being that if an account is biased then, in principle, an unbiased account is possible) instead of seeing in psychoanalysis a method of reading and interpreting (where questions of truth, bias, and verification are not relevant). Like

Mitchell, she is unable to recognize the role of signification in the production of individuals as subjects. Admittedly, Chodorow does discuss language, but her account seems to rely on an empiricist understanding of language as a system of *naming:*

> Research on the development of gender identity and gender identity disturbances further qualifies the Freudian clinical claim. These studies confirm that gender identity is with rare exception firmly and irreversibly established for both sexes by the time a child is around three. Gender identity receives its major input from social ascription of sex that begins at birth and is cognitively learned concomitantly with language (Chodorow 1978: 150)

Chodorow largely concentrates on psychoanalysis as a mode of explaining sexist discrimination in social and family life, and on formulating programmes for alternatives, such as shared parenting, in the socialization of children. Her focus on the unequal relations between the sexes means that, unlike a number of later psychoanalytic feminists, she leaves the structures of patriarchal, and particularly phallocentric, oppression intact and unexplained. In other words, while her position may well explain the ways in which women are induced to take on the role of mothering – as it aims to do – it leaves the question of the underlying meaning and value of sex roles unasked. The relevant issue here is not simply who parents, or how to equalize the input of both parents, but to examine the meanings ascribed to the behaviours of each sex in parenting.

Mitchell is less interested in using psychoanalysis to explain sexism or inequality, and more interested in using it to explain our culture's reproduction of structural or patriarchal forms of oppression. Instead of sexist acts of discrimination, Mitchell focuses on the underlying (or unconscious) patriarchal structures, the structures which make these acts possible, and provide social validation or support for them.

Both Chodorow and Mitchell leave the functioning of discursive and signifying systems – the domain of phallocentrism – unquestioned. This dimension of representations, the symbolic, the most alien to Anglo-Saxon intellectual traditions, becomes the focus of many feminist concerns developed in France. Feminists such as Luce Irigaray, Julia Kristeva, and Hélène Cixous analyse and criticize psychoanalytic models of subjectivity in terms of sexual differences. As a pervasive mode of representing women, phallocentrism ensures that even if, as Chodorow suggests, men and women equally share the functions of parenting, the meanings of their actions will remain different; and, in the case of challenges to patriarchy, such as Mitchell's, phallocentrism ensures that the patriarchal structure appears inevitable and unchangeable, coded as natural. This may explain Mitchell's commitment to the oedipus complex and women's 'castration' as socially universal and necessary (Mitchell, in Mitchell and Rose 1982: 18).

To return, then, to the question of which feminisms to use to highlight the interaction of feminist and psychoanalytic theory, I intend to focus only on those feminist accounts that maintain some sort of positive, even if critical, relation to Lacanian psychoanalysis. This means that pre- or anti-psychoanalytic feminisms will be avoided; also, given the vast numbers of feminist texts which today utilize psychoanalytic frameworks, I will further restrict discussion to those feminist texts that have some internal relation to Lacan's framework. This will rule out those positions, like Chodorow's, which rely on ego-psychology or object-relations versions of psychoanalysis antithetical to Lacan's position. Inevitably, some arbitrary decisions must be made in an area as complex and varied as this. The centrality of Lacan's particular version of Freud seems, in the context of this book, to provide a less arbitrary criterion than others.

In the next chapter, I will outline the range, scope, and relevance of Lacan's conception of the ego. Chapters 2, 3, and 4 focus on one of the three central loci in Lacan's contributions to the reading of Freud – the ego/mirror stage, sexuality, and the unconscious/language. In the final two chapters, I will look more directly at the peculiar, ambivalent relations that have developed between Lacanian psychoanalysis and feminist theory, particularly those now called 'French feminisms'.

2

The ego and the imaginary

Freud's two views of the ego

Freud vacillated between two quite different views of the ego. He used both conceptions intermittently throughout his career; it is by no means clear which represents his final or definitive position, whether he regards them as alternatives, or whether he aimed to replace one with the other. Both are useful in some explanatory contexts but not in others. I will describe them as the realist and the narcissistic views. In outlining each, I will focus on their differences, which will become significant in distinguishing Lacan's position from that of neo-Freudianism, revisionist Freudianism, or ego-psychology.

The realist view is sketched in rudimentary form in the post-humously published draft, 'The Project for a Scientific Psychology'. Freud couched his model of the psyche and its agencies in neuronal and neuro-physiological terms in this proto-psychoanalytic text. Later he 'translates' this model into psychological terminology in *The Interpretation of Dreams* (1900). In *The Ego and The Id* (1923), over a quarter of a century later, he returns to it. And at the very end of his life, in *An Outline of Psychoanalysis* (1938a), he affirms it yet again.

The narcissistic view is developed more in the middle period of Freud's work, yet it too has a similarly long and protracted history. In *The Three Essays on The Theory of Sexuality* (1905), Freud claims that an explanation of the genesis and development of the ego is needed, yet it was left unelaborated until his metapsychological papers, particularly 'On Narcissism: An Introduction' (1914a). In a related paper from the same period, 'Mourning and Melancholia' (1915a), he elaborates further details of the narcissistic account. He appears to abandon it in *The Ego and the Id;* but in fact returns to it in the last paper published in his lifetime, 'The Splitting of the Ego in the Process of Defence' (1938b).

Clearly a number of central questions need to be raised here: are the two views compatible, or contradictory? Which is to be preferred, and on what grounds?

The realist ego

In *The Ego and The Id,* Freud describes the ego as an agency which intervenes in the conflict between anti-social, endogenous, sexual impulses or wishes, which originate in the id, and the demands of reality, which impinge on the organism from the outside. The ego acts like a filter in both directions, from the id to reality and from reality to the id.

Freud likens the ego to the rider of a horse; the horse signifies the energies of the id, energies which must be correctly harnessed if the rider is to keep his/her seat. Reality is represented by the path or destination the rider must entice and control the horse to follow:

> In its relation to the id, the ego is like a man on horse back, who has to hold in check the superior strength of the horse; with this difference, that the rider tries to do so with his own strength while the ego uses borrowed forces. The analogy may be carried a little further. Often a rider, if he is not to be parted from his horse is obliged to guide it where it wants to go; so, in the same way, the ego is in the habit of transforming the id's will into action as if it were its own. (1923: 25)

The realist ego is motivated by principles of 'rational' compromise. It protects the rules and norms of (social) reality by modifying the 'unreasonable', impossible demands of the id, on the one hand; while on the other, the ego protects the id by shielding it from harmful or excessively strong stimuli coming from reality – from external criticism, harsh judgements, the absence of desired objects. In relation to the id's endogenous functions, it acts as a bearer or representative of reality. Here its role is unifying, homogenizing, and organizing the chaotic, pleasure-seeking impulses of the id. In relation to reality, its aim is to rationalize and justify many of id's demands, to represent it to social Law. It is a moderating influence on the strength and specificity of id impulses, bringing them into line with what is socially acceptable. As a rational mediator, it strives to protect the organism from threats and danger from the social; and at the same time, it strives to procure maximum satisfaction and pleasure for the wishes of id that it also serves, while ensuring the smooth reproduction of social norms and values. It is an agency serving two masters. It functions by means of expediency and compromise in attempting to gain maximum satisfaction in a pleasure-repressing social context.

On this model, the ego is thus a more or less stable agency or entity, identified with 'the self'; it modifies the pleasure-seeking id, influencing it in accordance with the dictates of the reality principle. It also modifies the demands of reality in accordance with the individual's psychic needs. It is identified with the 'higher' mental functions and achievements of the individual. The key features of the realist view can be indicated as follows:

1 the ego is a pre-given, natural, or innate faculty, the biological result of the interaction of psychical and social relations with the surface of the organism;

2 the ego is one 'agency' or system among a number of others which compete for gratification within the subject;

3 the ego is the 'reasonable' mediator intervening between antagonistic forces, arbitrating as an outsider between the demands of the id and the requirements of reality;

4 the ego's specific form is a consequence of the neuronal impact of external impingements on the subject's interiority. It also acts as a delegate for the id's wishes. It is the agency guarding and supervising the pleasure-seeking id and a hostile, repressive reality;

5 the ego, as mediator or rational harmoniser of psychical conflict, is thus responsible for the 'higher' mental accomplishments of culture;

6 the ego functions to inhibit psychical impulses and/or the force of social custom. Its role is to modify both, inducing compromises between these antagonistic interests by inhibiting their strength or impetus.

This realist view of the ego has been adopted by neo-Freudian orthodoxy, which Lacan has scathingly described as 'the psychology of free enterprise'.[1] The conceptualization of the ego as a bearer of reality is, he claims, fundamentally conservative: the two terms between which it mediates are *given* and unquestioned, the id being a function of biology, and reality an unalterable, ahistorical system, 'civilization'. On such a model, it is not surprising that the most plastic, manipulable agency is precisely the ego. The ego can thus be considered 'weak' in so far as the balance between pleasure and reality tilts in either one direction or another. The function of psychoanalytic therapy in this case is to strengthen and reinforce the ego, thus enabling it to accept and satisfy some of the id's wishes while conforming to social expectation.

Lacan's most biting irony is reserved for ego-psychologists (including some of the best known contemporary analysts, Abraham, Hartmann, Kris, Erikson, Loewenstein, Segal, and others) who are committed both to the ideal of the 'autonomous ego', the ego functioning outside the influence of the unconscious, and to psychoanalysis as a mode of transmission of normative ideals. Psychoanalysis directs the analysand to a pre-selected goal – a strong, masterful, autonomous ego. For those whose egos are 'weak', the task of analysis is to model the analysand's ego on the analyst's (i.e. the analyst functions as the ego-ideal with whom the analysand identifies).

> Lacan . . . naturally opposed the idea that there is a *whole* self that serves as an agent of strength, synthesis, mastery, integration, and adaptation to realistic norms. Lacan perceives partisan analysts pushing analysands towards an ideal of health which merely defined group norms. (Ragland-Sullivan 1986: 119)

For Lacan, these 'popularized' or 'consumerist' versions of psychoanalytic therapy bring the analysand to a pre-set destination – being a better wife and mother, a more successful businessman, a child who can 'cope' with the demands of schooling, and so on. In his view, by contrast, there can be no guarantee of where psychoanalysis will lead, no given point of termination, no promise of 'cure', no assurances of 'normality' (cf. Schneiderman 1983). Psychoanalysis, for Lacan, is resolutely disconnected from medicine; it is not an analysis of the 'self', consciousness, or the ego, aimed at boosting its performance. If the analyst acts as the role model, judge, ego-ideal or superego for the analysand, psychoanalysis is reduced to a form of (re-)socialization, patching up those areas of 'breakdown' or unsuccessful socialization of the subject.

> What happens when the subject begins to speak to the analyst? . . . It is to him that is offered something that will first, necessarily, take the form of a demand. Everyone knows that it is this that has oriented all thinking on analysis in the direction of a recognition of *the function of frustration.* But the subject knows very well that, *whatever his needs may be, none of them will find satisfaction in analysis.* (Lacan 1977b: 269, emphasis added)

Psychoanalysis neither strengthens nor weakens the ego. It is not a system of 'cure'. It doesn't provide a 'deeper' understanding of the 'self'.[2] These are descriptions more appropriate to therapy than analysis. Psychoanalysis is no more – nor any less – than an analysis of the unconscious which belies the subject's ego or consciousness (Schneiderman 1983). It subverts, renders ambiguous, and resists the ego's conscious ideals. The ego cannot judge reality, or mediate between reality and desire because it is always marked by error, (mis)recognition or lack:

> We have learned to be quite sure that when someone says 'It is not so' it is because it is so; that when he says 'I do not mean' he does mean; we know to recognise the underlying hostility in most 'altruistic' statements, the undercurrent of homosexual feeling in jealousy, the tension of desire hidden in the most professed horror of incest, we have noted that manifest indifference may mask intense latent interest . . . . Our view is that the essential function of the ego is very nearly that systematic refusal of reality which French analysts refer to in talking about the psychoses. (Lacan 1953: 12)

The narcissistic ego

Where ego-psychology refers to the realist view, Lacan relies on Freud's second or narcissistic account of the ego. The realist ego is considered innate or natural; by contrast, the narcissistic ego is the effect of non-biological social/familial and meaningful interventions into biological development. Freud sketches the bare outlines of an account of the genesis of the ego by linking it to the operations of infantile or primary narcissism. The phenomenon of narcissism, whereby the ego is able to take itself as its own libidinal object, poses a problem for the realist view; in so far as the latter relies on sharp cleavage between ego-instincts and sexual instincts, this makes it difficult to explain how the ego is able to take a part of itself as a sexual object, how it is simultaneously subject and object. The relation between the procedures governing the individual's psychical or internal functions (ego-instincts) and those directed outward to external objects (sexual instincts) must be much more confused and mutually defining than this model allows.

In the narcissistic view, narcissism must be distinguished from auto-eroticism: 'A unity comparable to the ego cannot exist in the individual from the start; the ego has to be developed . . . . There must be something new added to auto-eroticism – a new psychical action – in order to bring about narcissism' (Freud 1914a: 76–7). The realist ego is given, a 'psychic substance', whose outlines are biologically preformed. It is structured by impingements from external reality on the subject's sensory/neuronal structure which modify the 'surface' of the id through perception. By contrast, the narcissistic ego is an entirely fluid, mobile, amorphous series of identifications, internalizations of images/perceptions invested with libidinal cathexes. Where the realist ego stands out over and above the two combatants (reality and the id), the narcissistic ego cannot be readily separated either from its own internal processes (e.g. the flow of libido) or from external objects (with which it identifies and on which it may model itself). It is thus no more 'rational' or 'conciliatory' than any other psychical or social force. Narcissism, the ego's ability to take itself as a libidinal object, cannot be explained on the realist account.

Freud conceives of the narcissistic ego as a storehouse of libido, a kind of psychic repository or dam where libido can be stored from its various sources throughout the body in the anticipation of finding appropriate objects in which it could be invested. Libidinal tributaries flow out of this reservoir into external objects (including its own body), or are absorbed back from external objects. The 'shape' of the ego is, as it were, contingent on the degree or amount of libido invested in others or stored in the ego. In this hydraulic model, Freud presumes that the ego has a more or less fixed quantity of libidinal cathexes at its disposal. It is able to either invest libido in objects (object-libido), or to retain libido within itself (ego-libido): 'The more of one is employed, the more the other becomes depleted' (ibid.: 76). On this model, the ego has no direct relation to reality and no privileged access to the data of perception. Its primary relations are libidinal, based on pleasure rather than the dictates of reality. It is not an entity, agency, or psychical content, for the ego is constituted by relations with others. Indeed, its self-identity is not given through feeling, sensation, or experience, but is always mediated by others. If the ego is based on relations between others and its own body then its 'plasticity' of form is easy to understand: the ego is dependent on various libidinal investments for its outline and features:

> Thus we form the idea of there being an original cathexis of the ego, from which some is later given off to objects, but which fundamentally persists and is related to object-cathexes much as the body of an amoeba is related to the pseudopodia which it puts out. (ibid.: 75)

The amoeba-like ego does not establish libidinal relations with external objects distinct from itself. Its relations to its objects, like the 'pseudopodia' of the amoeba, incorporate the object, transforming its own outlines to accommodate what is introjected.

Two extremes illustrate the ego's dependence on its libidinal investments in others – falling in love and illness. When the subject falls in love, the ego invests libido in its privileged love-object, depleting its 'reserves' of ego-libido. The process of falling in love risks the safety of the ego in order to (over-)estimate the beloved. In those fortunate circumstances where the relation is reciprocated, the depleted ego is, in its turn, reinvested with cathexes proceeding from the beloved. Being loved provides libidinal nourishment for the ego and thus an elevation of its self-esteem. A kind of happy balance between projection and introjection occurs. However, more frequently, where such a reciprocal desire is not sustained, the unrequited love for the other severely lowers feelings of self-regard or self-worth. At its most extreme, for example, in the case of the death or loss of the beloved, the ego undergoes an intense process of mourning, brilliantly analysed by Freud in 'Mourning and Melancholia' (1915a). Mourning is the (gradual) process of disinvesting or de-cathecting the lost object of the intensity of all memories, impulses, and libidinal investments associated with it. Mourning is a reclamation of libido from unreciprocated investments which have emptied the ego. The ego gradually replenishes its libidinal reserves by reinvesting narcissistic cathexis in the subject's own body. Only after the associative networks of the lost, mourned object are sufficiently disinvested, and the body reinvested, is the ego able to seek substitutes for the lost object. Illness also demonstrates the pliable, see-saw relation between ego and object-libido. The more that is invested in objects, the less there is invested in the ego. When the subject is ill, the ego is unable to sufficiently invest external objects to give them attention. Instead, libido is directed towards the subject's own body, appearing to replace an external love object with its own body or, at least, its pain.

The narcissistic model of the ego implies that the ego can take itself, its own image, parts of its own body as an 'object', and invest them as if they were external or 'other'. It is constituted as an ego only through alienation, through the creation of a necessary rift between lived immediacy of perception/sensation, and mediated reflection or self-distance. Its identity is bound to relations with others. It is a sedimentation, a locus, of images of others which form its self-image. To summarize the key features of the narcissistic view, we can say:

1 primary narcissism is a stage distinct from auto-eroticism. It is unpredictable from a biological point of view – a psycho-sexual intervention into biological development;

2 the narcissistic ego is simply the boundary that is established to surround the libidinal reservoir. For this reason, the narcissistic ego is able to take itself or a part of its body as one of its libidinal objects;

3 but this implies that, unlike the realist view, the narcissistic model of the ego is not an entity or agency within the subject;

4 the amount of libidinal energy, and consequently the shape or

contours of the ego itself are variable, not fixed. They are dependent on the kinds and forms of libidinal investment sent out from
the ego and received back by it, and thus vary over time and from
one relation to another;
5   far from being a self-contained or potentially autonomous
entity, the ego is paradoxically intersubjective; it depends on the
subject's relations with the other;
6   instead of being dominated by the demands of reality and a
logic of expediency and compromise, the ego is governed by
fantasy, and modes of identification, and introjection, which make
it amenable to the desire of the other;
7   rather than defending the id against the demands of reality, the
ego defends against a part of itself. The subject that takes itself as its
own object is fundamentally *split*, as a subject and an object.

This model is antithetical to the realist view, at least in its details.
Freud's commitment to the narcissistic model is very often ignored
in more conventional psychoanalytic circles. Lacan will develop his
own account of the ego using Freud's narcissistic model. He
challenges contemporary proponents of the realist view in developing his account of the mirror stage, to which we will now turn.

Lacan and the mirror phase

Lacan's account of the ego is chronologically his first, and most
accessible, intervention into the 'reading' of Freud. It is widely
recognized as the basis of his questioning and subversion of
dominant, i.e., humanist, social sciences and of the reign of the
Cartesian *cogito*. It is arguably the most 'interdisciplinary' of his
technical contributions to the reading of Freud.

The clue comes from Freud's comment that a 'new' psychical
action must occur for the genesis of the ego. Freud himself does not
provide any suggestions of what this 'new' action is, for his major
point seems to be the unnaturalness, the unpredicability that marks
the emergence of a unity such as the ego. The ego unifies the
heterogenous experiences and disorganized sensations of the
(proto-)subject. Yet it is produced in opposition to biological,
organic, or instinctual processes. Lacan's theory of the mirror stage
can be interpreted as his attempt to fill in the genesis of the
narcissistic ego, whose adult residues Freud so convincingly described.[3]

It is significant that for Freud, the ego is represented as a psychical map, a projection of the surface of the body.[4] In this case the
ego is the psychical representation of the subject's perceived and
libidinalized relation to its body: 'for every change in the eroto-

genicity of the organs, there might be a parallel change in the erotogenicity of the ego' (Freud 1914a: 84). Freud leaves these suggestive remarks unexplored. As we will see, his insights about the ego's form being the consequence of a projection of the body's surface will become important for feminist critiques of psychoanalysis and the development of concepts of sexual difference.[5]

The Real preconditions of the ego

As the threshold of a number of ruptures or divisions which govern the child's hitherto 'natural' existence, the mirror stage is conditioned on:

1   The child's first recognition of a distinction between itself and the (m)other/mirror-image (self-as-other);
2   The recognition of lack or absence, whether this is the absence of the mother, or an absence of gratification of needs;
3   Displacing the child's dependence on the (m)other with a self-reliance. The mirror stage is a compensation for the child's acceptance of lack. It provides a promise or anticipation of (self)mastery and control the subject lacks, and which the mother provisionally covered over in gratifying the child's needs;
4   The genesis of the ego coincides with the emergence of the child's first psycho-sexual drives – that is, with the substitution of a part of its own body and auto-erotic pleasure, for that originally given by the now absent mother;
5   The advent of an internalized psychic (as opposed to neurophysiological) sensory image of the self and the objects in the world. It marks the child's earliest understanding of space, distance, and position.

It marks a first stage in the child's acquisition of an identity independent of the mother, the genesis of a sense of self or personal unity, the origin of the child's sexual drives and the first process of social acculturation.

Libidinal relations establish the ego through a fantasized identification with others, particularly the mother (the child strives to be the object of the mother's desire), and an illusory corporeal cohesion, founded on a (mistaken) identification of the child with its visual *gestalt* in the mirror. The ego is partially a consequence of idiosyncratic and socially structured psychological relations between itself, others, and its body image.

Lacan hovers between seeing the mirror stage as a purely internal, biologically regulated process;[6] and as a linguistically structured, socially regulated relation. He utilizes a number of ethological and zoological examples, citing studes of the behaviour of migratory locusts, pigeons, chimpanzees, and insects as illustrations of the socializing effects of the internalization of the image of another of the same species on the individual. In this sense, his work could be interpreted as universalist both within and across species. Yet his work also relies on the work of a number of theorists who themselves actively destabilize the biologistic or naturalist presumptions of biological and ethological research. For example, he refers to the work of Roger Caillois, especially his paper 'Mimicry and Legendary Psychaesthenia' (1984) in several of his papers on the ego and interpersonal relations (Lacan 1953; 1977a: 3; 1977b: 73, 99–100, 109). Caillois claimed that the ability of an insect to mimic its environment is not an adaptive or defensive function, but 'a *luxury* and even a dangerous luxury' (1984: 25). Mimicry, even within animals, threatens to assimilate the individual into its environment at the cost of any 'identity'. We have here the effect of a 'depersonalization by assimilation into space' (1984: 7, 30).[7]

The child's ego development is paradoxically *naturally social*. Lacan argues that the mirror stage is grounded in a 'biological prematurity': it is based on an 'anatomical incompleteness' or 'organic insufficiency' (1977a: 4), which the child attempts to fill by means of an identification with the image of an other. Its biologically 'premature' birth, its organic dependence on others for its survival, its long-term 'unease and motor unco-ordination' indicate that the subject (-to-be) is vitally dependent on the (m)other for both physical and psychical survival for a longer period than other animals, whose existence is instinctively regulated. Animal survival is contingent upon the operation of instincts relative to the harshness or generosity of the environment. By contrast, human survival is regulated by the *necessarily social* organization of human life. Each child is born into an already existent social and family structure (which it may share with some animal species); in place of the survival value of instinctual behaviour, the human must rely on language (which distinguishes it from animals). Language and law regulate its (social) existence. Lacan sees these two elements – our 'unnatural' natures, and our necessarily social existence – as two sides of the one coin. The social and linguistic orders function in place of the instinctual in human existence.

For many months, the child remains physiologically incapable of controlling its bodily movements and behaviour, 'stuck in his motor incapacity and nurseling dependency' (Lacan 1977a: 2). Its body is an unco-ordinated *aggregate,* a series of parts, zones, organs, sensations, needs, and impulses rather than an integrated totality. Each part strives for its own satisfaction with no concern for the body as a whole. It has no experience of corporeal or psychical unity or of occupying a stable position within a corporeally delimited space. Sensory/perceptual impingements, which may animate certain organs and bodily parts, cannot be attributed to a continuous, homogenous subjectivity. The child, in other words, is born into the order of the Real.[8] The Real is the order preceding the ego and the organization of the drives. It is an anatomical, 'natural' order (nature in the sense of resistance rather than positive substance), a pure plenitude or fullness. The Real cannot be experienced as such: it is capable of representation or conceptualization only through the reconstructive or inferential work of the imaginary and symbolic orders. Lacan himself refers to the Real as 'the lack of a lack'. It is what is 'unassimilable' (1977b: 55) in representation, the 'impossible' (167). Our distance from the Real is the measure of our socio-psychical development. The Real has no boundaries, borders, divisions, or oppositions; it is a continuum of 'raw materials'. The Real is not however the same as reality; reality is lived as and known through imaginary and symbolic representations.

The child experiences its body as fragmented. Some parts of its body are more perceptually available to it than others. The sensations coming from its hands are more developed, for example, than those from its feet for many weeks, due to the later myelinization of nerve fibres. The right hand matures more quickly than the left (cf. Merleau-Ponty 1964: 123). The body matures unevenly, forming the basis of the child's experience of 'the body-in-bits-and-pieces'. This image helps explain adult fantasies of corporeal disintegration or decomposition manifested in dreams of dismemberment and peculiar bodily organization (Lacan 1977a: 4–5).

The experience of unco-ordination and fragmentation is a theoretical inference; it cannot be known except through a retrospective reconstruction. The child forms a syncretic unity with the mother, and cannot distinguish between itself and its environment. It has no awareness of its own corporeal boundaries. It is *ubiquitous,* with no separation between itself and 'objects', for it forms a 'primal unity' with its objects. It cannot recognize the absence of the mother (or breast). Freud mentions the baby's *hallucinatory* reactivation of its previous perceptions of satisfaction where the Real object of satisfaction (e.g. milk) is absent. Sucking re-evokes in hallucinated form the feeling of contentment from milk even in the absence of milk (Freud 1911b: 219).

The child's recognition of absence is the pivotal moment around which the mirror stage revolves. The child is propelled into its identificatory relations by this first acknowledgement of lack or loss. Only at this moment does it become capable of distinguishing itself from the 'outside' world, and thus of locating itself *in* the world. Only when the child recognizes or understands the concept of absence does it see that it is not 'one', complete in itself, merged with the world as a whole and the (m)other. In other words, its recognition of itself as a (potential) totality is correlative with its recognition that the world as a whole is *not* its own. This marks the primitive 'origins' of the child's separation of inside and outside, subject and object, self and other, and a number of other conceptual oppositions which henceforth structure its adult life.

The child can only give up this hermetically sealed circuit of need and satisfaction by accepting that the (m)other is not within its control, being a separate object. The 'fullness', the completeness that the child experiences through the maternal supplementation of its needs is interrupted by lack. The child is no longer in that happy state of satisfaction, protected by and merged with the (m)other. From this time on, lack, gap, splitting will be its mode of being. It will attempt to fill its (impossible, unfillable) lack. Its recognition of lack signals an ontological rift with nature or the Real. This gap will propel it into seeking an identificatory image of its own stability and permanence (the imaginary), and eventually language (the symbolic) by which it hopes to fill the lack. The child loses the 'pure plenitude' of the Real and is now constituted within the imaginary (i.e. the order of images, representations, doubles, and others) in its specular identifications.

Vision and the specular image

Dating from around six months, the mirror stage lasts until around eighteen months and is only, if ever, dissolved with the oedipus complex. Lacan claims that it must be distinguished from reflex actions and non-conscious or uncontrolled behaviour. It is an intellectual act, an act of (re-)cognition. The child notes its own image in a mirror with great delight and pleasure. The recognition of itself is a complex act involving, over and above the registration and perception of sensations, an apperception: an act of attributing perception to an underlying perceiver. Specular recognition (the child's recognition of its mirror-image) will significantly distinguish it from the animal: where the latter functions on the Real level of need or instinct, the former is specifically founded by the subsumption or tracing of need by verbal demand, an effect of its immersion in the imaginary:

This act [of recognition] rebounds in the case of the child in a series of gestures in which he experiences in play the relation between the movements assumed in the image and the reflected environment, and between this virtual complex and the reality it reduplicates – the child's own body and the persons or things around him. (Lacan 1977a: 1)

Lacan here compares the child's development to that of a chimpanzee, as outlined in the work of Wolfgang Köhler (in *The Mentality of Apes* 1951). In spite of an intellectual advantage the chimpanzee of the same age has over the child, once the animal recognizes that the image in a mirror is simply an image and not another chimpanzee, it loses interest and develops an instrumental relation to it.[9] By contrast, the child retains its fascination with the image, indeed even intensifies it, when it learns of its representational status. A drawing or photograph may be even more pleasing than what it represents. The child joyously celebrates the recognition of its specular image or the form of others.

We must not, however, assume that this process of recognition occurs instantly or that it is immediately comprehended as such by the child. Its capacity for specular perception is mastered only gradually. For example, the child is more likely to understand the doubling effect of the mirror when it perceives others than in its self-perceptions. In Henri Wallon's study, *Les origines du caractère chez l'enfant* (1949), cited many times by Lacan (1953; 1977a: 3; 1977b: 73, 99, 109) he suggests that an infant smiles in recognition of its father's image in the mirror. When the father speaks to the child, the child seems shocked and turns from the image towards the father supporting him. The child is surprised that the voice emanates from a different place to the image. This indicates that it has not yet grasped the differences and connection between its father's physical presence and his specular reflection. In his penetrating analysis of the earliest psychical relations with others, Merleau-Ponty claims that:

> One cannot say that the child comes into possession of a perfectly clear relation between the image and the model, that he learns to consider the mirror image as a spatial projection of the visible aspect of his father, the experience of which we are speaking occurs at about 5 or 6 months and does not give the child possession of a stable conduct. Just as the child studied by Wallon turned away from the specular image towards the father after a week, so several weeks later, he still tried to grasp the image in the mirror with his hand; this means that he had not yet identified this image as a 'simple image' that was nothing other than visible. (Merleau-Ponty 1964: 128)

The child's fascination with its mirror-image coincides with its recognition of lack. Wallon argues that to begin with the child responds to the specular image of others rather than to its own mirror-reflection. This is largely because it is easier to recognize the differences between the two visual experiences of the other (one virtual, the other real) than it is to compare their correlates in the self. In the example cited above, the child has two visual images of its father, one derived from the 'real' father holding it, the other, specular. In the case of the self-reflecting image, the child only has one visual image (a virtual one) of itself, necessarily partial and incomplete; and a sensory or kinaesthetic image, which may be difficult to compare with the visual. Rephrasing Wallon, Merleau-Ponty claims:

> Thus for him, it is a problem first of understanding that the visual image of his body which he sees over there in the mirror is not himelf since he is not in the mirror but here, where he feels himself; and second, he must understand that, not being located there in the mirror, but rather where he feels himself introceptively, he can nonetheless be seen by an external witness *at the very place at which he feels himself to be* with the same visual appearance that he has from the mirror. (Merleau-Ponty 1964: 129)

The external perception of the self – 'autoscopy' – is not built up by a point-for-point mapping of felt experiences onto the visual image, but on a wholesale adoption of the visual image in its totality. It is incorporated into the child's organization of its experience of the body. On a global level, the coincidence of the image with the experience of self (extroception and introception, respectively) is not guaranteed: there is no *cenesthesia* (images directly projected from bodily zones, organs, and sensations and thus capable of representing them directly for consciousness). The child, according to Wallon, does not distinguish between perceptions provided by introception and those provided by extroception or perception.

It gradually understands that the reflection is an image of itself. It reacts with a delight which, for Lacan, is an ensnarement and lure as much as a pleasure. The child is fixated by the image, enamoured and captured by the specular double. The child's triumphant delight and fixation prefigures the dynamics involved in all imaginary relations. These residues will later become defined as erotic/ libidinal and aggressive impulses or drives when they become more clearly differentiated.

The mirror stage relies on and in turn provides a condition for the body-image or imaginary anatomy, which in turn helps distinguish the subject from its world. By partitioning, dividing, representing, inscribing the body in culturally determinant ways, it is constituted as a social, symbolic, and regulatable body. It becomes the organizing site of perspective, and, at the same time, an object available to others from their perspectives – in other words, both a subject and an object.

The child sees an image of itself as an organized and integrated totality. The image is positioned in a physical environment. It comes to have a fixed but partial, limited perspective on itself through the externalization provided by the mirror; and it is or can become the object of another's perspective. In spite of 'a contrasting size that fixes it [the image] and a symmetry that inverts it, in contrast to the turbulent movements that the subject feels are animating him' (1977a: 2), the child's recognition of its own image means that it has adopted the perspective of exteriority on itself. The capacity of representing oneself to oneself, mirror-reversals, the obsession with symmmetry, and the division of the subject into both subject and/or object are later reactivated in the dreams of adults or, in a more extreme form, in psychoses (1977a: 4).

The primacy of the visual in this phase is not altogether surprising, if we understand the genesis of the ego as a specifically social process, one that is culturally and historically variable in its structure. Of all the senses, vision remains the one which most readily confirms the separation of subject from object. Vision performs a distancing function, leaving the looker unimplicated in or uncontaminated by its object. With all of the other senses, there is a contiguity between subject and object, if not an internalization and incorporation of the object by the subject. The tactile, for example, keeps the toucher in direct contact with the object touched; taste further implicates the subject, for the object must be ingested, internalized in order for it to be accessible to taste. As Sartre (1974) recognized, the look is the domain of domination and mastery; it provides access to its object without necessarily being in contact with it. Moreover, the visual is the most amenable of the senses to spatialization. Clearly all the other senses are capable of providing a concept of space – the child's sense of touch and taste, during the oral phase provided what Merleau-Ponty described as a 'buccal space', a space mapped by oral incorporation (Merleau-Ponty 1964: 122).[10] This space is hierarchically organized and structured in terms of a centralized, singularized point-of-view by being brought under the dominance of the visual.

The tactile, auditory, and olfactory sense organs depend on some spatial representation, which, in our culture if not in all civilizations, is hierarchically subordinate to the primacy of sight. Thus, the sense of sight is the only one of the senses that directs the child to a *totalized* self-image. Other senses can, at best, lead to a body-image conceived as an aggregate – precisely the body-in-bits-and-pieces. Only the simultaneity afforded by sight confirms the integrity of a cohesive self and body. None of the other senses have this ability to perceive 'synchronically', in a non-linear and non-temporal fashion.

Although the visual is privileged in Lacan's account of the formation of the ego, it is not the only kind of perceptual identification possible. Clearly the congenitally blind have egos and conceptions of space. Yet it is significant that the particular details and limits of bodily organization – indeed, the corporeal or postural schema of the body, one's image and experience of one's own body, the limits or boundaries of one's corporeality – may vary considerably from that of sighted subjects. The body's felt orientation, its position in space, the ways it takes up that space, the relations between the body's positions and that of others, the subject's capacity to identify with other subjects, must be perceptually different in the blind.

Lacan's ocularocentrism – his vision-centredness – in complicity with Freud's, privileges the male body as a phallic, virile body and regards the female body as castrated. Although I will later examine the charge of phallocentrism directed by many feminists at Lacan's work, we should note here that the female can be construed as castrated, lacking a sexual organ, only on the information provided by vision. The other sensori-perceptual organs would have confirmed the presence of a female organ instead of the absence of a male organ.

The child sees itself as a unified totality, a *gestalt* in the mirror: it experiences itself in a schism, as a site of fragmentation. The child's identification with its specular image impels it nostalgically to seek out a past symbiotic completeness, even if such a state never existed and is retrospectively imposed on the pre-mirror phase; and to seek an anticipatory or desired (ideal or future) identity in the coherence of the totalized specular image. Lacan claims that the child is now enmeshed in a system of confused recognition/misrecognition: it sees an image of itself that is both accurate (since it is an inverted reflection, the presence of light rays emanating from the child: the image as icon); as well as delusory (since the image prefigures a unity and mastery that the child still lacks). It is the dual, ambivalent relation to its own image that is central to Lacan's account of subjectivity. If the child simply *recognizes* the image, we would have another version of Freud's realist view of the ego – an ego essentially in contact with reality. But if, on the other hand, the child merely misrecognizes its image, it is the subject of error and falsehood, unable to produce knowledge, a subject of ideology. Instead, Lacan posits a divided, vacillating attitude that is incapable of a final resolution. This 'divided' notion of self and the problem of self-recognition are crucial in so far as they may explain processes of social inculcation and positioning. Neither ignorant nor aware of its own socialization, the child must be both induced to accept social norms and values as natural, and yet to function as an agent within a social world, an agent who has the capacity for rebellion against and rejection of its predesignated social place.

In identifying with its mirror-image, the child introjects it into the subject's ego; yet the subject's relation to the image is also alienated. The image both is *and* is not an image of itself:

> this *gestalt,* by these two aspects of its appearance, symbolises the mental permanence of the I, at the same time as it prefigures its alienating destination; it is still pregnant with the correspondences that unite the I with the statue in which man projects himself, with the phantoms that dominate him, or with the automaton in which, in an ambiguous relation, the world of his own making tends to find its completion. (Lacan 1977a: 2–3)

The child identifies with an image of itself that is always also the image of another. Its identification can only ever be partial, wishful, anticipated, put off into the future, delayed. Its internal or felt reality can only ever be incompletely approximated or represented by the mirror-image. This constitutive identification is necessarily alienating. Lacan posits two 'poles' or functions around which the ego is oriented – an *affairement jubilatoire,* and a *connaissance paranoiaque,* that is, between a joyful, affirmative self-recognition (in which the ego anticipated the unity of its image), and a paranoiac knowledge produced by a split, miscognizing subject. In short, the ego is torn between the demand for pleasure, gratification, and self-aggrandizement; and a jealousy and frustration Lacan sees in terms of an intra-subjective aggressivity.

Lacan elaborates some key elements of this primordial aggressivity in his paper on this theme (1977a: chapter 2). This frustration is a function of the inevitable awkward, uncontrolled relation the child has to, and in, its disunified, incapable body:

> What I have called the *mirror stage* is interesting in that it manifests the effective dynamism by which the subject originally identifies himself with the visual *Gestalt* of his own body: in relation to the still very profound lack of co-ordination of his own motility, it represents an ideal unity, a salutory *imago;* it is

invested with all the original distress resulting from the child's intra-organic and relational discordance during the first six months . . . (Lacan 1977a: 19)

Infantile transitivism and primordial jealousy

The mirror stage is the phase of libidinal investment in the image of one's own body and the stage in which a primordial frustration and aggressivity are manifested. The child invests the specular image of itself or another with all the hostility directed towards its own lack of satisfaction, the very motivation for internalizing the image in the first place. The *imago* or internalized image becomes an intrapsychic object of aggression (for example, in narcissistic self-deprecation). Its aggressivity is also an effect of its particular relation to its specular image. The child identifies with an image that is manifestly different from itself, though it also clearly resembles it in some respects. It takes as its own an image which is other, an image which remains out of the ego's control. The subject, in other words, recognizes itself at the moment it loses itself in/as the other. This other is the foundation and support of its identity, as well as what destabilizes or annihilates it. The subject's 'identity' is based on a (false) recognition of an other as the same. (Is this the 'origin' of phallocentrism?)

In this context, Lacan cites the work of Charlotte Bühler and the Chicago School on the psychotic (in adults) but 'normal' (in children) phenomenon of transitivism (1977a: 17; and 1953). In the text, *Sociological and Psychological Studies on the First Year of Life* (1927), Bühler discusses the relation of transitivism between pairs of children whose ages are relatively close but separated by at least three months. She documents pairs of children in the appropriate age categories playing dichotomous roles without direct consultation. For example, one child is active, the other passively looks on at his or her antics; or one occupies the role of master, the other takes on the position of the slave. In these cases we have a kind of complementary transitivism. The roles of master and slave, actor and audience, doctor and patient are complementary, a relation of active to passive. There is also commonly a transitivism of similarity, where one child imitates the behaviour of the other (cf. Spitz 1965). For example, when one child is punished the other also cries. In both cases, the identity of the one remains indistinct from, confused with, the other. It occurs when the borders separating them are affirmed and simultaneously confused. Lacan claims that:

It is in this erotic relation, in which the human individual fixed upon himself an image that alienates him from himself, that are to be found the energy and form on which this organisation of the passions that he will call ego is based. (1977a: 19)

Jealousy finds its explanation in this context. It is in part a result of the structure of transitivism (occurring from around seven to nine months). The structurally active and passive roles – actor/audience, orator/auditor, seducer/seduced, etc. provide jealousy with its ground: the jealous child is the one who wishes to occupy the role of its double or counterpart, to be the one watched, rather than the one watching:

One might say that the jealous person sees his existence invaded by the success of the other. It is the attitude of the one who sees no life for himself other than that of achieving what the other has achieved, who does not define himself by himself in relation to what others have . . . All jealousy, even in the adult, represents a non-differentiation of that kind between oneself and the other, a positive inexistence of the individual that gets confused with the contrast that exists between others and himself. (Merleau-Ponty 1964: 143)

If the ego is basically ruptured or split in its identity, divided between a body it claims as its own, and an other it strives to be like, this rupture also generates a knowledge that is paranoiac, divided between recognition and miscognition:

What I have called paranoiac knowledges is shown . . . to correspond in its more or less archaic forms to certain critical moments that mark the history of man's mental genesis, each representing a stage in objectifying identification. (Lacan 1977a: 17)

The mirror stage both affirms and denies the subject's separateness from the other. If we look more directly at the privileged stage for the acting out of the drama of the mirror stage – that is, at the mother-child relation, in which the mother takes on the position of specular image and the child that of incipient ego, the mirror stage is an effect of the discord between the *gestalt* of the mother, a total, unified, 'completed' image, and the subjective, spatially dislocated, positionless, timeless, perspectiveless, immersing turmoil the child experiences. The mirror stage is a necessarily alienating structure because of the unmediated tension between the fragmented or 'fragilized' body of experience; and the 'solidity' and permanence of the body as seen in the mirror. 'It is the stability of the standing posture, the prestige of stature . . . [which] sets the style for the identifications in which the ego finds its starting point and leave their imprint in it forever' (Lacan 1953: 15).

The ego sees itself in its relations with others. Its fascination with specular reflections will forever orient it in an imaginary direction. Imaginary identifications, the identifications of self with other and other with self, vary widely, ranging from the so-called 'normal' attitude of falling in love (see chapter 5), to psychoses. The imaginary is the order of identification with images. It is the order of dual, narcissistic relations with others (see Wilden 1981), of libidinal pleasure unregulated by law, and indistinguishably intra- and inter-psychical aggression. In the psychoses of 'cenesthesia' (where the subject hears voices in his or her head or bodily parts), we have the obliteration of a tenuous boundary between self and other. If the subject hears another's voice from within his or her own body, this is because the self and other remain confused; the boundaries of the skin which 'normally' outline the subject's spatial-corporeal limits have become permeable (cf. Merleau-Ponty 1964: 134).

If it places the subject's tumultuous, unlocatable experiences within its corporeal boundaries and organs, the mirror-stage also engenders social relations with others with whom the subject identifies. These two effects are not clearly separable, particularly if the metaphor of the mirror represents the child's relation to the mother. It is by identifying with and incorporating the image of the mother that it gains an identity as an ego. The image is always the image of another. Yet the otherness of the other is not entirely alien. The subject, to be a subject at all, internalizes otherness as its condition of possibility. It is thus radically *split*, unconscious of the processes of its own production, divided by lack and rupture. The ego illusorily sees itself as autonomous and self-determined, inde-pendent of otherness. It feels itself to be its own origin, unified and developed *in/by nature*. There is thus a form of fixity built upon misrecognized dependencies. It is an attempt to arrest rigidly the tensions of the opposition between the fragmented perceived body and the unified, specular body.

The imaginary anatomy

For Lacan, the ego is a product of the internalization of otherness. It is also a psychical projection of the body, a kind of map of the body's psycho-social meaning. Lacan's account of the founding role of what he calls 'the imaginary anatomy' is perhaps one of the most productive and under-developed features of his work. The body as it is perceived or experienced by the child is the fragmented

43

body-in-bits-and-pieces. This is an uncoordinated, discrete assemblage of parts exhibiting no regulated organization or internal cohesion. Out of this largely biological chaos of neuronal prematurity will be constructed a lived anatomy, a psychic/libidinal map of the body which is organized not by the laws of biology but along the lines of parental or familial significations and fantasies about the body – fantasies (both private and collective) of the body's organization, Bound up within parental fantasies long before the child is even born, the child's body is divided along lines of special meaning or significance, independent of biology. The body is lived in accordance with an individual's and a culture's *concepts* of biology. This imaginary anatomy has been called a number of other names elsewhere – in Schilder's work, it is the 'postural schema of the body', in Merleau-Ponty's, it is the 'body-subject' or 'body-image', in Wallon, the 'corporeal schema':

> If the hysterical symptom is a symbolic way of expressing a conflict between different forces, what strikes us is the extra-ordinary effect that this 'symbolic expression' has when it produces segmental anæsthesia or muscular paralysis unaccountable for by any known grouping of sensory nerves or muscles. To call these symptoms functional is but to profess our ignorance, for they follow a pattern of a certain imaginary Anatomy which has typical forms of its own. In other words, the extra-ordinary somatic compliance which is the outward sign of this imaginary anatomy is only shown within certain limits. I would emphasize that the imaginary anatomy referred to here varies with the ideas (clear or confused) about bodily functions which are prevalent in a given culture. It all happens as if the body-image had an autonomous existence of its own, and by autonomous I mean here independent of objective structure. (Lacan 1953: 13)

To illustrate the existence of an autonomous body-schema, Lacan cites the phenomena of the phantom limb and hysteria. The limb that has been surgically removed continues to induce sensations of pain in the area where it used to be. While this pain cannot be located in the 'real' anatomy of the body, it inhabits the space occupied by the imaginary body. The absence of a limb can constitute a narcissistic investment as readily as its presence. The phantom limb is a symptom of mourning for the lost bodily totality. Hysterical symptoms also conform to a 'morphology', a psychical anatomy at odds with biology, indicating that the imaginary body is the consequence of the meaning of biology rather than biology itself.

Schilder has stressed that the body-*gestalt* is structured by 'psychological' or 'morphological' not anatomical requirements. Its 'laws' function according to a *desire,* a *nostalgic* phantasy of wholeness and completion. The phantom limb is a kind of memorial to bodily autonomy:

> The phantom in the beginning usually takes the shape of the lost extremity but in the course of years, it begins to change its shape and parts of it disappear. Where there is a phantom of the arm, the hand comes nearer to the elbow, or in extreme cases may be immediately in the place of amputation. Also the hand may be smaller and be like the hand of the child . . . The position of the phantom is often a rigid one, and . . . it is often in the position in which the patient lost his limb. It is as if the phantom were trying to preserve the last moment in which the limb was present. (Schilder 1978: 63–4)

Hysterical paralyses follow a 'logic' that relates more to the body's visible form than its biological makeup. An arm that is hysterically paralysed will, in all likelihood, be paralysed from a joint – shoulder, elbow, or wrist – rather than from muscular groupings as would occur in the case of physical injury. The hysteric's symptoms approximate what a culture and individuals conceive anatomy to be, rather than what it is. The anorexic's body-image as overweight is structured in part by what is considered the 'correct weight'; the neurotic differs more in degree than kind in the radical rupture between the imaginary and physiological anatomies. Moreover, in many dreams there is evidence of the pre-oedipal body-image, particularly in dreams about the dissolution of bodily unity and control. The body is often divided or 'fragilized' along lines of pre-oedipal significance, with organs appearing in odd places and unusual arrangements.

> Such typical images appear in dreams, as well as in fantasies. They may show, for example, the body of the mother as having a mosaic structure like that of a stained glass window. More often, the resemblance is to a jig-saw puzzle, with the separate parts of the body of a man or animal in disorderly array. Even more significant for our purposes are the incongruous images in which disjointed limbs are rearranged as strange trophies; trunks cut up in slices and stuffed with the most unlikely fillings, strange appendages in eccentric positions, reduplications of the penis, images of the cloaca represented as a surgical excision, often accompanied in male patients by fantasies of pregnancy. (Lacan 1953: 13)

The ego regresses to its earliest phases in some dreams. Its fragmentation is represented through hallucinatory reactivation of memory traces, especially of the body and its fragmenting impulses. There is always the possibility of the subject's collapse back into the chaos out of which it was formed, given the ego is thus a libidinal repository made up of the internalized images of others, including its own body. The ego can thus be seen as an intrasubjective relation founded on inter-subjectivity. It is the coagulation and residue of internalized images of others.

The structure of the imaginary body-image is the result of a number of principles, as Schilder argues, including the following:
1   the body-image is a function of libidinal cathexes, which circulate through the child's body. These are particularly concentrated in the erotogenic zones (mouth, anus, genitals, eyes, ears), and at points of greatest contact between the introceptive sensations and extroceptive perceptions – in the hands, especially the fingers, the feet, the face, the orifices, and the skin's surface;
2   the body-schema has a relation to organic and biological functions. Thus the amputation of limbs, lesions, and organic disorders create the possibility of a 'somatic compliance' with psychic meanings, enabling afflicted areas/zones to take on hysterical characteristics and meanings by deferred action: hysterogenic zones rely on the imaginary anatomy;
3   the corporeal schema is the result also of the internalization of the corporeal schema of others (the nurturer in particular). The body-image of others is of major significance in the transmission of gestural and postural schema – explaining perhaps the tendency of close friends or family to share body-habits;
4   the body-image is an effect of the highly particular, indeed, idiosyncratic meanings with which bodies have been endowed within the confines of the nuclear family;
5   neither mind nor body, neither purely individual nor purely social, neither natural nor cultural, the body-image is a *threshold* term, undecidably occupying both positions.

Relations between self and other thus govern the *imaginary order*. This is the domain in which the self is dominated by images of the other and seeks its identity in a reflected relation with alterity. Imaginary relations are thus two-person relations, where the self sees itself reflected in the other. This dual, imaginary relation – usually identified with the pre-oedipal mother-child relationship – although structurally necessary, is an ultimately stifling and unproductive relation. The dual relationship between mother and child is a dyad trapping both participants within a mutually defining structure. Each strives to have the other, an ultimately, to *be* the other in a vertiginous spiral from one term or identity to the other. In Lacan's view, this is an effect, ultimately, of the child's biological prematurity and dependence on the mother. He refuses to understand its constricting force as a product of a specifically patriarchal containment of women in maternity, which supposedly satisfies all their desires but gives women no autonomy as women. Therein lies the limit of imaginary identifications. There is no way out of the vacillation between two positions and the identification of each with the other ('s desire). Each strives to fill the impossible lack in/of the other. The *I* truly is an other.

The dual imaginary relation needs to be symbolically regulated or mediated. This occurs with the help of a term outside this dual structure, a third position beyond the mother-child dyad. This 'third term' is the Father; not the real, or rather, the imaginary father, who is a person, an other, to whom the child may relate. The imaginary father usually takes on the symbolic function of law, but in any case these laws and prohibitions must be culturally represented or embodied for the child by some authority figure. It is generally the father who takes on the role of (symbolic) castrator and the Name-of-the-Father.[11]

Through the 'name-of-the-father', the child is positioned beyond the structure of dual imaginary relations within the broader framework of culture, where genuine exchange may become possible (exchange requires the third term, the object exchanged between the subject and the other). However, the resolution of the oedipus complex or the assumption of the name-of-the-father, is rarely if ever entirely successful. The imaginary returns, being only partially or unsuccessfully repressed, resurfacing in both pathological and 'normal' forms in adult life as symptoms, dreams, and amorous relations, in those relations where the self strives to see itself in the other.

Summary

The ego is split, internally divided between self and other. It can represent the person as a whole (as in the realist view) only in so far as it denies this internal rupture and conceives of itself as the source of its own origin and unity. It maintains an active, aggressive, and libidinal relation to the other on whom it depends. It comes to distinguish itself as subject from its own body, over which it establishes a hierarchical distance and control. It gains from, as well as loses itself in, the other. It develops a paranoiac relation to what it knows, for what it knows is bound up with the order of images, the domain of the ego, and not the Real. Self-knowledge, indeed, the identity of the speaker and object spoken about – autobio-graphy – are no longer possible.[12]

To sum up the key elements of Lacan's account of the mirror stage:

1 it marks the child's first recognition of lack or absence;

2 it signals the moment of the child's recognition of the distinction between self and other;

3 it represents the child's first concerted attempts to fill the lack by identifying with its own specular image;

4 the specular image is a totalized, complete, external image – a *gestalt* – of the subject, the subject as seen from outside;

5 the visual *gestalt* is in conflict with the child's fragmentary, disorganized felt reality;

6 the discordance of the visual *gestalt* with the subject's perceived reality means that the specular image remains both a literal image of itself and an idealized representation, more complete than it feels. The mirror-image thus provides the ground for the *ego ideal,* the image of the ego, derived from others, which the ego strives to achieve or live up to;

7 the specular image positions the child within a (perspectivally organized) spatial field, and, more particularly, within the body, which is located as a central point within this field;

8 the mirror stage initiates the child into the two-person structure of imaginary identifications, orienting it forever towards identifica-tion with and dependence on (human) images and representations for its own forms or outline;

9 the ego can be seen as the sedimentation of images of others which are libidinally invested, through narcissism, by being internalized;

10 the ego does not uphold *reality* to the demands of the id; it systematically misrecognizes reality.

In this outline, Lacan displaces the ego as the central and most secure component of the individual, unsettling the presumptions of a fixed, unified, or natural core of identity, and the subject's capacity to know itself and the world. The certainty the subject brings with it in its claims to knowledge is not, as Descartes argued, a guaranteed or secure foundation for knowledge. It is a function of the *investment* the ego has in maintaining certain images which please it. Rather than a direct relation of recognition of reality, the ego only retains a pre-medi(t)ated, i.e., imaginary or precon-structed, Real.

Lacan's conception of the ego as *inherently* alienated has had considerable critical effect on any theory that presupposes Cartesian or post-Cartesian views about the subject and its role in the production of knowledges. Perhaps more than Lacan, the implications of the psychoanalytic notion of subjectivity for other branches of western knowledges have been spelled out in the work of Julia Kristeva and Luce Irigaray, as we will see. Relying heavily on Lacan's understanding of the ego, and its modes of denial of the unconscious, they point to a series of underlying assumptions governing the structure of knowledges. Kristeva focuses on linguistics and literary theory, but it is clear that her arguments apply equally to most other social sciences, if not the natural sciences. Irigaray directs her claims to the discipline of philosophy. Both claim that literary and linguistic theory presuppose an unproblematic pre-constituted subject – the speaking/writing subject – who is simply presumed as a knowing subject.

Attempts to universalize and naturalize the subject, taking the modern, forms of western (male) individual as norm, characterize most contemporary science. But if, as Lacan argues, the subject is constituted as such by processes of internalization, introjection, projection, and identification, then there cannot be a universal, general subject, but only concrete, specific subjects who are produced within a concrete socio-symbolic and family structure. In order to make this clear, the psychoanalytic account of oedipal processes and the unconscious produced by its resolution need to be elaborated. This will be discussed in chapters 3 and 4.

3

Sexuality and the symbolic order

The imaginary represents the child's earliest entry into social life. Through an intense, mutually defining relation with the mother, the child gradually understands that it is distinct from her, and has an identity of its own, an identity which is fundamentally alienated. The child is constituted as a libidinal subject and confined to the limits of its body through the establishment of the ego. Its identity is thus always incomplete, dependent on the other. The other is thus not simply an external, independent other, but the internal condition of identity, the core of the self.

The ego or sense of self – which Lacan designates as a *moi*, a me, the self as object/other – is precipitated in a game (*le jeu*), through which an I (*je*), that is, the self as subject, is formed. The game of mirror-doubles is the child's attempt to master its own lack (the absence of a fixed or given identity) through a libidinal investment in its own specular image. While prerequisite to the child's acquisition of a social place independent of the family, the identificatory structure of narcissism does not adequately account for the child's social and symbolic construction. The mirror stage positions the child within a physical, psychical, and familial space, but it does not empower the child to act as an agent or subject in a larger linguistic and economic community. In other words, while the child remains bound to the other as its *double*, it cannot participate in social or symbolic exchange with others.

If left to itself, the mother-child relation would entail a vicious cycle of imaginary projections, identifications, internalizations, fantasies, and demands that leave no room for development or growth. Lacan claims that if the child and mother form an enclosed, mutually defined relation, relations with a third, independent term become impossible. (This may be what Guillaume and others have described as the 'eighth month anxiety syndrome'.)[1] The unmediated two-person structure of imaginary identifications leaves only two possibilities for the child, between which it vacillates but cannot definitively choose: being overwhelmed by the other, crowded out, taken over (the fantasy of the devouring mother/voracious child); and the wretched isolation and abandonment of all self-worth by the other's absence or neglect (the fantasy of the bad or selfish mother/child).

I will examine Lacan's account of the child's acquisition of a symbolic, and thus a social, verbal, and economic, position within culture. This will involve outlining Freud's concept of the oedipus complex, and Lacan's hypothesis of the socially regulatory function of the name-of-the-father. As a starting point, we need to turn to Freud's account of the genesis of sexual drives in the pre-oedipal phase, and then to the ways in which the oedipus complex regulates, orders, and represses them. In describing the constitution of the sexual drive in infantile life, I will be describing modes of social inscription and regulation which construct a subject adequate to the requirements of social production and organization. Oedipalization will ensure the production of a socially functional and sexually differentiated individual, whose behaviour and desires are regulated by the dictates of conscience and whose energies are directed to socially valued outlets. Lacan's understanding of the name-of-the-father, on which the child's entry into the symbolic order depends, is a reading and rewriting of Freud's oedipal model in linguistic and socio-cultural terms.

Freud's two theories of sexuality

Freud developed two quite different accounts of the development of infantile sexuality. Unlike his two views on the ego, however, they can be located in two distinct periods of his writing, and, in this case, there is a clear indication that Freud meant one to supersede the other. These two accounts of infantile sexuality can be called the seduction theory and the oedipal theory.[2] The first posits the intrusion of an external, alien sexuality which initiates the child (usually 'prematurely') into adult forms of sexuality; the second is a developmental and quasi-biological account of the various infantile stages of endogenous sexual maturation. Both remain problematic as they stand; moreover, controversy surrounds Freud's motives in moving from one account to the other.[3] Nevertheless, it is at the intersection of these two views that Lacan develops his own understanding of the acquisition of social identity and a speaking position.

In the *Studies on Hysteria* (1893–5), Freud and Breuer demonstrated that there is a connection between psychical trauma and neurotic defence. A psychical trauma, 'any experience which calls

51

up distressing affect – such as those of fright, anxiety, shame, or physical pain . . . ' (1895: 6), is the catalyst for the appearance of neurasthenic, hysterical or obsessional symptoms. Freud does not claim that the trauma *causes* the symptom; rather, it acts as an irritant, a 'foreign body', an 'invading alien', utilizing the invaded body's own defensive responses. These may overdetermine the appearance of symptoms but they do not explain them.

He claims that an intolerable idea or experience confronts the subject from outside. As a result of defensive processes, the idea or memory is repressed – that is, it is rendered incompatible with the subject's other conscious ideas and is thus separated off from them. The unacceptable idea, however, accumulates other ideas around it. This means that

> For the first time there comes into being a nucleus and centre of crystallisation for the formation of a psychical group divorced from the ego – a group around which everything which would imply an acceptance of the incompatible idea subsequently collects. (ibid.: 123)

The traumatic idea remains unintegrated into consciousness, existing in a kind of preconscious zone (prefiguring Freud's later notion of the unconscious). Its effect is not immediate, but delayed or deferred. The seduction theory supposes that only a sexual trauma activates repression and the subsequent appearance of hysterical symptoms. The aetiology of neurotic symptoms is thus considered to date from the act of (unsuccessful) 'repression' of a sexual trauma.

In *The Project* Freud develops the theory that hysterical repression results in a 'symbol-formation', capable of representing the trauma or seduction. He elaborates this with the help of an enigmatically brief case study of Emma:

> Emma is subject at the present time to a compulsion of not being able to go to shops *alone* [agoraphobia]. As a reason for this she produced a memory from the time when she was 12 years old (shortly after puberty). She went into a shop to buy something, saw the two shop-assistants (one of whom she can remember) laughing together and ran away in some kind of *affect of fright*. In connection with this, she was led to recall that the two men were laughing at her clothes and that one of them had pleased her sexually . . .
>
> On two occasions when she was a child of eight she had gone into a shop to buy sweets and the shopkeeper had grabbed at her genitals through her clothes . . . (Freud 1895: 353–4)

Emma's neurotic symptoms are a consequence of two scenes. The first occurred when she was eight; it is a scene of 'seduction' or rather, sexual attack. An innocent child is 'seduced' or attacked by a sexually mature adult. This first scene is not necessarily considered sexual *by the child*, given her (or less frequently, his) sexual naivety and lack of understanding. Nor does it provoke a traumatic response at the time of its occurrence. As Freud suggests in a letter to Fliess, 'Although sexual in terms of objectivity, it has no sexual connotation for the subject, it is "presexually sexual" ' (Letter 30, quoted by Laplanche and Pontalis 1968: 4).

The second scene, when she is twelve, occurs after the onset of puberty, and is in no way traumatic. Nothing happens in this scene that could constitute a trauma. It is related to the first scene by two seemingly trivial similarities – 'laughter' and 'clothes'. It is only after this second scene that her symptom appears. The second scene provokes a traumatic reaction only because it has the power to retroactively recall the first scene. In short, intervening at some time between the first and second scene, the child comes to know, or be able to understand, the *meaning* of the first scene. The memory of this scene has been repressed or removed from consciousness. When the second scene occurs, and recalls the first, the child reacts retrospectively to the latter's *meaning*. The intervention of the processes of sexual maturation associated with puberty intensifies and makes meaningful an event which had little or no meaning at the time of its occurrence, and which remained dormant until the second reactivated it or provided it with an innocuous mode of expression.

Clearly there are serious problems with this account. Freud himself recognized in *The Three Essays* (1905) that he had assumed a non-sexual infant. He presumed that the onset of puberty led to a new *biologically ordained* sexuality, but neglected infantile (i.e. oedipal and pre-oedipal) factors in the aetiology of the neuroses. He gradually abandons this theory over the next five years to replace it with the developmental account, where sexuality arises 'spontaneously, from internal causes' (1905: 190–1). In spite of abandoning the seduction theory, he continues to refer to the psychical reality of seduction in the aetiology of the neuroses. Now, however, it takes on a contingent rather than a necessary status. (In analysing the Wolf-Man twenty years later, Freud again invokes a sexual trauma – in this case, witnessing the 'primal scene' when he was eighteen months old – coupled with a second scene, his sister's 'seduction' of him when he was three and a quarter in the aetiology of his phobia (1918).)

Freud sets out the reasons why he gives up the hypothesis of sexual seduction in Letter 69 to Fliess written in 1897. First, he claims that the hypothesis of a trauma as a real event has not effectively explained the symptom. He came to believe that 'what we are faced with is a falsification of memory and phantasy' (1892–9: 258). From 1897 on he regarded seduction not so much as a real event as a wished-for or fantasized one. Second, Freud argues that he is not prepared to accept the overwhelming, indeed near universal, perversion of fathers, to whom seduction is usually attributed. Third, he argues that unconscious memories carry no index of the veracity or truth of their contents. A memory may have originated either as a perception or as a wish. The unconscious cannot distinguish between fantasies and 'real events' in so far as wishes have as much force as 'real' events in the subject's psychical life. Fourth, he recognizes that in the most severe, psychotic cases, where one would expect a particularly powerful traumatic event, there appeared little evidence of sexual seduction.

Freud writes to Fliess in 1897 that 'I no longer believe in my neurotica . . . ', thus 'officially' abandoning the seduction theory to replace it with an early account of infantile sexuality. By 15 October, he had begun the first outline of what would become the theory of the oedipus complex. He claims that 'I have found, in my own case too, falling in love with the mother and jealousy of the father, and I now regard it as a universal event of early childhood' (1892–9: 265). His account of the development of sexuality thus dramatically shifts from a sexuality imposed from outside by a sexually threatening adult (usually a father, uncle, or brother); to an account of a sexual desire emanating from the child who fantasizes or desires seduction, albeit in infantile terms. This is not quite a shift from 'reality' to 'fantasy', nor from adult to infantile; for reality is not clearly separable from fantasy in this definitive way (see Freud's paper 'Screen Memories' (1899)), nor is the child, even in the earlier seduction theory, as naive or ignorant as it may seem. Even so, there has been much speculation regarding the motivation for Freud's reorientation, suggesting an (unconscious) evasion on his part: when being a son is less significant than being a father, he shifts orientation from the father to the son.

The Three Essays represents Freud's most clearly elaborated developmental account of infantile sexuality. His analysis is primarily, though not exclusively, directed by biological and universal considerations. Sexuality can also, secondarily, be seen as a function of social and educative practices:

> In reality this development is organically determined and fixed
> by heredity . . . it can occasionally occur without any help at all

from education. Education will not be trespassing beyond its appropriate domain if it limits itself to following the lines which have already been laid down organically and to impressing them somewhat more clearly and deeply. (1905: 178)

His account here implies a developmental unfolding of infantile psycho-sexual stages, which successively follow each other: oral drives give way to the primacy of anal drives, which in turn give way to phallic impulses, and so on in a series of universal, biologicially regulated phases. Biological stages can thus generate a series of norms, ideals, or goals directed towards the end of heterosexual genital and reproductive sexuality.

For Freud, the oral stage consists in a process of rhythmical repetition or mimicry of the processes of sucking and incorporation of the nutritive object, milk. In the first instance, oral pleasure is derived from the instinct for nourishment. In its *instinctual* form, sucking takes milk as its object, and ingestion and incorporation as its aim; its goal is the quelling of the unpleasure generated by the sensations of emptiness or hunger and its replacement by satisfaction, for a time at least.

It was the child's first and most vital activity, his sucking at his mother's breast, or at substitutes for it, that must have familiarised him with this pleasure . . . To begin with, sexual activity attaches itself to functions serving the purpose of self-preservation and does not become independent of them until later. No-one who has seen a baby sinking back satiated from the breast and falling asleep with flushed cheeks and a blissful smile can escape the reflection that this picture persists as a prototype of the expression of sexual satisfaction in later life. (ibid.: 181–2)

While oral pleasure originates in sensations of satisfaction provoked by milk which gratify the hunger instinct, it should not be identified with such purely instinctual, processes. On the contrary, what seems threatening about Freud's account is the fact that the oral drive is determined by biology only in its outlines and at its limits. The physiological maturity and control over the operations of oral, alimentary, bowel, sphincter, and bladder muscles and organs provide the preconditions of the emergence of the infantile psycho-sexual drives, but do not cause them. The drives (in Freud's German text, *trieb*) are a deviation of the (natural) instinct (for Freud, *instinkt*; cf. Strachey's introduction to 'Instincts and their vicissitudes', 1914b; see also Laplanche 1976, chapters 1 and 2). The emergence of erotic and libidinal relations from self-preservative instincts is a function of *lack* or *absence,* the lack or absence of a given or predetermined object. Such a lack would be intolerable and constitute a life-endangering denial in the case of an instinct-proper; yet it is the precondition of the drive.

It is only at a time when the child is capable of recognizing the absence of the breast or mother – at the time of the mirror stage – at around six months – that the phenomenon Freud describes as 'sensual sucking' or orality, the first *sexual* stage, emerges.

> the sexual instinct has a sexual object outside the infant's own body in the shape of the mother's breast. It is only later that he loses it, just at a time perhaps, when he is able to form a total idea of the person to whom the organ that is giving him satisfaction belongs. As a rule, the sexual drive *then* becomes auto-erotic . . . The finding of an object is in fact the re-finding of it. (1905: 222)

The drive is distinguished from earlier (instinctual) oral needs by its object. In the case of the oral sexual drive, it is not milk so much as the process of sucking that gives the child pleasure. It is distinguished from hunger by its indifference to or playfulness with nourishment.

Freud presents three defining features of sensual sucking: 'At its origin it attaches itself to one of the vital somatic functions; it has as yet no sexual object, and is thus auto-erotic; and its sexual aim is dominated by an erotogenic zone' (ibid.: 182–3). The instincts ('vital somatic functions') provide the grounds or traces for a series of neuronal pathways traversing the body which will later mark out the pathway of impulses facilitated by the drive. The drive is, as it were, a second-order system based on first-order instincts. The drive is not simply a psychical reflection of or delegate for a biological instinct (this would ensure the drive is as rigidly unchangeable as any instinct). The drive is based on a corporeal mimicry of the instinct. According to Laplanche (1976), the drive is propped up on or supported by the instinct. It is impossible to ascertain at what point the instinct ends and the drive 'begins': the defining features of all drives – aim, object, source, and pressure (see Freud 1915b) – are difficult to distinguish from their instinctual antecedents because there is a fundamental ambiguity at the level of their aims and objects in the child's acquisition of oral (and anal, and genital) pleasures.

The object to which the hunger instinct is directed is milk; the object of the oral drive, in the first instance, is the breast – which is metonymically linked to milk. The drive borrows the sites, sources, and techniques of satisfaction generated by instincts to develop its own modes of (sexual) satisfaction. Once the digestive system, for example, has demonstrated its usefulness to the drive, any aspect of the biological process may be utilized sexually, to express the subject's desires. This is why oral neuroses like anorexia nervosa or globus hystericus are the results of the hystericization or sexualization of what was once (but is no longer) a biological, or Real, process.

Infantile sexuality in all its forms is localized in particular regions of the body – the erotogenic zones – including mouth, anus, penis or clitoris, eyes, etc. The corporeal sites or sources from which erotic drives emanate are thus psychically privileged. As well as the usual sexual zones, Freud also includes as potential sexual zones the cutaneous-mucous layering of the orifices, the entire surface of the skin, the internal organs, and even the processes of mental functioning or thought: 'After further reflection and after taking observations into account, I am led to ascribe the quality of erotogenicity to all parts of the body and to all internal organs' (ibid.: 184 fn.). He claims that the drive to knowledge, the 'epistemophilic' impulse, shows that even the brain itself can function as a sexual 'organ'. In 'Leonardo da Vinci and a Memory of his Childhood' (1910), he argues that intense intellectual effort is a form of sexual excitation. This means that sexuality is not only a series of *places* or zones marked out on/in the body; it must now be understood as a mode of functioning, a rhythmical tracing that could occur in any part of the subject's body (see *Totem and Taboo* 1913: 89).

In accounting for the genesis of adult forms of sexuality from their infantile and oedipal stages, Freud moves perilously close to biological determinism. His work on infantile development is frequently couched in biological, quasi-biological, and functionalist terms. Yet if we pay careful attention to brief, sometimes obscure passages in his work, passages that are often at variance with the overall argument within which they are embedded, his work deconstructs the oppositions with which it began. Instead of deciding between a biological and an environmental explanatory model, Freud posits an environmental, or sociofamilial tracing, mapping, or mimicking of biological processes. These are infused with psychical meanings quite independent of biological functions.

At first, Freud presumed a theory of infantile development in which sexuality is imposed from outside, initiating a sexually innocent child into a new world of pleasure. His second theory is an analysis of biologically pre-structured stages that unfold with an internal logic and wishful structure that projects the child's desires onto reality. The first, seduction, theory denies the child a sexuality and desire (while recognizing the genuine disparity between adult and infantile sexual wishes); the second, developmental, theory denies a social/familial imposition on the child, seeing the child itself as the source or origin of sexual impulses. The first claims sexuality is initiated accidentally; the second that it is constitutional in origin. The differences between the two positions seem to hinge on the status of the seduction: in the seduction theory it is a literal event, a concrete empirical experience which the child passively undergoes; in the developmental account, it is a fabrication or wishful fantasy the child actively produces. Yet it is not at all clear that the distinction is as clear-cut and decisive as this: in most (but certainly not all) cases neither a literal nor a fantasized seduction occurs. Or, if there is a 'seduction', it is not the kind envisaged by either of Freud's models. In between the oppositions of real and fantasy, active and passive positions, endogenous and externally imposed development, is a third: seduction is not (usually, at least) initiated by an adult onto a naive child; nor does the child simply project its wishes onto the adult in fantasized form. Rather, the adult enacts a 'seduction' that unavoidably arises in the relations of nurture and care, corporeal contact and desire bestowed upon it by its mother or nurturer. Freud recognizes this but doesn't attempt to incorporate it as an explanatory principle in infantile sexual development:

> A mother would be horrified if she were made aware that all her marks of affection were arousing her child's instinct and preparing for its later intensity. She regards what she does as asexual, 'pure' love, since, after all, she carefully avoids applying more excitations to the child's genitals than are unavoidable in nursery care. As we know, however, the sexual instinct is not aroused only by direct excitation of the genital zone. What we call affection will unfailingly show its effects one day on the genital zone as well. Moreover if the mother understood more of the high importance of the part played by instincts in mental life as a whole – in all its ethical and psychical achievements – she would spare herself any self-reproaches even after her enlightenment. (1905: 223)

Sexuality and signification

Both of Freud's conceptions of infantile sexuality remain problematic. The seduction theory presumes the mechanical imposition of sexuality from outside the child; and the developmental theory relies on an endogenous, hydraulic model of drives, tension, release, and satisfaction. Lacan avoids these problems, while at the same time relying heavily on Freud's texts. Where Freud locates the 'germs' of sexual drives in ontogenesis, species survival, and predetermined biological development, treating sexual drives as *given*, Lacan analyses sexual drives always through the functioning of language and linguistic processes. Where Freud develops an aetiological model of sexual maturation from the child's first psychosexual impulses to adult forms of genital sexuality, Lacan rarely uses a developmental model, analysing sexuality instead as it is manifested in the transferential relation between analysand and analyst – in, that is, the data of the analysand's speech. His object is sexuality in so far as sexuality is the 'reality of the unconscious' (Lacan 1977b: 152). For Lacan, the drive cannot be regarded as *Real,* biologically determined, or natural, but is a function and effect of the field of the Other (1977b: 180). It is, in short, of the order of language and the symbolic: it is a 'sexuality in the defiles of the signifier' (see 1977b, esp. chapter 12).

Lacan asserts that the psychoanalytic notion of sexuality is radically different from everyday concepts. It is not concerned with feelings, attitudes, emotions, performance, orgasmic intensity, etc. (although these may play some role in its functioning). It is not a form of marriage guidance, counselling, or personal advice. It deals only with speech, the analysand's discourse, and the demands and desires this discourse articulates. The sexuality about which the analysand talks is in fact the sexuality or desire manifested by and hidden in language. Psychoanalysis functions to restore the analysand to his or her desire, which lies unacknowledged within his or her demands. Lacan's account of sexuality relies on a distinction between need, demand, and desire (which, incidentally, can be placed over the Freudian developmental grid).

Need, demand, and desire

Need, demand, and desire are expressions or effects of the orders of human existence Lacan defines as the Real, the imaginary, and the symbolic. These three orders are the 'raw materials' of psychoanalysis. The child's 'development' from need to demand and desire is congruous with its movement out of the Real and into the imaginary and symbolic.

Need is the experiential counterpart to nature. Need comes as close to instincts as is possible in human existence. Needs are more or less universal or constant in human life, they are the requirements of brute survival: nourishment, shelter, warmth, freedom of movement, a minimal community, and so on. They require objects whose attainment is the precondition of the individual's survival and well-being. Need requires real, tangible objects for its satisfaction. Milk, for example, satisfies the child's hunger *needs* or instincts, even if feeding must occur in cyclical movements of deprivation/hunger and satisfaction/satiation. An instinctually triggered series of impulses and behaviour, need is always in principle capable of, indeed requires, satisfaction. The child needs objects which, even if it is not able to attain them itself, can be obtained through others. The objects of need must be more or less available continuously, or at the least, with a rhythmic regularity. This (western ?) presumption of a reliable and available source of satisfaction creates habits, expectations, or patterns of need and satisfaction that enable the child, as it matures and becomes more dexterous, to gratify itself. Need, as purely natural or instinctual, is short-lived; it is rapidly overlaid by a structure of meaning and significance that envelops it in imaginary and symbolic relations, transforming it into demand and desire. When the child recognizes the absence of the mother, biological or instinctual need becomes converted into social, imaginary, and linguistic functions.

The Fort! Da! game Freud describes in *Beyond the Pleasure Principle* (1919b) represents the child's first attempt to articulate in verbal or proto-verbal form the needs it feels animating its body. Freud observed his young grandson playing a game with a cotton reel. The boy throws the reel outside his cot, uttering a sound approximating the German for 'gone' (*fort*); then, to his delight he draws it back by holding on to the thread, accompanying his actions with the term for 'here' (*da*). The child's earliest entry into verbalization is in fact closer to the articulation of a primitive binary opposition – the opposition between 'ooo' and 'aaa'. The inarticulate cry, which comes closest to representing the unspeakable need, is now specified and narrowed down by means of a binary pair of phonemes. The child symbolically represents the perceived loss of the mother by the cotton reel and, in turn, represents the cotton reel (already a representation of a representation) by the binary pair of elementary phonemes. Following Freud, Lacan interprets this as the child's attempt to control the mother's presence and absence through language, substituting a linguistic relation, which it may control, for the mother's presences and absences, which it does not control. The game converts the child's passivity into activity through language and play.

A relation of pure difference between (linguistic) signifiers, the opposition between 'ooo' and 'aaa', replaces the child's immediate or lived relation to the mother's presences and absences. Signification insinuates itself in place of the absent object, the object engendering desire. As Lacan claims, 'the symbol manifests itself first of all as the murder of the thing'. Language is substituted for the satisfaction of need, which is consequently transformed into demand. It has become fundamentally insatiable. Instead of the need, which is represented by its 'natural sign', the indeterminate cry, demand is always formulated in language. Demand takes the form of the statement, 'I want . . .' or the command 'Give me . . .'. In Lacan's understanding, the demand is always transitive for it is always directed to an other (usually the mother). By being articulated in language, a language always derived and learned from the (m)other, demand is always tied to otherness. The other to whom demand is addressed is the imaginary other, the alter-ego or double precipitated in the mirror phase. Demand articulates and thereby narrows down and specifies the amorphous need by tying it to a concrete object, thus particularizing it. It converts the need from a quasi-biological status to a linguistic, interpersonal, and social phenomenon.

Demand is able to borrow the forms of instinctual need because of its fundamental ambiguity: demand always has two objects, one spoken, the other unspoken: the object or thing demanded (this or that object), and the other to whom the demand is ostensibly addressed. The thing demanded – food, attention, a 'cure' from the analyst, the undying love of another – are all relatively insignificant, or rather, they function as excuses for access to the second object, the (m)other. The thing demanded is a rationalization for maintaining a certain relation to the other. Where need aims at an object which satisfied it, demand appeals to an other in such a way that even if the demanded object is given, there can be no satisfaction. This is because the demand is really for something else, for the next thing the other can give, for the thing that will 'prove' the other's love. Demand requires the affirmation of an ego by the other to such a degree that only an imaginary union or identification with them, an identity they share, could bring satisfaction – and only then with the annihilation of the self, for it is now invaded by and exists as the other:

> it is in the oldest demand that the primary identification is produced, that which is brought about by the mother's omnipotence, that is to say, the identification that not only *suspends the satisfaction of needs* from the signifying apparatus, but also that which fragments them, filters them, models them upon the defiles of the structure of the signifier.
>
> Needs become subordinated to the same conventional conditions as those of the signifier in its double register: the

synchronic register of opposition between irreducible elements, and the diachronic register of substitution and combination, through which language, even if it does not fulfil all functions, structures everything concerning relations between human beings. (Lacan 1977a: 255)

Demand enshrouds the various objects of the need's satisfaction, using them as the basis for a battery of signifiers which can now be fired, directed to the other who provides for the need's satisfaction. These objects (food, warmth, movement, etc.) can be pointed to, articulated and specified. But when they become bound up with the order of language, they veer off from their appetitive or instinctual function to acquire social meanings and thus act as messages directed to or received from the other. As demand, they form a circuit to and from the (m)other.

The child thus addresses a series of demands to the mother. She may respond to them with a variety of specified objects, but none will satisfy the child's wants. One demanded toy, for example, is rapidly replaced by another, and the entire list of substitute objects is ultimately unsatisfying. The child wants everything, an impossible plenitude; it wants to be filled by the other, to *be* the other, which is why no determinate thing will do. It demands a love that paradoxically entails its own annihilation, for it demands a fullness of the other to stop up the lack that conditions its existence as a subject:

[The subject] . . . is also the locus of this want, or lack. That which is given to the Other to fill, and which is strictly that which it does not have, since it too lacks being, is what is called love, but which is also hate and ignorance. It is also what is evoked by any demand beyond the need that is articulated in it, and it is certainly that of which the subject remains all the more deprived to the extent that the need articulated in the demand is satisfied. (1977a: 263)

Demand is the consequence of the subjection of the need to the regulation of language. The transcription of the need into a dyadic and (proto-)personal or interpersonal register, transforms it and brings it into the structure of demand. As a result, a (metonymic) chain of objects, substitutable for each other, stand as signifiers of the other's desire. Needs, even instinctual ones, can be deferred, displaced, or even abandoned (leading in some cases to death – for example, in anorexia). The object of demand is always *an imaginary object*. It lacks a tangible form and the organization or regularity of the object of 'natural' need. Demand functions on a conscious level, yet it exists in a limbo region where the subject is neither fully animal (natural need is alienated by its articulation) nor fully human (not yet regulated by and positioned within a signifying and social order):

> [The signifier] . . . proceed[s] from a deviation of man's needs from the fact that he speaks, in the sense that in so far as his needs are subjected to demand, they return to him alienated. This is not the effect of his real dependence . . . but rather the turning into signifying form as such, from the fact that it is from the locus of the Other that its message is emitted.
>
> . . . Demand in itself bears on something other than the satisfaction it calls for. It is demand of a presence or of an absence – which is what is manifested in the primordial relation to the mother, pregnant with that Other to be situated *within* the needs that it can satisfy. Demand constitutes the Other as already possessing the 'privilege' of satisfying needs, that is to say, the power of depriving them of that alone by which they are satisfied. This privilege of the Other thus outlines the radical form of the gift of that which the Other does not have, namely, its love.
>
> In this way, demand annuls *(aufhebt)* the particularity of everything that can be granted by transmuting it into a proof of love, and the very satisfactions that it obtains for need are reduced *(sich erniedrigt)* to the level of being no more that the crushing of the demand for love . . . (1977a: 286)

Demand is thus addressed to the (pre-oedipal, phallic) (m)other. It is insatiable, a correlate and function of the mother's phallic, omnipotent position *vis-à-vis* the child. Demand is the result of the ego's self-idealization and aggrandisement – a measure of the magnitude of the ego-ideal (the psychic double or ideal of otherness to which the ego aspires). Demand always addresses an other. It consciously demands concrete, particular objects. The only 'things' capable of satisfying it are generalities or absolutes (ultimately, it is a demand for *everything)* which, in the end, boils down to nothing. Need or instinct is robbed of the security of its access to a given object of satisfaction, and is subjected to the 'defilements' of signification. Demand is the effect of the association of signifying relations with a sexual drive or impulse, a coupling of libidinal cathexis, and a series of signifiers (which, however, can never adequately represent the drive's somatic force):

> Psychoanalysis touches on sexuality only as much as in the form of the drive, it manifests itself in the defile of the signifier, in

which is constituted the dialectic of the subject in the double stage of alienation and separation. (Lacan, quoted by Macey 1978: 122)

The demand for food is not simply the demand for satisfaction of nutritive need. It is also a demand for *love*. The demand operates in the interplay of the demanded object, and the other who, in delivering up the object, affirms the subject as loved. This may explain why the anorexic, in functioning in the oral register, demands the *positive presence* of the absence of food: she demands 'no thing', 'no food'.

If need is a function of the Real and demand is a product of imaginary identifications, the third term in Lacan's libidinal trilogy is *desire*, the symbolic 'equivalent' or counterpart of need and demand. Rather than rely simply on Freud's two basic views of erotic desire, libido, and the structure of the wish just outlined, Lacan derives his conception of desire from Hegel, particularly from *The Phenomenology of Spirit,*[4] where Hegel posits desire as a lack and absence. Desire is a fundamental lack, a hole in being that can be satisfied only by one 'thing' – another('s) desire. Each self-conscious subject desires the desire of the other as its object. Its desire is to be desired by the other, its counterpart. Following Hegel, Lacan assumes a concept of desire as the *difference* or gap separating need from demand. Desire participates in elements of both need and demand: it re-establishes the specificity and con-creteness of the satisfaction of *need;* while it participates in demand's orientation to the other:

> It is necessary . . . that the particularity [of need] . . . abolished [by the demand] reappear *beyond* demand. It does, in fact, reappear there, but preserving the structure contained in the unconditional element of the demand for love . . . For the unconditional element of the demand, desire substitutes the 'absolute' condition: this condition unties the knot of that element in the proof of love that is resistant to the satisfaction of a need. Thus desire is neither the appetite for satisfaction, nor the demand for love, but the difference that results from the subtraction of the first from the second, the phenomenon of their splitting. (ibid.: 287)

Like both need and demand, desire exhibits the structure of the wish; it is based on the absence or privation of its object. Like demand, it preserves an absolute or unconditional element and an orientation towards the other. In opposition to demand (and in accordance with need), desire is beyond conscious articulation, for it is barred or repressed from articulation. It is structured like a language, but is never spoken as such by the subject. Its production through repression is one of the constitutive marks of the unconscious, upon which it bestows its signifying effects. Desire undermines conscious activity; it speaks through demand, operating as its underside or margin:

> desire is situated in dependence on demand – which, by being articulated in signifiers, leaves a metonymic remainder that runs under it, an element that is not indeterminable, which is the condition of both, absolute and unapprehensible, an element necessarily lacking, unsatisfied, impossible, misconstrued, an element that is called desire. (1977b: 154)

In spite of Lacan's disdain for the unifying function of the dialectic, which supersedes contradictions in a higher order unity, his notion of desire is remarkably close to that of Hegel. For Hegel, desire requires mediation. It is intrinsically inter-subjective. Consciousness desires the desire of another to constitute it as self-conscious. Desire desires the desire of an other. Desire is thus a movement, an energy that is always transpersonal, directed to others:

> It must be posited that, as a fact of an animal at the mercy of language, man's desire is the desire of the Other. [This formulation] concerns a quite different function from that of the primary identification . . . for it does not involve the assumption by the subject of the *insignia* of the other, but rather the conditions that the subject has to find the constituting structure of his desire in the same gap opened up by the effect of the signifiers in those who come to represent the Other for him, in so far as his demand is subjected to them. (Lacan 1977a: 264)

Demand attempts to guarantee the ego its self-certainty and self-knowledge. Because it is directed to others who can either comply with or refuse to satisfy it, it is submitted to an interpersonal and familial pressure that prefigures social morality and the norms governing the superego. It is thus proto-social, for the other is the child's first point of access to the social. Desire threatens to subvert the unity and certainty of conscious demand. As unconscious, desire cares little for social approval or the rewards and punishments consciousness offers to demand. Desire is concerned only with its own processes, pleasures, and internal logic, a logic of the signifier. While such a logic can support social laws and values, it is also able to subvert or betray them, based as it is on expelled, socially inappropriate, repressed wishes.

The indeterminate need which can be satisfied by a wide variety of socially specified objects, is alienated in being formulated as demand. The element of need that is articulated becomes the designated object of demand; and the remainder or residue left over from this articulation is subjected to a primal repression, a founding repression that constitutes the unconscious as such (see Freud 1915b). Primal repression is not the obliteration of articulation, but rather a particular kind of articulation by means of a signifier whose relations to other signifiers, and to the discourse of consciousness, is carefully regulated and controlled. Primal repression fixes a drive to a signifier or representation which acts as its delegate in the functioning or expression of the unconscious. Primally repressed wishes reappear in and as unconscious desire, preserved in a timeless unchangeable limbo where they are rendered relatively inactive in conscious life:

> Desire is produced in the beyond of the demand in that, in articulating the life of the subject according to its conditions, demand cuts off the need from that life. But desire is also hollowed within the demand, in that, as an unconditional demand of presence and absence, demand evokes the want-to-be under the three figures of the nothing that constitutes the basis of the demand for love, of the hate that even denies the other's being, and of the unspeakable element in that which is ignored in its request. (Lacan 1977a: 265)

Demand is a verbalization of imaginary subject-object, self-other relations. Desire opens the subject to a broader world of signification or infinite semiosis: a world in which it has access to systems of meaning unregulated by any individual or group, and unrestricted in the range of its possible messages. Desire thus institutes a new relation to and in language. Demand initiates the child into the categories and terms of discourse, but it does not position the subject in a stable enunciative position as a speaker or discursive 'I'. In regulating its primitive entry into language and coupling this with the mechanism of repression, desire marks the child's entry into the domain of the Other – the domain of law and language, law-as-language. The symbolic is the domain or order of the signifier's primacy over the subject:

> Desire begins to take shape in the margin in which demand becomes separated from need: this margin begins that which is opened up by demand, the appeal of which can be unconditional only in regard to the Other . . . A margin which, linear as it may be, reveals a vertigo, even if it is not trampled by the

elephantine feet of the Other's whim. Nevertheless, it is this whim that introduces the phantom of the Omnipotence, not of the subject, but of the Other in which his demand is installed . . . and with this phantom, the need for it to be checked by the Law. (Lacan 1977a: 311)

Like demand, desire is in principle insatiable. It is always an effect of the Other, an 'other' with whom it cannot engage, in so far as the Other is not a person but a place, the locus of law, language, and the symbolic. The child must find his or her place within this order to become a speaking being. Indeed, as far as Lacan is concerned, the relation between desire and language constitute the twin axes of psychoanalytic interpretation. Together they serve to locate the subject as *split* and divided, a being who fades in the unfolding of discourse:

> it is only through a speech that lifted the prohibition that the subject has brought to bear upon himself by his own words that he might obtain the absolution that would give him back his desire.
> But desire is simply the impossibility of such speech, which, in replying to the first can merely reduplicate its mark of prohibition by completing the split which the subject undergoes by virtue of being a subject only in so far as he speaks. (ibid.: 269)

Desire is an effect of language and the unconscious. The lack (of object, in representation) characterizing desire is based on the lack, conditioning the chain of signification which Saussure defined as *langue,* the general structure of language. This will be further elaborated in chapter 4. Desire is the *reality* of the unconscious, the way in which the unconscious and sexuality have become coextensive: 'The function of desire is a last residuum of the effect of the signifier in the subject. *Desidero* is the Freudian *cogito*' (1977b: 154).

Oedipus, the name-of-the-father, and the Other

The dual imaginary mother/child relation is bound up with a narcissistic structure of mutual identifications. Each defines the identity of the other in a closed circuit. This relation does not provide the conditions for social, linguistic, and economic exchange relations, although it provides some of their preconditions. The imaginary is the order of demand and appropriation: exchange is not possible between two individuals for whom there is no third term. In order for the dyadic structure to give way to the plurality constituting the symbolic order, the narcissistic couple must be submitted to symbolic regulation. Within the confines of the nuclear family, this order is initiated by a third family member – the father – who most easily (because, presumably, of his frequent absence from day-to-day nurturing rather than from any biological necessity) can represent law, order, and authority for the child. It is not, however, the *real* or genetic father, but the *imaginary father* who acts as an incarnation or delegate of the *Symbolic Father*. In the case of his absence or failure to take up the Symbolic function, other authority figures – the teacher, headmaster, policeman, or ultimately, God, – may take his place in instilling in the child the sense of lawfulness and willing submission to social customs.

Freud described the father's (construed or real) intervention into the mother-child relation as 'the oedipus complex'. The father regulates the child's demands and its access to the mother by prohibiting (sexual) access to her. The boy perceives his father as a potential castrator, an (unbeatable) rival for the mother's affections and attentions. He construes the father's (or mother's) prohibitions as castration threats, and these eventually lead him to renounce his desire of the mother because of his fear of the organ's loss, i.e., because of the father's authority and power as 'possessor' of the phallus. This renunciation is only temporary; he gives up the mother in exchange for the promise (a 'pact' between father and son) of deferred satisfaction with a woman of his own. This pact, in other words, founds patriarchy anew for each generation, guaranteeing the son a position as heir to the father's position in so far as he takes on the father's attributes. In exchange for sacrificing his relation to the mother, whom he now recognizes as 'castrated', the boy identifies with the authority invested in the father. He internalizes the symbolic father's authority to form the superego, by means of which he 'shatters' his oedipal attachment by repressing his desire. This founds the unconscious through the act of primal repression. A metaphoric relation between father and son is instituted, for the boy must be like his father (i.e., acquire the characteristics of masculinity the father represents) while also *not* being like him (by not desiring the woman the father desires).[5] This may explain why, instead of resting the power of the complex on the personage of the father, Lacan speaks of the 'paternal metaphor' or 'the name-of-the-father'. The father with whom Lacan is concerned is the father Freud invokes in *Totem and Taboo* (1912–13) as the 'dead father', the 'father of individual prehistory', whose death leads to the prohibition of incest. The real father's authority is never so strong as in his absence or death. The dead father, murdered by the primal fraternal horde, founds an inexorable law, more powerful and effective than his supervising presence: 'if this murder [of the father] is the fruitful moment of the debt through which the subject binds himself for life to the Law . . . the symbolic father, in so far as he signifies this Law, is certainly the dead Father' (Lacan 1977a: 199).

We must leave aside for the moment the status of Freud's 'primal myth', which he believes provides a reconstruction of the origins of patriarchy. It is significant that this myth does not in fact explain patriarchy, for it already presupposes it. For the father to have control of all the women, for the sons to be dominated by him, patriarchy must already exist. One must postulate an earlier 'event' at the origin of patriarchy which explains the father's pre-eminent position. This is less likely to be a parricide than a matricide: the authority of fathers is already symbolic in so far as paternity remains uncertain and requires representation. The father's authority over women and children is a consequence of his usurpation of the immediacy of the mother's ('umbilical') authority over the child. His name and law supplant the blood and matter of the mother's connection to the child.

The Freudian/Lacanian framework is more problematic and less plausible in describing the 'corresponding' processes of oedipalization for the girl. For Freud, the girl's oedipus complex is structurally different from and complementary to that of the boy. For her, the oedipus complex involves no rewards, no authority, no compensation for her abandonment of the mother; rather, it entails her acceptance of her subordination. It involves the 'discovery' that what the boy has been threatened with – castration – has already taken place in the girl. He believes that she and the mother are castrated. In her 'recognition' of her narcissistic inadequacy, the girl abandons the mother as a love-object, and focuses her libidinal drives on the father, now recognized as 'properly' phallic. The girl has quickly learned that she does not have the phallus, nor the power it signifies. She comes to accept, not without resistance, her socially designated role as subordinate to the possessor of the phallus, and through her acceptance, she comes to occupy the passive, dependent position expected of women in patriarchy. Crucial to her subsequent development is the question of who *has* the phallus, and who *is* the phallus. I will discuss this further in chapter 5.

In summary, for Freud, the oedipus complex brings about four major functional changes in the child's pre-oedipal relations:

1   it introduces the sexually indifferent or polymorphous child to the (sexual/genital) differences between the sexes, in recognition that it must take on the role of one or other, but not both;

2   it attempts to 'match' the child's 'biological' sex with its socially

determined 'gender', correlating male bodies, with a penis, to active social agency and the attributes of masculinity, and female bodies 'lacking' a penis, castrated, to passivity and the attributes of femininity;

3 it introduces the reality principle, social law, and considerations of material existence to the pleasure-seeking, gratification-dominated child, who has hitherto been ruled only by the primary processes; and

4 it severs the constricting mutuality binding the child to its parents, especially the mother, enabling the child to establish relations, including sexual relations, with others outside the family.

The oedipus complex mediates the imaginary, pleasurable, erotic, symbiotic, mother/child relation, from which the child cannot and does not want to escape. Ideally, it creates a sense of individual autonomy or 'identity', regulating and hierarchically organizing libidinal flows and energies into socially authorized (heterosexual, genital) adult outlets. These require a 'resolution' of the castration complex, that is, repudiation of the mother as love object and the submission of the child's desire to the law prohibiting incest. The 'Law of the Father', as Lacan sees it, is the threshold between the 'Kingdom of culture' and 'that of nature abandoned to the law of copulation'. It is not a function of Real, biological blood relations, but of systems of nomenclature or kinship systems. One is forbidden sexual access to those who one *has named* as family. The question of paternity is in fact a matter of *naming,* of the Father's Name, not his blood.

Instead of the Freudian commitment to a phylogenetic, pseudo-biological explanation of the oedipal structure,[6] Lacan will use social, unconscious, and linguistic explanations. While agreeing with Freud that the castration complex is the pivot of the child's entry into culture, Lacan confirms Freud's conflation of patriarchy with culture in general, yet he refuses to see women as castrated in any *Real* or anatomical sense. The mother is denigrated from her position as the all-powerful phallic mother, not because of the child's perception of an anatomical lack. Instead, the child perceives her powerlessness in terms of the mother's relation (of desire for, of subordination to) the father:

> It will be said that the accent is placed precisely on the link of love and respect, by which the mother does or does not put the father in his ideal place. Curious, I would reply at first, that one hardly takes account of the same link the other way around . . . we should concern ourselves not only with the way in which the mother accommodates herself to the person of the father, but

also with the way she takes his speech, the word let us say, of his authority, in other words, in the place that she reserves for the Name-of-the-Father in the promulgation of the Law. (Lacan 1977a: 218)

The mother carries the Law of the Father within her, in the very form of her unconscious desire (for the phallus). She invokes 'his' authority on loan whenever she threatens or punishes the child for wrong-doing. She requires the authority of he who is absent. Thus she does not lack in any anatomical sense. This is to attribute lack to the Real, which, as Lacan defines it, is the 'lack of the lack', a pure, unspeakable, pre-representational plenitude. Instead, she is positioned in relation to a signifier, the phallus, which places her in the position of *being* rather than *having* (the phallus, the object of the other's desire):

Castration may derive support from *privation,* that is to say, from the apprehension in the Real of the absence of the penis in women – but even this supposes a symbolization of an object, since the Real is full and lacks nothing. In so far as one finds castration in the genesis of neurosis, it is never real but symbolic and is aimed at an imaginary object. (Lacan 1966: 512)

Both sexes must accept the mother's castration; each must give her up to develop an exogamous libidinal relation and a symbolic and speaking position independent of her. The child's sacrifice of its primary love-object in conformity with the law must be compensated, (more for boys, less for girls!) by means of the acquisition of a position, a place as a subject in culture. The child becomes a subject only with reference to the name-of-the-father and the sacrificed, absent body of the mother: 'It is the *name-of-the-father* that we must recognise as the support of the symbolic function, which, from the dawn of history has identified his person with the figure of the law' (Lacan 1977a: 67).

In introjecting the name-of-the-father, the child (or rather, the *boy*) is positioned with reference to the father's name. He is now bound to the law, in so far as he is implicated in the symbolic 'debt', given a name, and an authorized speaking position. The paternal metaphor is not a simple incantation but the formula by which the subject, through the construction of the unconscious, becomes an 'I', and can speak in its own name. What occurs in the case of the girl is less clear and explicable. In one sense, in so far as she speaks and says 'I', she too must take up a place as a subject of the symbolic; yet, in another, in so far as she is positioned as castrated, passive, an object of desire for men rather than a subject who

other (represented by the dotted line from Es to autre). In the mirror stage (represented by the triangle, *Es-autre-moi)*, the child enters an imaginary relation with the other, with others, including the mother, father, nurturer, or mirror-image (represented by *autre)*. This *autre* is the 'real' (i.e. imaginary) other, a concrete individual, and not here a delegate or agent of the Other. The mirror stage generates the child's ego or *moi*, which is built upon its imaginary identification with the other. The *moi* is necessarily caught up in/as the other. The Other (represented by *Autre)* enters the oedipal triangle as a point outside the dual imaginary structure. As the law of symbolic functioning, the Other is embodied in the figure of the symbolic father, who intervenes into the narcissistic, imaginary, and incestual structure of identifications and gratifications. The relation between self/*moi* and other is necessary for the initiation of social exchange, and the articulation of the unconscious. The locus of the Other is at the same time that site within the subject known as the unconscious, (hence the direct connection between *Autre* and *Es)*. Through this interaction, the Es now represents, not the id, but the 'I', the subject of the discourse of the unconscious.

In synchronic terms, this diagram must be read as a model of the intra-psychic relations and tensions comprising the subject. The Es is the id, a given, biological, endogenous psychical input. The *autre* can be seen as the ego-ideal, the internalized representative of the other; the *moi* is the ego (which takes itself to be the whole of the diagram.) The *Autre* is the superego, which engenders the unconscious, now represented by the *Es,* in so far as the id is subjected to repression. Taken together, they represent the agencies or systems constituting the 'decentred subject'.

The drive and the signifier

Lacan stresses throughout his work that the sexual drive cannot be assimilated to the instinct or any natural or biological process. For one thing, he argues that biological instincts always follow rhythmical or cyclical patterns of deprivation or lack and temporary satisfaction, while the drive 'has no day or night, no spring and autumn, no rise and fall. It is a constant force' (1977b: 165). The drive is not an instinct because, unlike the instinct, the drive is subjected to what Freud has called 'vicissitudes', fluctuations and transformations in aims and the renunciation of (some) of its objects (which is strictly impossible in the case of an instinct). The drive gains satisfaction even in the deflection of its aim, as is the case in the vicissitude of sublimation (see Freud 1915b). The drive is motivated by but always falls short of satisfaction. There is an ambiguity in its *aim (ziel)*: the aim of the drive is always both the attainment of its object, *and* ultimately, a gain in satisfaction. In spite of renouncing its object, as in the process of sublimation, the drive is still able to gain satisfaction:

> In other words – for the moment, I am not fucking, I am talking to you. Well, I can have exactly the same satisfaction as if I were fucking. That's what it means. Indeed, it raises the question of whether in fact I am not fucking at this moment. (Lacan 1977b: 165–6)

Lacan suggests here that even when the subject has renounced a certain satisfaction through the attainment of its aim, there is still a satisfaction. There can be satisfaction, in other words, at giving up satisfaction. The symptom always satisfies something even if this satisfaction thwarts or frustrates the drive. This satisfaction functions only in the category of the impossible, which is defined by the field of the Other. The drive is indifferent to its object: it is not an object that satisfies it, for this object reveals only another want, another satisfaction for which it yearns:

> Even when you stuff the mouth – the mouth that opens in the register of the drive – it is not the food that satisfied it, it is, as one says, the pleasure of the mouth . . . it is obvious that it is not a question of food, nor the memory of food, nor the echo of food, nor the mother's care, but of something that is called the breast . . . *la pulsion en fait le tour* [the drive moves around, or tricks its object]. (1977b: 168)

The 'object' providing satisfaction is not the object *of* the drive. It is always a divergence, a metonym, a lack of the real, displaced onto a substitute. The object of satisfaction is represented by Lacan's formulaic expression, the *objet a*. The *objet a* is not the drive's *objekt,* but the *cause of desire.*

The *source* of the drive also reveals a duplicity. The source of a biological instinct is the corporeal pathway traced by one of the 'vital functions': the mouth, digestive tract, stomach, and anus, in the case of hunger; the intestines and bowels, in defaecatory processes. Yet the source of the sexual drive is only a part, a metonym, of these more encompassing pathways or traces. Lacan asserts that the drives' source is always defined by the erotogenic rim, the orifice, or a cut on the body's surface that marks a threshold between its interior and its exterior, and thus also a site of exchange between the subject and the world.

The cut on the body's surface, the gap or hole, draws towards it

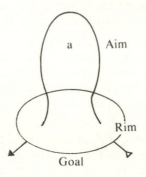

Figure 2

an object that may fill it but does not satisfy it. This (double) gap or void is the condition of the compatibility, the complicity of sexuality and the unconscious: 'The drive is precisely that *montage* by which sexuality participates in the psychical life, in a way that must conform to the gap-like structure that is the structure of the unconscious' (Lacan 1977b: 176). The drive thus strives for an (impossible) object to satisfy its bivalent aims by filling the lack or gap. It is because of its essential lack of an essence, its capacity to substitute one object for another to gain satisfaction, that the drive is the field in which desire is manifested:

> with regard to the agency of sexuality, all subjects are equal, from the child to the adult . . . they deal only with that part of sexuality that passes into the networks of the constitution of the subject, into the networks of the signifier . . . sexuality is realized only through the operation of the drives in so far as they are partial drives, partial with regard to the biological finality of sexuality. (1977b, 176–7.)

To represent the rim-like structure of the erotogenic zone and its relation to its object, the *objet a,* Lacan presents the diagram shown in Figure 2 (from Lacan 1977b: 178).

The erotogenic rim on the surface of the body reveals a *béance* which the drive aims to fill by means of the 'a', that object that is the counterpart or other to the ego. The *objet a* is impossible to incorporate, but also impossible to sever. It *hovers* between the self and the other. The divergence of the goal from the aim is what distinguishes the drive from the instinct; it renders the *objet a* into an imaginary object. To quote Lacan:

> When you entrust someone with a mission, the *aim* is not what he brings back, but the itinerary he must take. The *aim* is the way taken . . . in Archery, the *goal* . . . is not the bird you shoot, it is having scored a hit and thereby attained your *but*, (aim/goal). (1977b: 179)

The drive can be satisfied without having attained its goal. The trajectory of the arrow is the circuit between the erotogenic rim and its object, its pathway being regulated by the *drang* or pressure the drive exerts, an endogenous pressure seeking external satisfaction. This circuit of the drive interlocks with the domain of the *quelle,* the source of the drive, the rim: 'The tension is always loop-shaped and cannot be separated from its return to the erogenous zone' (1977b: 179).

The aim, then, is always a return, a reintegration into the circuit of a perfectly self-enclosed auto-eroticism which has succeeded in replacing the lost object with its own processes and parts. The drive describes the residue or remainder left over of the primal object that ensures no substitute (even the Real itself) will ever plug the rim, fill it to completion. Lacan refers here to Freud's postulate of an intermediate stage in between the active and passive forms of the (scopic or aggressive) drive; voyeurism/exhibitionism and sadism/ masochism, the self-reflexive position represented by Freud's dazzling metaphor of the mouth kissing itself.

> In the drive, is not this mouth what might be called a mouth in the form of an arrow? – a mouth sewn up, in which, in analysis we see indicating as clearly as possible, in certain silences, the pure agency of the oral drive, closing upon its own satisfaction. (1977b: 179)

A mouth kissing itself – this is no mere auto-erotic pleasure. It implies that the subject is already a being at the mercy of language, a subject positioned as such through language. What designates sadism/voyeurism as active and masochism/exhibitionism as passive forms of sexual drives is not the amount or kind of energy invested in the process (passivity involves as much activity as activity!); but the fact that they are governed rather by a grammatical function, which is itself mediated by the self-reflexive position: 'I look', 'I am looked at', mediated by 'I look at myself'.

The drive involves the process in which the subject detaches part of itself from itself, and, in attempting a reincorporation, returns this movement back to the subject's body. This movement outside and back again is only capable of being sustained if the object, the *objet a,* is not a Real object, but the 'presence of a hollow, a void, which can be occupied . . . by any object' (1977b: 180). The absence that sustains the drive, the absence of a real object, is produced only through the other. Lacan's question, then, is: what is the voyeur trying to see? To what is his gaze directed?

> what he is trying to see, make no mistake, is the object as absence. What the voyeur is looking for and finds is merely a shadow, a shadow behind the curtain. There he will phantasize any magic presence, the most graceful of girls, for example, even if on the other side there is only a hairy athlete. What he is looking for is not . . . the phallus – but precisely its absence . . .
> What one looks at is what cannot be seen. If, thanks to the introduction of the other, the structure of the drive appears, it is really completed only in its reversed form, in its return form, which is the true active drive. In exhibitionism what is intended by the subject is what is realized in the other. The true aim of desire is the other, as constrained, beyond his involvement in the scene. It is not only the victim as referred to some other who is looking at him. (1977b: 182–3)

For Lacan, the drive is located somewhere *between* the eye and the gaze.[9] The scopic drive must be distinguished from vision. The gaze demonstrates the *excess* of the drive over geometrical or in Lacan's term, 'geometral' or flat optics, a perspectival optics. Perspective represents the reception of *light*, a light which conforms to the laws of physics and the rules governing projection and the point-for-point representation of space (see 1977b: 86). This may explain why it is so difficult to map the gaze: at best, one can represent how seeing occurs. Lacan refers here to Diderot's observation, in *Lettre sur les aveugles à l'usage de ceux qui voient,* that the geometral perspective of the Cartesian subject is a perspective understandable even by the blind, for whom the gaze is not experienced:

> the geometral space of vision – even if we include those imaginary parts in the virtual space of the mirror, of which, as you know, I have spoken at length – is perfectly reconstructible, imaginable, by a blind man.
> What is at issue in geometral perspective is simply the mapping of space, not sight. (1977b: 86)

This may be why Lacan resorts to topological figures, Escher objects, objects represented from *impossible* perspectives to capture something of the enigma of the gaze. Lacan exemplifies the failure of perspective to capture the desire entailed by the gaze in the peculiar fascination of the spectator with anamorphic images, images that distort, stretch, and contort perspective in their remapping, reprojection of perspectival space: he refers to Hans Holbein's painting of 1533, 'The Ambassadors'. Between the two figures in the foreground hovers a barely discernible ghostly distortion of death's head, the image of the skull to which the spectator is irresistibly drawn. ('The Ambassadors' is reproduced on the front cover of *The Four Fundamental Concepts,* Lacan 1977b.)

For Lacan, the formula best capturing the complexity of the scopic drive is the statement, from Paul Valéry, 'I saw myself seeing myself' (ibid.: 74, 80). This makes clear that the subject cannot be reduced to the sum of its anatomical functions:

> *I warm myself by warming myself* is a reference to the body as body – I feel that sensation of warmth which, from some point inside me, is diffused and locates me as body. Whereas in the *I see myself seeing myself,* there is no such sensation of being absorbed by vision. (1977b: 80)

Referring to Merleau-Ponty's *The Visible and the Invisible*, in which seeing is defined in terms of what it is impossible to see, Lacan affirms that seeing is a function both of the subject looking from a singular, perspectival point – in which case, what it sees is located *outside* itself ('Perception is not in me, . . . it is on the objects that it apprehends', 1977b: 80); it is also contingent on the *possibility of being seen*. The gaze is thus, like the phallus itself, the drive under which the subject's identity and certainty fail. The subject is necessarily alienated, for it is defined on Lacan's model as *seeable, shown,* being seen, without being able to see either its observer or itself. Sartre's definition of the Look implies the in-principle reversibility of observer and observed. But Lacan's point is quite different: for him the possibility of being observed is always primary. To occupy a place in the scopic field is to be able to see, but more significantly, to be seen. The gaze is what ensures that when I see, at the same time, 'I am *photo-graphed*' (1977b: 106).

> we are beings who are looked at, in the spectacle of the world. That which makes us consciousness, institutes us by the same token as *speculum mundi* . . . . The spectacle of the world, in this sense, appears to us as all-seeing . . . . The world is all-seeing, but it is not exhibitionistic – it does not provoke our gaze . . . not only does it look, *it* also *shows* . . . . It shows – but here, too,

some form of 'sliding away' of the subject is apparent. (1977b: 75)

The gaze must be located outside the subject's conscious control. If it is outside, for Lacan, unlike Sartre, this means that the gaze comes always from the field of the Other. It is only the gaze which can, as Sartre astutely observed, reduce me to shame at my very existence. But it is not the gaze of an other; it is the Other's gaze. It is the result of being located in the field of the Other.

Together with the other sexualized drives, including oral, anal, and invocatory drives, the object of the gaze is the paradigm of Lacan's *objet a*. The scopic drive takes the *objet a* as its object. This means that the object is simultaneously part of the subject (e.g. the eyes) and something detachable from the subject, a part of itself not identical with itself:

> At the level of the scopic dimension . . . is to be found the same function of the *objet a* as can be mapped in all other dimensions.
> The *objet a* is something from which the subject, in order to constitute itself, has separated itself off as organ. This serves as a symbol of the lack, that is to say, of the phallus, not as much, but insofar as it is lacking. It must, therefore, be an object that is, firstly separable, and secondly, that has some relation to the lack. (1977b: 103)

Sexuality is thus the privileged field in which desire is played out. Desire always refers to a triangle – the subject, the other and the Other. The other is the object through whom desire is returned to the subject; the Other is the locus of signification which regulates the movement by which this return is made possible. The subject's desire is always the desire of the Other.

Summary

To round off Freudian and Lacanian hypotheses about the drive, we can say:

– sexual drives are not the effects of nature or biology, but are the consequences of the introduction of a gap, lack, or absence in the child's life. Sexual drives are marked by the lack (of a fixed object). Sexuality is pleasure that is dominated by the lack;
– the sexual drives nevertheless mimic or simulate the biological processes and organs marked as significant by biological instincts. It is for this reason that the drive can be considered anaclitically dependent on the instinct; it moreover accounts for the apparently

instinctual form of drives. If the drive imitates the instinct, it is not surprising that it will appear to be biologically regulated;

– thus, although they appear to be innate and predetermined in aims, objects, and sources, sexual drives are highly malleable, variable, and culturally specific. The aims and objects the drive develops are effects of the social and familial meaning of the child's body and pleasures;

– processes of biological maturation, including the development of auto-erotic capacities, form the preconditions and the outlines later to be traced or recathected by the sexualized drive;

– the drives always exhibit a diphasic structure. But where, for Freud, pre-pubertal sexuality is to be distinguished from its post-pubertal forms, in his more considered judgement, as in Lacan's, sexuality is split into pre-oedipal (imaginary) and oedipal (symbolic) forms;

– in its pre-oedipal forms, sexual drives are chaotic, anarchic, and circulate throughout the child's body, in many regions that, from the adult point of view, have little to do with copulative sexuality; in its oedipalized forms, sexual drives become hierarchized under the primacy of the genitals and the aims of heterosexual genital reproductive sexuality;

– sexual drives always take the *objet a* as their privileged object: the *objet a* is both a part of the child's body, and what can be detached from the body in order to become an external object;

– thus the objects of sexual drives are interchangeable in so far as all are forms of the *objet a;*

– if sexuality is pleasure marked by a lack, this lack is not given, but an effect of signification. It is for this reason that sexuality, desire, is marked by the search for particular meanings. What we love and desire is what is meaningful to us in our social context;

– sexuality is a consequence, among other things, of the necessity of representing (biological) needs in signifying systems. Sexuality always operates according to the 'defiles of the signifier';

– the constitution of the subject as a sexual and desiring being at the same time produces subjects as *sexually differentiated,* i.e., as active and therefore masculine or passive and thus feminine;

– by means of oedipalization, the child of either sex is separated from its first love object, the mother, and positioned within the larger social and symbolic environment of its culture;

– it is by means of the control, or the repression of sexual drives that the unconscious is formed. The unconscious is the residue of repressed and renounced pre-oedipal drives.

4

Language and the unconscious

The Freudian unconscious

In his earliest works, Freud considered the 'contents' of the unconscious, its memories, perceptions, and sensations, as a series of neuronal impingements. In later texts, he sees them more in terms of a series or chain of 'ideational representatives' (*Vorstellungsrepräsentanz*), 'representational representatives'[1] of sexual drives. He specifies that the ideational representative is 'a succession of inscriptions and signs' – not signs *of* a drive, but signs by means of which the drive is delegated a place in the unconscious (1914c). The energetic component of the drive and its ideational representative become 'fixed' together during the act of primal repression which constitutes the unconscious as a system distinct from consciousness, separated by a barrier of censorship. Ideally, with the resolution of the oedipus complex, the newly formed superego represses the forbidden desire for the mother. If primal repression is conditioned on the formation of the superego, this means that in the case of the pre-oedipal child, there is no barrier of repression to prevent a perceptual impulse from gaining access to consciousness: the conscious and the unconscious are not yet distinct systems governed by two forms of organization or two separate libidinal economies (the primary and secondary processes):

> we have reason to assume that there is a *primal repression*, a first phase of repression, which consists in the psychical (ideational) representative of the instinct being denied entrance to the conscious. With this, a *fixation* is established, the representative in question persists unaltered from then onwards and the instinct remains attached to it. (1914c: 148)

In primal repression, a particular (psychical) sensation, action or memory becomes attached to and symbolizes a drive. This memory or sensation is frozen – preserved and fixated – as a memory trace, inscribed in/as the (timeless) unconscious. The quota of affect or energy of the threatening experience, which is intimately connected to the drive, is separated from the memory or image, leaving a smaller quota associated with the idea. The idea continues to strive for conscious expression and motility in the form of a *wish*. The wish is nothing but this process of striving towards consciousness and motility or 'discharge'. The drive is thus bound up with representation or signification as soon as it is capable of *psychical* registration. Indeed this is its condition of psychical existence. The drive can be lived or experienced only in so far as it acquires a significance.

Primal repression lays down a primarily infantile nucleus or kernel for the unconscious, a series of key memory traces which, from this time on, attract other perceptual traces or experiences associated with them towards the unconscious. These are also repressed, 'pulled' into the unconscious by ideas already contained there. These later repressions – 'repression-proper' – constitute the bulk of unconscious contents. They are selected according to their proximity to the primally repressed. The unconscious is largely composed of infantile, oedipal, memories and wishes. The unconscious remains infantile in its aims and wishes, governed by impulses that are laid down in our individual (pre-)histories, permanently preserved, unchanged by the passage of time. The criteria for 'selection' of unconscious contents remains within the order of representation: the proximity of terms to the primally repressed nucleus of the unconscious is determined not by any real relation between one idea and the repressed term, but on the basis of usually verbal or signifying relations.

The topography of the unconscious

In chapter 7 of *The Interpretation of Dreams* (1900), Freud elaborates what he describes as a topographical model of the unconscious, one that represents in spatial terms processes that in fact occur temporally. He asks us to look at the pysche as a 'compound instrument', a series of components within a machine, like a camera, where the components are spatially related in real or virtual space (1900: 536-7). He develops the idea, first formulated in *The Project*, of representing the passage of an external stimulus or perceptual impingement, first in sensory terms, then in its passage through the various psychical agencies and systems that mediate between sensation and conscious expression. *The Project's* neurological terminology is translated into psychological terms in his later account, but it will be useful for understanding the nerve-endings ---> *Φ* system ---> *μ* system ---> *ω* system

(sense organs)   (non-conscious perception)   (memory)   (motility)

quantities: i.e. neuronal motion   permeable neurones   impermeable neurones   consciousness qualities

Figure 3

complexity of Freud's account, and of Lacan's contributions to it if we remain close to his earlier formulations. As we will see later in this chapter (p. 96), if we substitute the signifier, the basic unit of sign-systems, for the neurone, the basic unit of the nervous system, we come closest to an outline of Lacan's position.

A stimulus from the external world impinges on nerve endings at the surface of a sense organ. To become conscious, this impulse must undergo a number of inscriptions and transformations. The unconscious resides in that gap or instant between a perception's impingement on the nervous system and its (deferred) conscious registration. We can reconstruct Freud's account in diagrammatic form (Figure 3: see Freud 1888: 234, 307ff.).

The *Φ* system is the first, perceptual, registration of the impingement. Freud postulates that the neurones composing this system must be different from those composing the *μ* system: its neurones are unable to retain memory traces because they have a *permeable* barrier or threshold that is only temporarily altered by the impingement (this is because, Freud explains, this system must retain its capacity to register fresh sensations, and hence must be pliable, 'as new', for each new perceptual or sensory impingement). By contrast, the *μ* system is a memory system, so its neurones must have impermeable barriers which are permanently modified by each perceptual impulse. They must retain these neuronal transformations permanently in order to act as a permanent record of (past)

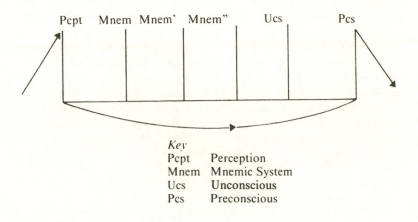

Key
Pcpt   Perception
Mnem   Mnemic System
Ucs   Unconscious
Pcs   Preconscious

Figure 4

perceptions. The perception however, is not yet psychically represented. It functions only on a neurological and energetic level, traversing neuronal pathways in its progress to consciousness. For memories to acquire psychical significance, their quantitative force or degree of energy, must be converted into qualitative terms. This is the function of the ω system, which, Freud argues, is sensitive to the *periodicity* or frequency of quantitative impingements. It 'translates' impulses into 'ideas' or 'ideational contents' which are only then capable of psychical, preconscious, or conscious, registration and are eventually able to be expressed in action.[2]

This early model forms the basis of his more psychologically oriented account in *The Interpretation of Dreams*. Here he distinguishes a sensory (perceptual) from a motor pole of the psychical apparatus. The movement of a stimulus from sensation to motility is precisely structured by the form of the wish: the path of an impulse from passive reception to active expression *is* the wish-form. His most elaborated picture of the psychical apparatus is represented in his diagram (Figure 4, 1900. 340).

'Pcpt' here represents the first neurophysiological registration of a sensory impingement. Freud again separates the perceptual function from memory by granting each its own agency. The impingement must be of sufficient strength to traverse the neuronal pathways or threshold comprising the perceptual system to become a memory. Freud clearly wishes to avoid conceiving of memory as a monolithic, unorganized aggregate of past perceptions. It is for this reason he posits not one but several mnemic systems through which the impulse must pass. It is thus recorded several times within different mnemic systems (ibid.: 539), according to different associative principles. He suggests that one system may be based on associations of simultaneity. Other associative principles – e.g., similarity, homophony, antipathy, cause and effect, etc. – may form the basis of further mnemic systems, much like a cross-referenced index file. The same perception is represented many times over in different associative connections, the centre of several dense webs of perceptions. It is only after the impulse is registered in mnemic systems (which are quantitative) that an impulse is capable of psychical (qualitative) registration.

Freud then turns to the motor end of the apparatus, which is largely unexplained in his earlier papers. He argues that the critical agency must be closer to consciousness than that which it criticizes (ibid.: 340). This means that once the impulse passes through mnemic systems, it is translated into psychical terms and registered unconsciously. If it passes the censor, the impulse is able to enter the preconscious system, and from there the passage to consciousness is relatively easy.

Perhaps more interesting is the fate of the repressed impulse, the one which is prohibited in its passage to consciousness. It is prevented from entering the Pcs. system and cannot form part of the network of memories at the subject's conscious disposal. Yet it strives for expression with a more or less constant energy against which the prohibitive barrier must be vigilant. For this reason Freud maintained a strong interest in dreams. In sleep, the supervising activities of the censor can be relaxed to the extent that the subject is asleep and the wish is thereby denied access to conscious motility. The unconscious wish strives to break through the barrier, but is barred from entry. It moves – 'regressively' (i.e. in the reverse direction to perception) – towards the sensory end of the apparatus, instead of towards the motor end. It thus reactivates a perceptual image (a memory) in hallucinatory fashion. The hallucination provides the dream with its manifest content. Moreover, Freud claims, its topologically regressive character also accounts for the dream's inability to express logical and grammatical relations (which are preconscious functions). As Freud suggests: 'in the case of regression, [wishes] would necessarily lose any means of expression except perceptual images. In regression the fabric of the dream thoughts is resolved into its raw materials' (ibid.: 543). The unconscious wish reactivates a memory (either recent or infantile) which will serve to express or represent it in the manifest dream. This may enable it to gain a (compromise, disguised) access to consciousness.

The primary processes: condensation and displacement

How are memories able to represent the unconscious wish? How is the wish able to transfer its particular messages to these memories? How can both significant and indifferent memories act as delegates for the unconscious wish? It is only if we understand the peculiar procedures the unconscious utilizes to gain expression that these questions can be answered, and dreams and symptoms interpreted.

The unconscious has only limited techniques at its disposal to gain even a partial pleasure through distortion and disguise. Freud cites the two primary techniques of disguise as condensation and displacement. With condensation, a compression of two or more ideas occurs, so that a composite figure, image or name, drawing on and leaving out features of both, is formed. In this way, a single image in a dream is able to represent many different wishes or thoughts through compression of common features and elimination of (relevant) differences. In the case of displacement, the significant, unconscious wish is able to transfer its intensity or meaning to an indifferent term, allowing the latter to act as its delegate, thus disguising it. The insignificant idea is able to represent the more significant one without the repressed features of the significant idea breaching the barriers of censorship. These two processes, which are the governing procedures of the psychical primary processes, function together to create the manifest dream and all other symptoms that so cleverly disguise and express the unconscious wish.

> the elements which stand out as the principal components of the manifest content of the dream are far from playing the same part in the dream-thoughts. And, as a corollary, the converse of this assertion can be affirmed: what is clearly the essence of the dream-thoughts – its content has different elements as its central point. (1900: 305)
>
> Dream-displacement and dream-condensation are the two governing factors to whose activity we may in essence ascribe the form assumed by the dream. (ibid.: 308)

Condensation and displacement are means by which the intensity of one or more elements is transferred onto other elements – essentially by delegation. In addition to condensation and displacement, Freud argues that there are other techniques the unconscious has at its disposal. As a third category of unconscious expression, Freud adds what he calls 'considerations of the means of representability', a series of ingenious devices the unconscious has at its disposal for representing logical, causal, and grammatical relations, given that the unconscious wish has no access to preconscious representations.

The dream must rely largely on visual images/perceptions through which it can express various logical or causal relations. (In this sense the dream's problem is analogous to that of the film: how to represent negation, or contradictory and conditional relations, i.e., logical, grammatical, or causal relations, without resorting to verbal means?) In other words, it must rely on visual material to represent verbal and logical relations. It does so in the manner of a charade, using 'hieroglyphs', formulaic terms, and shorthand devices. It is the ability to use visual material (signifiers) in verbal form that enables the possibility of a rigorous and precise interpretation of dreams. The 'considerations of representability' recast the (visual and auditory) memories into the form of linguistic propositions, treating visual elements by verbal techniques. This explains why Freud likens the dream to the rebus, which is a picture representing or expressing a statement. Dream elements are treated like words:

> Let us say, then, that the dream is like the parlour-game in which one is supposed to get the spectators to guess some well known saying or variant of it solely by dumb-show. . . . That the dream runs up against a lack of taxematic material for the representation of such logical articulations as causality, contradiction, hypothesis, etc., . . . proves they are a form of writing rather than of mime. The subtle processes that the dream is seen to use to represent these logical articulations, in a much less artificial way than games usually employ, are the objects of a special study in Freud in which one sees once more confirmed that the dream-work follows the laws of the signifier. (Lacan 1977a: 161)

Freud gives the following examples to help explain the dream's ingenious modes of expression: the expression of contrary relations, or the expression, 'just the reverse' is illustrated by a dream in which the 'up above' or 'less than' may be represented by sensory intensities, by the vividness of impressions; relations of cause and effect may be represented by two dreams occurring in sequence, the first representing the cause and the second, the effect, and so on. The dream's expressive devices function like those operating in film, where, for example, the passage of time, expressing the relation of 'earlier' and 'later' is represented by the whirring hands of a clock. This indirect mode of expression highlights the problem of both cinema and the dream: both must use iconic or visual images as if they were verbal signs.

The unconscious wish may use secondary revision to blur the status of what it has expressed. This consists in various statements or thoughts, usually stated in the form, 'it is only a dream'. They enable the unconscious content which has inadvertently breached the barrier of censorship to be left unscrutinized by consciousness. The dream's content has been rendered acceptable only by a retrospective judgement diminishing its status or coherence.

Dream interpretation

The dream is essentially composed of images derived from the subject's current and past experiences, memories which are often not readily accessible to waking consciousness. These are used by the dream-work, the labour involved in a dream's production, to provide a manifest content for the dream, disguising the real source and explanation of dreams, their latent or unconscious contents. The images used in the dream are recalled from stratified mnemic systems because of their direct or indirect connection to the unconscious wish. They provide the dream with a bland or confusing appearance which protects unconscious wish(es) from detection.

The 'work' of the dream, its 'economy', consists in transforming latent dream-thoughts and wishes (which may be expressed in propositional form) into manifest dream images (which are usually visual) using the four techniques of distortion just elaborated. Condensation ensures that dream images are overdetermined. They take on the significance of several latent wishes or thoughts. Displacement ensures that apparently trivial, indifferent, and insignificant material can represent highly significant uncon-scious elements. Together, they ensure that 'the essence of the dream is, as it were, differently centred from the dream-thoughts' (ibid.: 305).

As thoughts, wishes, and associations are condensed into singular dream images, the dream is always capable of being situated within the subject's associative chains and memories, thus providing the possibility of interpretation. As a compressed, laconic, evasive yet systematically regulated effect of the primary processes, the dream – or at least the subject's verbal report of it – can be deciphered through free associations. Yet, as Lacan will affirm, what seems most threatening and subversive about Freud's understanding of the unconscious is the peculiar, unsettling mode of deciphering or interpretation he developed, an approach to reading/interpreting the dream that problematizes more traditional notions of literary and textual interpretation. As we shall see, in place of the totalizing approach of literary forms of interpretation, Freud posits a mode of interpretation that more closely resembles the unravelling of cross-word puzzles, particularly cryptic crosswords than it does literary criticism. An offensive method, no doubt, to those respecting the 'integrity' and 'autonomy' of texts instead of elaborating their intertextual dissolution.³

Unconscious dream-thoughts are composites of various unconscious memories or wishes, usually of an oedipal or pre-oedipal kind. In a sense, this means that one can more or less 'guess' that the wish expressed in any dream will always be the renounced oedipal wish. What is significant, though, is not this claim in its generality, but the particular experiences and memories by which each individual is able to tie the wish to the concrete elements of the dream – that is, the dream-work, whose methods of unconscious representation are, for Freud, the essence of dream-interpretation.

How the dream work utilizes the unchanging unconscious wish and the subject's recent and past experiences to form the dream's manifest appearance is the really interesting and individualizing psychological question. It displaces the intensity and meaning of the unconscious elements onto their conscious delegates, and links the manifest dream-images, through multiple connections, to a number of associated terms in the preconscious and the unconscious.

The dream report, rather than the dream itself, is the object of psychoanalytic interpretation. It should not be read as a narrative, in which the integrity of the plot as a whole must be respected. Instead, the report is to be treated more as a list or aggregate of images, like the rebus.⁴ The dream report must be broken down into simpler units, each of which must be regarded as autonomous. Each is embedded with mutiple associative chains. Where these chains overlap, nodal points of the dream are to be found, which prove crucial to its interpretation:

The associations to the dream are not yet latent dream-thoughts. The latter are contained in the associations like an alkali in the mother-liquor, but not yet completely contained in them. On the one hand, the associations give us far more than we need for

formulating the latent dream thoughts, namely all the explanations, transitions, and connections which the patient's intellect is
bound to produce in the course of his approach to the dream-
thoughts. On the other hand, an association often comes to a
stop precisely before the genuine dream-thoughts. (Freud 1933:
12)

Latent dream-thoughts are highly rational, intelligible,
preconscious thoughts. These are in sharp contrast to the associative chains, which are chaotic, apparently random and linked by
'superficial' connections. Freud mentions that relations of asson-
ance, ambiguity, contiguity, similarity, puns, and jokes are all used
in recalling associative links. From this vast, potentially infinite,
network of terms, the dream work will select those most amenable
to visual representation. These representable elements are then
thrown together in a relatively random way to form a composite
scene: 'the whole mass of these dream-thoughts is brought under
the pressure of the dream-work and its elements are turned about,
broken into fragments and jammed together – almost like an ice-
pack' (1900: 312). Secondary revision then submits the dream to
further modifications in order to evade censorship. Wishes left over
from the day preceding the dream serve as a cover for infantile and
repressed sexual wishes. They provide the impetus for the dream's
manifest form.

In tracing the paths from the manifest dream to the unconscious
wish, we will be disappointed if we expect to find a clearly
crystallized wish structure, a coherent wish. What we find, instead,
are chains of associations, overlapping memories, linkage between
elements, repetitions, and nodal points, which are highlighted
against the mass of other associative connections. The dream does
not, strictly speaking, have *an* unconscious meaning, for there is
little more than an arrangement of manifest terms. Analysis
consists in mapping out the connections between these terms, and
the context from which they are derived. In this network of terms,
Lacan will see the fundamental 'play of signification', the movement of linguistic elements governed by their own 'logic' and not by
the law-like operations of grammar and syntax.

The unconscious structured like a language

Does the dream have a meaning in the same way that conscious
speech is meaningful? What are the relations between a language of
the unconscious and that of consciousness? Freud directed himself
to these questions in the metapsychological text, 'The Unconscious'

(1914c). There, he regards repression as a 'failure of translation'; he sees the various mnemic systems as forms of notation (see Freud 1910: 220). He talks in terms of inscriptions, transcriptions, registrations, and translations. He claims that a 'linguistic' model of the unconscious may help solve some of the dilemmas associated with the topological account. For example, if we regard consciousness as composed of 'thing-presentations' (perceptions or sense-impressions), combined with their 'word-presentations' (their verbal 'translations'), and the unconscious as composed only of thing-presentations severed from their word-presentations, there remains the question of whether an impression is registered once or twice in the psyche. The question of whether the 'same content' is reproduced in two locations – conscious and unconscious – or is a single content which undergoes a functional change in its passage to consciousness is solved:

> we now seem to know all at once what the difference is between a conscious and an unconscious presentation. The two are not, as we supposed, different registrations of the same content in different psychical localities; nor yet different functional states of cathexis in the same locality; but the conscious presentation comprises the presentation of the thing plus the presentation of the word belonging to it, while the unconscious presentation is the presentation of the thing alone. (1914b: 201-2)

Lacan's most highly respected intervention into Freudian psychoanalysis is his rigorous use of the linguistics developed by Saussure (and appropriately modified by Lacan) to explain the functioning of the unconscious. If the 'unconscious is structured like a language', then it is plausible to claim that linguistics and semiotics are necessary for an understanding of the unconscious. He regards the contents of the unconscious as signifiers; the primary processes the unconscious relies upon to express and distort itself – i.e. condensation and displacement – he represents in terms of Jakobson's notions of metaphor and metonymy; and the subsidiary means of unconscious expression he defines by the rhetorical devices or figures outlined by Quintillian.

As the 'talking cure', psychoanalysis has nothing but the analysand's speech as its object, nothing but literary/linguistic procedures of interpretation, and no diagnostic or prognostic tools other than language. Freud's frequent references to literature and language were, Lacan claims, not coincidental, for his notion of the unconscious is conceived in terms of language. Yet, Lacan argues, when Freud formulated his account of the unconscious in 1900, linguistics as such had not yet developed. Saussure's lectures on semiology and general linguistics took place from 1906 to 1911, and were not published until 1916. Even if, as Benvenuto and Kennedy argue (1986: 15–16), Saussure's son, Raymond, became a psychoanalyst under Freud, and Freud was aware of Saussure's work, still, Saussurian semiology is at best a *post hoc* knowledge that Freud did not use at the time of his formulations. Lacan's intervention in any case does not require this justification. It will be of value in so far as it elucidates features of psychoanalytic therapy and theory that remain otherwise unexplained.

The signifier

The smallest unit of analysis in semiotics, the sign, is composed of two components, which Saussure called the signifier and the signified. The signifer is the material (phonic, graphic) component and the signified is the conceptual (meaningful) component, and together, they are the bases of all languages and representational systems. For Saussure, the sign is not the attachment of a label or name to a pregiven concept. Rather, the sign is active in constituting its ingredients. Neither the signifier nor the signified pre-exist their relations in the sign. The sign is in fact the coupling of a difference in/as the signifier with a difference in/as the signified. Saussure claims, in other words, that the elements composing the sign, as well as the sign itself, can only have identity by virtue of their *pure difference*.[6] Neither the signifier nor the signified have any positive identity. Each can only be defined in terms of what it is *not*. The signifier is that element of the sign that is not the signified; each sign has meaning and value only in relation to other signs similar to it, which it is *not* (what defines 'tree', for example, is not pointing to the leafy green object growing in the garden; rather, it is the fact that, in any given (verbal) context, 'tree' is *not* 'bush', 'shrub', 'flower', 'hedge', etc., etc. Its mode of difference within similar i.e. substitutable, terms is what gives it its specific value).

For Lacan, one problem with Saussure's understanding is his tendency to *psychologize* the concept of the sign. While he regards the sign as a two-sided term where one side is material and the other conceptual, he also stresses that the terms 'material' and 'conceptual' are only relative. Both terms are to be understood psychically. The signifier is not simply the sound of a word, but rather, the 'sound-impression', the impression the 'sound makes upon our senses'. The sign, for him, is situated internal to the subject, within the realm of thought. Saussure regards the sign as mutually and reciprocally defined by its parts. This may explain why, in his

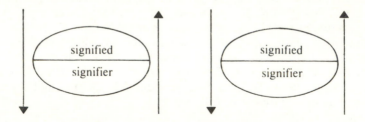

Figure 5

diagrams, he represents their relation as reversible (indicated by the twin arrow, see Figure 5).

Lacan argues that psychoanalysis is founded on this distinction: 'A psychoanalyst should find it easy enough to grasp the fundamental distinction between signifier and signified and to begin to use the two non-overlapping networks of relations that they organise' (Lacan 1977a: 126). He transforms the Saussurian system into a materialist account. While acknowledging the sign's fundamentally layered structure, Lacan reverses Saussure's formula, signified/signifier, giving primacy to the material element (the signifier) in the genesis of the concept (the signified). His own formula for the sign is thus 'S/s', 'which is read as: the signifier over the signified, "over" corresponding to the bar separating the two stages' (1977a: 149). The signifier is granted priority because, in Lacan's understanding, the signified is in fact simply another signifier occupying a different position, a position 'below the bar' within signification:

> One cannot go further along this line of thought than to demonstrate that no significations can be sustained other than by reference to another signification: in its extreme form this amounts to the proposition that there is no language in existence for which there is any question of its inability to cover the whole field of the signified . . . (ibid.: 150)

The signifier must be understood *literally, to the letter*; it is a material object. It is for this reason that the French edition of the *Écrits* opens with his analysis of Poe's short story, *The Purloined Letter*, which represents a fable of the literal: 'But how are we to

$$S \dashrightarrow S \dashrightarrow S \dashrightarrow S \dashrightarrow S$$

$$s \dashleftarrow s \dashleftarrow s \dashleftarrow s \dashleftarrow s$$

Figure 6

take this letter here? Quite simply, literally. By "letter", I designate the material support that concrete discourse borrows from language (langue)' (ibid.: 147).

As a material unit, whether in phonic or visual form, the signifier's operations define the structure of the unconscious. If the discourses of consciousness are composed of *signs*, then the discourses through which the unconscious is articulated are composed only of signifiers, detached, as it were, from their signifieds: 'the pretensions of the spirit would remain unassailable if the letter had not shown us that it produces all the effects of truth in man, without involving the spirit at all' (ibid.: 158).

For Lacan, as for Saussure, if any particular signifier refers to any given signified, it does so only through the mediation of the whole chain of signifiers. It is only the *totality* of signifiers that corresponds with the *totality* of signifieds; no single signifier is definitively attached to a single signified. Their only direct relation is one described as a relation of *glissement* or sliding. The chain of signifiers incessantly slides over the chain of signifieds (Figure 6).

There is a continuous evacuation of meaning as soon as the signifier moves out its concrete relations, its syntagmatic bonds in a given speech act, back into the signifying chain. This signals a *constitutive lack* at the core of language, a lack which marks the absence of a fixed anchoring point, the absence of a solid core of meaning for any term – its necessarily open, ambiguous potential. The sliding of the signifier over the signified is only momentarily arrested in specific contexts. This lack of a founding sign – a signifier tied firmly to a given signified – means that if each term is founded on *pure difference* and thus already requires another term to be understood, all terms can only be understood relative to language as a whole. This 'indefinite sliding of meaning' constitutive of signification is, however, halted in the operations of the symptom, dream, or unconscious manifestation. These could be seen as 'stuck' or 'congealed' signs, where the signifier is not free to form other connections and meanings, but is tied to a particular significance:

> the pinning down or stopping point I speak of is mythical, for never has anyone been able to pin a meaning to a signifier and see what happens. But, in any case, something new always results . . . namely the appearance of a new meaning. (Seminar, 22 January 1958 in Wilden 1972: 33)

The bar separating signifier from signified in Saussure's formulation (see Figure 3) is used by Lacan to designate a fundamental break or discontinuity between the two chains. There are two orders of discourse always separated by a barrier, a censorship, which cannot be traversed. Moreover, being a condition of signification, the bar itself cannot be represented. This provides him with both a metaphor and a model of the unconscious based on purely linguistic concerns. The unconscious consists in signifiers which have fallen below the barrier, i.e., submitted to a repression, preventing them from traversing the bar and gaining access to consciousness. Freud's neurological model is transposed into linguistic form.

The signifier and the signified are thus two hierarchically structured networks in which the signifier always has primacy over the signified. Relations between signifiers generate the signified:

> The first network, that of the signifier, is the synchronic structure of the language material insofar as in that structure each element assumes its precise function by being different from the others . . .
>
> The second network, that of the signified, is the diachronic set of concretely pronounced discourses, which react historically on the first, just as the structure of the first governs the pathways of the second. The dominant fact here is the unity of signification, which proves never to be resolved into a pure indication of the real, but always refers back to another signification . . . (1977a: 126)

On this conception, the chain or network of signifiers is regulated by the play of pure difference. Pure difference defines the possible linguistic identities of each term. By linguistic double articulation, smaller units can be combined to form larger or higher level units, and the larger units in turn provide a context for each of the smaller or lower order units.[7]

The chain of the signified consists in the bulk of historical texts (systems of signifiers), which, in some sense regulate and render the drift of signifiers comprehensible. In turn, the laws of the signifier determine what is possible and meaningful in those texts. But if, *contra* Saussure, Lacan equates the chain of signifieds with historical texts and not with mental concepts or conceptual meanings, the chain of signifieds is nothing but the historically given arrangement of signifiers. The signified is not an ontologically distinct order from the signifer; its function, its position (i.e., its latent position 'under' the signifier) is what distinguishes these two orders.

His conception of the primacy of the signifier in representation correlates with Lacan's subversion of the primacy of the subject in his account of the mirror phase. He problematizes the common presumption of consciousness or intentionality regulating discourses. For him, language does not represent the subject's pre-existing intentions or ideas; the subject no longer constitutes language or functions as its master, but conversely, is constituted as a subject by language.

A subject does not represent an idea by means of a signifier for another subject (a version of the commonly held communicational model of language, whereby the sender transmits a message to a receiver); rather, a signifier represents a subject for another signifier. While the sign may function in the act of communication between subjects, the signifier subverts the subject's intentions and undermines the possibility of communication, the transmission of messages between sender and receiver. It subjects the subject to its dominion (see Lacan 1977b: 157).

> A signifier is that which represents a subject: for whom? – not for another subject, but for another signifier. . . . In order to illustrate this axiom, suppose that in the desert you find a stone covered with hieroglyphics. You do not doubt for a moment that, behind them, there was a subject who wrote them. But it is an error to believe that each signifier is addressed to you – this is proved by the fact that you cannot understand any of it. On the other hand, you define them as signifiers by the fact that you are sure that each of these signifiers is related to each of the others. And it is this that is at issue with the relation between the subject and the field of the Other . . . . The subject is born insofar as the signifier emerges in the field of the Other. But by that very fact, this subject – which was previously nothing if not a subject coming into being – solidifies into a signifier. (1977b: 198–9)

The subject cannot be considered the agent of speech; it is

(through) the Other (i.e. the unconscious) that language speaks the subject. The subject is the effect of discourse, no longer its cause.

Metaphor and metonymy

Lacan relies on the work of Roman Jakobson to elaborate Freud's account of the primary processes of condensation and displacement. For Jakobson, the two fundamental poles around which all languages and systems of signification must revolve are selection and combination. Here Jakobson elaborates and elevates Saussure's conception of the syntagmatic (combinatory) and paradigmatic (selective) relations.[8]

From a large repertoire of terms, only some can be selected in any particular situation; selections occur between terms which are similar, and thus capable of substituting for each other. Jakobson aligns selection, similarity, and substitution. The terms selected must then be combined to form a larger unit (such as the sentence, formed from the combination of signs). Combination operates with terms related by contiguity. It results in the creation of a context for the terms selected. Combination, contiguity, and context are thus associated together as well.

Jakobson defines the pole of selection or similarity as metaphoric and the pole of combination or contiguity as metonymic. He claims that both are necessary for meaningful language. The absence or impairment of one of the other (e.g. as a result of cerebral lesion) may result in the linguistic disturbance of aphasia.[9] Aphasia, for Jakobson, falls into two categories – one an impairment of the pole of selection, the other, of combination: 'The relation of similarity is suppressed in the former, the relation of contiguity in the latter . . . Metaphor is alien to similarity disorder, and metonymy to the contiguity disorder' (Jakobson and Hallé 1956: 76). Not only are these two poles or processes necessary in all signifying systems, they are also the two major means by which new meanings, ambiguities, and extended usages occur. They account for the productivity of language and its capacity to change, develop, alter within the closely guarded constraints of *langue*.

In 'The Agency of the Letter' (1977a), Lacan outlines his own view of the role of the signifier in psychical life. Metaphor and metonymy are probably the two central terms in his analysis of unconscious production. Yet he stresses that when he speaks about language and discourse, his interest is not that of a literary critic, nor of a hermeneutic interpreter. A psychoanalyst is uniquely *uninterested* in meaning *per se*, but must instead address the fluid ambiguity and multiple meaning of terms, the duplicity of a language that allows itself to be used in indeterminate, open-ended contexts with several meanings at once.

Language has no place in the Real. It neither corresponds to nor represents to the Real. It signifies, not because it expresses thoughts or pictures reality, but because it constitutes subjects as historically and geographically, culturally specific beings.

Language alone is capable of positioning the subject as a social being, because it is a self-contained system which predates any subject and must be assumed by each subject individually. Language is thus a referential system only in so far as it refers to its own terms and categories. Lacan presents his powerful anti-realist and non-referential position through his gloss on the Jakobsonian distinction between metaphor and metonymy.

Metonymy is not based on any real relation of contiguity between objects. The contiguity on which it depends is purely linguistic. In Lacan's example, 'thirty sails' (1977a: 156) (which is, technically speaking, synecdoche rather than metonymy) the fact that 'sail' can represent 'ship', or 'crown' 'monarch' is not grounded on any real relations (although there *are* real relations between ships and sails, or crowns and monarchs); in this case, we could not understand 'thirty sails' to mean 'thirty ships'. A real relation would forbid us the assumption that each ship has only one sail! The metonym is created only through the word-to-word connection between 'sail' and 'ship'. It is the relation between two terms linked by contiguity, where one takes the place of or represents the other. (In more typical contexts, only words related by similarity are capable of being substituted for each other.) In the case of metaphor, once again, the metaphor is not based on any real similarity or resemblance between objects. The metaphor, 'the mouth of a river' is not based on any resemblance between mouths and rivers, but on the purely linguistic relation between similar terms. In Lacan's example, taken from Victor Hugo, 'his sheaf was neither miserly nor spiteful', 'his sheaf' comes to represent 'Booz' (Lacan 1977a: 156) not because of a real relation of cause and effect, or property and possession; 'his sheaf' can represent 'Booz' because they are signifiers and thus able to be linked through a third term which constitutes the condition of possibility of their similarity. Metaphor is the relation between two terms linked by similarity where one takes the place of the other:

> The creative spark of metaphor does not spring from the presentation of two images, that is, of two signifiers equally actualised. It flashes between two signifiers one of which has taken the place of the other in the signifying chain, the occulted

> signifier remaining present through its (metonymic) connection
> with the rest of the chain . . . (Lacan 1977a: 157)

Metaphor, the substitution of one term for another, is identified
by Lacan with the Freudian process of condensation. He equates
metonymy with the process of displacement, that 'veering off of
signification' which primary processes utilize to evade the censor.
The metaphoric process, the submersion of one term underneath
another, provides the general model for the unconscious symptom:
the term having 'fallen below the bar', becomes repressed, and the
signifier which replaces it or becomes its symptom. In metonymy,
unlike the hierarchical, repressive structure of metaphor, relevant
connections are not so much modelled to the relation between
latent and manifest as based on the connection between a term and
what substitutes for it. In this movement from one term to its
substitute, Lacan will recognize the movement of *desire*. Desire too
is based on a chain of substitution whereby the first (lost) object of
desire generates a potentially infinite chain of (only partially
satisfactory) substitutes.

Where Freud talks of the separation of the thing-presentation
from the word-presentation as his preferred model of repression, in
Lacanian terminology this could be redescribed as the isolation of
certain (usually visual) signifiers and their relegation to the position
of signifieds, restricting their associative freedom, their normally
unlimited possibilities of connection with other signifiers.
Repression ensures a more-or-less fixed connection between a
repressed content (a signifier acting in the position of the signified)
and the conscious symptomatic behaviour it engenders (the dream
or symptom as signifier of the unconscious signified). Without the
process of repression, the signifier could take on the function of the
signified only momentarily, while it is being spoken. Repression
places key infantile signifiers into the position of more or less
permanent signifieds by casting them into the unconscious where
their relations are no longer governed by the basic principles of
arbitrariness, double articulation, and pure difference.[10]

Metaphor or condensation freezes and privileges repressed
signifiers, leaving them active but confined to their own realm.
They are no longer subject to change, being unrelated to and
unmodified by relations with other signifiers. Metonymy or
displacement ensures, by contrast, that the repressed term always
remains in associative relations to the rest of the subject's language,
explaining how the unconscious is able to intervene into or speak
through consciousness at symptomatic moments. It enables the
links between the unconscious terms, their preconscious/conscious

representatives, and networks of free associations to be unravelled enough to facilitate interpretation (in spite of the potentially 'unplummetable navel' at the heart of every dream) (Freud 1900: III, 525; Weber 1977).

Lacanian algorithms of the unconscious

Lacan claims that the topography of the unconscious can be represented by the formula S/s. Using this as his founding 'axiom', he attempts to develop a series of 'algorithmic' representations of the metaphoric and metonymic processes harnessed by the unconscious. His formulae are fundamentally incoherent as mathematical or logical hypotheses. They are irresolvably obscure if taken seriously as formulae. However, if they are taken as symptoms or dreams (a rebus?) they can suggestively detail the processes by which the unconscious reaches conscious expression, i.e., evades censorship by disguise and distortion. These formulae must, in effect, be read as diagrams, visual representations which need to be read term by term rather than as equations.

The first postulate of the Lacanian algebra is the formula S/s. 'S' represents the signifier, 's' the signified, and '/' the barrier which resists being traversed or represented (i.e. the barrier between unconscious and preconscious systems). Signifiers can be transformed into the following form by simple mathematical expansion:

$$F (S) \ 1/S$$

This 'axiom', which designates the replacement of one signifier by another, which is cast into the unconscious, is the formula of the sign and is the cornerstone for his 'algorithms' for metaphor and metonymy. His formula for metonymy is:

$$F (S. . .S) = S (-) S$$

to which Lacan adds the following gloss:

> it is the metonymic structure, indicating that it is the connection between signifier and signified, that permits the elision in which the signifier installs the lack-of-being in the object relation, using the value of 'reference back' possessed by signification in order to invest it with desire aimed at the very lack it supports. The sign – placed between ( ) represents here the maintenance of the bar . . . (Lacan 1977a: 164)

Displacement or metonymy replaces the original (lost) object of a drive with a substitute. This is the same movement as the *glissement* of the signifier over the signified. The loss of the primal object creates a lack which the child will attempt to fill using language to signify its demands. The language at its disposal replaces an ontological lack (lack of nature, lack of identity, lack of fixed objects) with a lack at the level constitutive of language (the lack of anchorage between the signifier and the signified: the lack constitutive of each sign). This lack is the most basic feature of desire and is both assumed and covered over by signification. The child is propelled into its (imaginary and symbolic) capture in/by signification.

The left-hand side of Lacan's formula can be read as a functional representation of the relation between two contiguous signifiers '(S. . .S¹)', two signifiers on the same level – in short, metonymy. And, as Lacan indicates, the right hand side can be interpreted as a relation between signifiers, 'S', and a signified 's' which does not traverse the barrier of censorship. The '=' indicates a relation of congruence. In its expanded form, this formula is transformed into the following:

$$\frac{S. . .S^1}{s} \cdot \frac{S}{S} = \frac{S}{s}$$

To take the position of the signifier 'S', its substitute, 'S¹' must metonymically displace the original, which was placed there by primal repression. In the displacement or transposition of value from one signifier to another, the substitute signifier replaces the rudimentary, infantile connection between the signifier and the drive by carrying the significance of the original, plus its own. A compromise formation results, which subverts preconscious censorship. The displacement results in a new term taking on the rigidity of the old, replacing it in conscious representations from which the original was expelled. Lacan's formulaic representation of metaphor is also obscure. It is:

$$F (S^1/S)S = S (+) S$$

He explains this in his text by saying:

> it is in the substitution of signifier for signifier that an effect of signification is produced that is creative or poetic or in other words, which is the advent of the signification in question. The

sign + between ( ) represents here the crossing of the bar [i.e. the relegation of the signifier to the level of the signified] – and the constitutive value of this crossing for the emergence of signification. This crossing expresses the condition of passage of the signifier into the signified. (Lacan 1977a: 164)

In his formula for metaphor, the left-hand side represents the original signifier 'S' vertically suspended underneath a substitute, 'S¹ ', which has taken its place in representation. It becomes thus the signified for a new signifier. It does not abolish the original but covers over it. The right hand side here represents the process by which the barrier is crossed, that is, the movement barring a signifier from consciousness and placing it in the (unconscious) position of signified, 's'.

Metaphor and metonymy are differentiated both in terms of linguistic orientations and psychical strategies. Metaphor functions on the (vertical) axis of selection, choosing signifiers which are substitutable for each other, while metonymy operates on the (horizontal) axis of combination, bringing together signifiers thus selected. While metonymy does not traverse the barrier (its aim is not to engender the signified, as metaphor does, but to establish a signifying context for the signifier), metonymy operates between two terms within a single order, the preconscious/conscious system; while metaphor, in breaching the barrier (in only one direction), makes what was once a signifier into a signified. Metaphor requires two hierarchically distinguished orders or levels, generating a signified by replacing it with another which represents it. The first signifier is now the implicit signified of the second.

If the metaphoric process generates the signified from the chain of signifiers, and the metonymic process ensures that each signifier has multiple connections and associations which relate it always to other signifiers and thus give it meaning, then it becomes clear these two processes must work hand-in-hand. They are not readily separable but could be seen as two elements of one process, since every condensation is also a displacement from S to S¹, and every displacement relies on terms generated by condensation (Laplanche 1976: 161; Wilden 1972).

The paternal metaphor

Lacan will utilize his 'algebra' of metaphor in reformulating the oedipal dynamic in terms of the child's submission to the name-of-the-father. In his understanding, the prohibition of incest and the establishment of paternal authority which Freud invoked in *Totem and Taboo*, can be understood as the child's submission to the *paternal metaphor*. The paternal metaphor diagrams the child's entry into the symbolic order and the social world beyond the family structure, as regulated by the Other. The paternal metaphor names the child and thus positions it so that it can be replaced discursively by the 'I', in order to enter language as a speaking being. The child can only accede to the paternal metaphor by means of acknowledging (maternal) castration or privation.

In his outline of the structure of psychosis, Lacan claims that the psychotic has *foreclosed*, failed to register or represent the paternal metaphor, and has thus been unable to position him or herself within the general formula of signifying substitution:[11]

$$\frac{S}{S^1} \cdot \frac{S}{X} \rightarrow S\ (^1/s)$$

Consequently, the psychotic is unlocated, symbolically positionless, and cannot be wrenched out of its imaginary confusion with the (m)other. Lacan formulates the paternal metaphor by substituting for the symbols of this formula the following terms:

$$\frac{\text{Name-of-the-father}}{\text{Desire of the mother}} \cdot \frac{\text{Desire of the mother}}{\text{signified to the subject}} \rightarrow \text{Name-of-the-father} \cdot \frac{(0)}{\text{phallus}}$$

This formulation of the metaphoric structure makes it clear that castration is crucial to the child's position in the symbolic. Like all metaphors, the paternal metaphor is able to generate new meanings, but in this case, it generates the signification of the subject itself. As a consequence of its operation, the child can represent itself as 'I'. Lacan claims that the crucial signifier in relation to which the child accedes to the 'I' is *the phallus*. The phallus as signifier is that by which the subject is placed as being or having. The subject, '(0)', is always positioned in relation to the phallus by the name-of-the-father (the right hand side of the metaphor). It is a zero, an 0, that becomes 'one' (if it does so) only through the mediation of, and as, two. The zero is not a subject, full and self-identical, a man [*un homme*]; rather, it is an 'hommelette', a 'little' man more closely resembling a scrambled egg than an identity.[12]

The left hand side of the formula maps out the process by which the child represses the signifier 'desire of the mother', relegating it to the position of signified for the signifier with which it is replaced, the 'name-of-the-father'. The oedipal renunciation of incestual desire of the mother, its replacement by the internalized authority of the father and the child's (boy's?) acquisition of a place within the social order (or Other) which authorizes the Father's Name are all encapsulated in short-hand in this formula. The child only resolves the complex and acquires a speaking position with respect to the Father's Name, i.e., the principle generating the phallus as threshold signifier to the symbolic order. The subject is positioned 'over' the phallus, that is, on one side (the masculine) or the other (the feminine), only because father's phallic status replaces the mother's. We will return to the paternal metaphor in dealing with the question of feminism's relation to psychoanalysis. For the remainder of this chapter, I will attempt to elaborate concretely Lacan's understanding of the unconscious as a language-like structure, and show how it can explain the mysterious procedures of dream interpretation on which psychoanalysis is founded by examining one of Freud's own dreams as he presents it in *The Interpretation of Dreams*.

Freud's dream of the 'Botanical Monograph'

This is one of only two dreams that Freud elaborated in any convincing detail and depth in *The Interpretation*. The other, 'Irma's injection', has been subjected to a good deal of commentary in recent years, so I prefer to deal with the less well-known but equally interesting analysis he presents regarding the dream of the 'Botanical Monograph'. Presumably these two dreams were elaborated in greater detail than others that were not Freud's own, because of his concern for discretion about living or recognizable individuals (see Freud 1900: 105 fn.).

The dream report is very short and simple, but the manner in which Freud interprets it will make clear the peculiar 'language' the unconscious uses to 'speak' through consciousness. Freud's report of the dream is as follows:

> I had written a monograph on a certain plant. The book lay before me and I was at that moment turning over a folded coloured plate. Bound up in each copy there was a dried specimen of the plant, as though it had been taken from a herbarium. (1900: 169)

Freud then breaks the dream into its simplest elements and free associates on each element individually. I will outline the associative chains, the chains of signifiers, that Freud recalls in connection with these elements, and how they explain the unconscious wishes and preconscious dream images the dream-work binds together. This will illustrate the 'rhetoric' on which the unconscious relies for its expression, the kinds of discourse it speaks and its relations to conscious discourse.

He recalls two experiences from the previous day, relatively fresh impressions which provide the dream with its innocuous manifest appearance. On the morning before the dream, he had been walking past a bookshop and noticed a monograph entitled *The Genus Cyclamen* in the window. This memory was the precipitating image of the dream; it is the 'datum' from which the dream image is derived. The second experience occurred on the evening of the same day. Freud had spoken to a Dr Königstein, a colleague who was an eye surgeon. They discussed a number of topics relevant to the dream. For example, Königstein had reproached Freud for being too absorbed in his favourite hobbies. His reproach, and Freud's repudiation of it, form the *preconscious* wish whose fulfilment the dream depicts. A number of other topics of discussion were also of direct relevance to the formation of the dream. Freud mentions them in passing, although he does not elaborate how they relate to the dream.

> All the trains of thought starting from the dream – the thought about my wife's favourite flowers, about cocaine, about the awkwardness of medical treatment among colleagues, about my preference for studying monographs and about my neglect of certain branches of science such as botany – all these trains of thought, when they were further pursued, led ultimately to one or other of the many ramifications of my conversation with Dr Königstein. (1900: 173)

During his conversation with Königstein, they are joined by a certain Professor Gärtner (Gardiner) and his 'blooming and healthy' wife. They talk together about, among other things, a mutual friend who was also one of Freud's patient's, called Flora. This associative chain may be called 'botanical' or 'flowery'. These two associative chains can be represented in diagram form (Figure 7). The dream effects a displacement from the more significant memories and events of the second scene to the less significant memories and events recalled by the first scene. The imagery and associations of the first scene serve as a *metonym* of the second. The dream's manifest content is thus derived largely from the botanical/herbal complex. It represents the fulfilment of a wish that arises in the second scene, a preconscious wish that Königstein be wrong in his estimate of Freud's abilities. This wish is a reply to Königstein's critical remarks: 'Once again the dream . . . turns out to be in the nature of a self-justification, a plea on behalf of my own rights' (1900: 173). In other words, the dream represents the preconscious wish that he produce a fertile piece of work. It represents the

First Scene	*Second Scene*
Botanical monograph	Eye-surgeon Königstein
bookstore	hobbies
genus cyclamen	Gärtner/blooming wife/Flora

Figure 7

fulfilment of his wish to produce, or be the author of a text, like the botanical monograph, which would prove his accuser wrong.

These two conscious recollections, residues from the previous day, form the centre of a wide-ranging series of associations which provide the links with the unconscious wish.

The first scene lends itself to a number of floral associations: first, Freud is led to recall that his wife's favourite flower is the cyclamen. He reproaches himself for forgetting to buy them for her, even though she never forgets to prepare *his* 'favourite flowers', artichokes. He then associates this with a story he had heard about a Frau L., whose husband used to bring her flowers on every birthday. The one year that he forgot the flowers, she saw it as a sign that he didn't love her any more, and burst into tears. Frau L., a former patient of Freud's, had spoken to Freud's wife two days before the dream. Second, Freud remembers that he had, many years earlier, written a monograph about a plant – not the genus cyclamen but the coca plant – during his researches on cocaine. Yet here too, as in the present, he remained largely unrecognized for his efforts, much to his disappointment: 'Cocaine had brought me a great deal of credit, but the lion's share had gone elsewhere' (*The Cocaine Papers*: 35).

Freud published his work on the anæsthetic properties of cocaine in local operations on the eye shortly after Karl Koller. Freud and Koller had in fact collaborated in their earliest work on the drug. It seems that Koller had read Freud's essay but realized, more rapidly than Freud, its implications for opthalmic surgery. When Koller began independent experiments, his assistant was Dr Gärtner, the same one Freud saw the night before the dream. When Freud began his experiments, some months later his assistant was none other than Dr Königstein, and it was the latter who suggested that cocaine might be useful in alleviating complaints such as trachoma and irritus. They published their research shortly after Koller. Freud was bitterly disappointed that the recognition he craved had been directed to Koller. He blamed himself for this failure: 'I had hinted that the alkaloid might be employed as an anæsthetic, but was not thorough enough to pursue the matter further' (ibid.). The presence of Königstein and Gärtner the day before the dream served as a reminder of this defeat. This event is already the repetition of an earlier scene in which Freud's teacher and mentor, Brücke, had been narrowly beaten in a race for publication. Through his identification with Brücke, the episode with Koller was the second time that fame had eluded him by a matter of days. In 1849 Brücke had recognized that: '[T]he red reflex from the eye came from the retina, but he had not the wit to put a lens in front of it so as to focus its vessels. In the following year, his friend, Helmholtz did so, and so was hailed as the discoverer of the opthalmascope' (ibid.: 34). 'Old Brücke', as Freud calls him, is a source of consolation through the latter's identification with him. Freud more than once 'consoled himself with the reflection that his revered master, Brücke, has suffered a similar fate' (ibid.).

In the 'dissection dream' Freud cites in *The Interpretation* (1900: 413, 452), he mentions Brücke as a father-figure, with whom he had a respectful and affectionate relationship. This associative chain will lead us directly to an unconscious paternal identification and complex of wishes directed to the father. Freud does not disappoint our expectations. After relating the Koller episode, Freud describes a fantasy he had the day before the dream. This fantasy will provide a direct connection with the dream's *preconscious* wish for fame and recognition: but also, more significantly, it will be overdetermined by its connections with the unconscious wish as well. Before relating this fantasy, we need some relevant background provided by Freud's self-analysis. Freud had been deeply affected, as he states, by a remark his father made to him when, as a seven-year-old, he had wet the bed. He was told, 'The boy will come to no good.' Freud's aspirations to fame and social recognition were powerful motivations throughout his adult life. He refers us back to another earlier and contrary scene, in which a fortune-teller tells him that he is destined for a great future, effectively retracted by his father's exclamation. His fantasy or day-dream is as follows:

> If ever I got glaucoma, I had thought I should travel to Berlin and get myself operated on incognito, in my friend's [Fliess's] house, by a surgeon recommended by him. The operating

surgeon, who would have no idea of my identity, would boast once again of how easily such operations could be performed, since the introduction of cocaine; and I should not give the slightest hint that I myself had had a share in the discovery. (1900: 170)

This fantasy clearly exhibits all the features necessary to fulfil the preconscious wish. As the famous discoverer of cocaine, Freud would be operated on using his own discovery, without the surgeon's awareness of his identity. He would have objective proof of his own greatness! This daydream, however, is already the reworking of a prior event, related to his father. His father had had trouble with his eyes and required surgery. This operation once again brings together the figures of Koller and Königstein: 'shortly after Koller's discovery, my father had in fact been attacked by glaucoma: my friend Dr Königstein, the opthalmic surgeon had operated on him . . .' (ibid: 171).

Freud's fantasy places him in the same position as his father, with one major difference: his father owed his cure to Freud, Koller, and Königstein ('Dr Koller had been in charge of the cocaine anæsthesia and had commented on the fact that this case had brought together all the three men who had a share in the introduction of cocaine' (ibid.)). Freud, by contrast, owed nothing to anyone. In his fantasy, he himself was the discoverer of cocaine. Represented here is the wished-for reversal of the oedipal structure where the son owes the father a (symbolic) debt in exchange for not castrating him. Freud's fantasy represents a reversal of this situation: here, his father owes Freud a debt for saving his *sight*. It is significant that Freud associates the symbolism of blindness, such as was the fate of Oedipus, with castration. The associative links only now begin to approach the unconscious sources of the dream.

The theme of the monograph leads Freud to a third set of associations related to a scene from his adolescence. Freud had worked on a herbarium when he was in secondary school. He had been given the task of redrawing some specimens, when it was discovered that the herbarium had been infiltrated by bookworms, which had eaten into the pages of the book. The term 'bookworm' triggers off an association for Freud, in which he sees himself as the bookworm. At seventeen, as if to confirm his father's prophecy, he overdrew his account at the bookshop, so voracious was his appetite for reading. This later manifested itself in his passion for reading monographs: 'While I was a medical student, I was the constant victim of an impulse only to learn things out of monographs' (ibid.: 172). Freud traces back this impulse for literary consumption to an infantile scene, covered over by a screen memory. The scene occurred when Freud was five and is the key to the dream's interpretation. Freud's father had given him a bible, which his father considered the dearest thing in the world to him, 'except his spouse'. Freud hurriedly devoured it. The bible was clearly highly significant, a gift from his father which the father loved most but gives up to his son. This is construed by the boy as the gift of the mother, for she is assimilated with 'the good book' and indeed, with all books. We can now understand why Freud is the bookworm! He desires to devour/rape any book/maternal body he is given.

This oedipal scene is covered over and represented by a screen memory dating from the same period. This (false) recollection has a formative role in the dream.

> It had once amused my father to hand over a book with coloured plates (an account of a journey through Persia) for me and my sister to destroy. Not easy to justify from an educational point of view. I had been five years old at the time and my sister was not yet three; and the picture of the two of us blissfully pulling the book to pieces (leaf by leaf, like an artichoke, I found myself saying) was almost the only plastic memory that I retained from that period of my life. (ibid.: 172)

As an explorer and discoverer of books, Freud devours them, rips them apart. He violates them. This seems to be a displacement of the desire for maternal rape (perhaps as an act of sexual revenge). His desire to ravage the mother is partially repressed and partially sublimated into a passionate interest in reading books and in scientific discovery – an epistemophilia that betrays its incestual origins. This impulse to know covers over the more primitive desire to know the mother's body. The dream can now be seen as the fulfilment of two wishes, one, the preconscious wish to become the author of a monograph; the other, the unconscious wish to procreate (become an author) with his mother – to give her a gift/book in the same way that his father had given him one. He gives back to the mother the debt of life he owes to her.

His image of himself as the bookworm now seems to make sense. The bookworm eats its way, leaf by leaf, into the heart of a book in the same way that the child yearns to enter or be incorporated into the mother's body. This dream provides a striking confirmation of the centrality of the oedipal dynamic to the unconscious wish motivating the dream. These associative connections relating the manifest dream images to the unconscious wish can be represented in Figure 8.

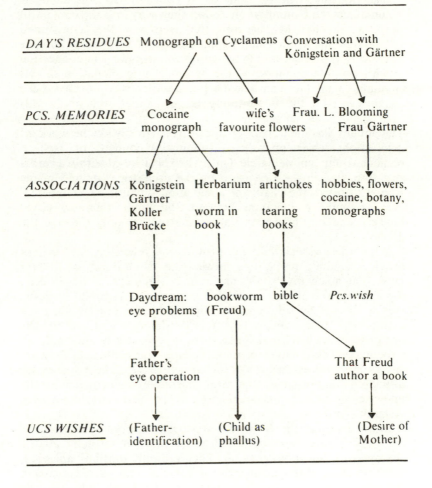

Figure 8

There are several overlapping associations or repeated elements in Freud's recollections: 'Königstein', 'Gärtner', 'hobbies', 'artichokes', and 'monograph', each representing a nodal point necessary for unravelling the dream's latent structure. Condensed into these nodal points are the meanings and intensities – the signifying traces – of the unconscious impulses. These nodal points are points of overdetermination, multiple meaning, and ambiguity in the dream. They indicate that there are a number of paths leading from the manifest dream to the unconscious signifiers:

The first investigation leads us to conclude that the elements 'botanical' and 'monograph' found their way into the content of the dream-thoughts, because, that is to say, they constituted 'nodal points' upon which a great number of the dream-thoughts converged and because they had several meanings in connection with the interpretation of the dream. The explanation of this fundamental fact can also be put another way: to have been represented in the dream-thoughts many times over. (ibid.: 283)

The dream has no meaning apart from this wide network of associations which provide its (linguistic) context. In itself, it remains strictly unintelligible. Only when positioned within a verbal structure, i.e., in the first case, by the dream report; and in the second, through the chains of association – can it be deciphered. We can make connections between the dream's largely visual imagery and its underlying linguistic structure only through the dream's verbalization.

While these associations are prolific and revealing, they do not provide anything resembling meaning in its ordinary or literary sense. The associative chains are webs of signifiers in non-sensical, a-grammatical, and a-syntactical arrangements. As Freud suggests, they exist side by side, each unaffected by the others. We must extrapolate from these key unassimilated signifiers to the unconscious wish. The wish-like form is generated by the libidinal, striving, yearning nature of these unconscious elements. They are wishes in so far as they strive for consciousness. These wishes are ultimately supported by fantasies, narratives constructed by the unconscious through its access to perceptual images in memory systems.

In the dream of the 'Botanical Monograph', Freud only presents us with the preconscious wish, as he does in virtually all the examples in *The Interpretation*. They are only partially analysed. He stops short of the unconscious in his explanations: 'I can assure my readers that the ultimate meaning of the dream, *which I have not disclosed*, is intimately related to the subject of a childhood scene' (ibid.: 191, emphasis added). Freud's wish to write a fertile text, which began with a metaphoric equivalence between the desire for the mother and desire for books, dates from the erotic scene in which he and his sister voluptuously tear up the coloured book leaf by leaf. This infantile scene provides connections with the repressed, oedipal wish for the mother, and prefigures his father's gift of the bible to his young son. This scene also mediates the two scenes comprising the day's residues, providing an intermediary link between the unconscious and the preconscious. The unconscious, oedipal wish is disguised by a preconscious ambition wish.

The dream has no meaning as such. It is not a narrative, a proposition, or a cohesive content. It does not convey a hidden meaning, but rather, it subverts the very processes by which meaning inheres in signifiers, rendering conscious signifiers, units of discourse, ambiguous and polyvalent. The dream's 'meaning' is thus closer to the play of language in poetry than in prose (cf. Kristeva 1976: 1984). It must be considered as signifying *matter* rather than the meaning signified, matter whose arrangement rather than contents are significant for analytic interpretation.

Summary

Freud posits four key characteristics of the primary processes and the unconscious system they serve:

– the unconscious admits no degrees of certainty or doubt, no forms of contradiction, no logical, grammatical, or causal relations. All that exists in the unconscious are positive contents, signifiers, cathected with more or less affect. Because they are usually visual in form, they can only be regarded as positive rather than differential terms, terms with *no* relations between them;
– unconscious processes are not temporally regulated – they are not arranged chronologically, and they are not subject to the normal processes of decay and fading. The unconscious is a permanent, unchanging, system whose dynamic comes from its individual contents striving for consciousness. The unconscious content has no index of age, and always functions as a current force;
– unconscious processes are regulated by the pleasure principle, not the reality principle. Unconscious ideas or signifiers have no 'indications of reality' which could guarantee a distinction between what is the product of fantasy, and what is an effect of reality; and
– the libidinal energies of the unconscious, although diminished through the processes of repression, have a relatively free mobility compared to preconscious/conscious wishes. By means of metaphor/condensation and metonymy/displacement, the libidinal cathexes of an unconscious idea can be shifted onto expedient substitutes, and through them it can gain some pleasure in compromise form through evasion of the censor.

To these can be added the specific contributions Lacan develops in his readings and elaboration of the unconscious:

– the contents of the unconscious can be regarded as signifiers, cast out from the signifying chain and thus unable to signify or to be integrated into conscious discourse;

– the primary processes by which the unconscious acquires a delegate in conscious life are metaphor and metonymy, the two fundamental axes of any system of signification;

– thus, even if the unconscious signifiers are primarily visual, they are treated as if they were verbal. The relations they represent are not based on their *visual* properties, e.g., resemblances seem to play little role in the interpretive process. They can only be interpreted when positioned in a verbal context by means of the chains of association;

– the symptom, as an expression of the unconscious, cannot be read as if it were a *sign*, a message directed from the subject to an interlocutor; rather, it is a signifier which fixes a subject for another signifier, a signifier which speaks through, not as, the subject;

– the discourse of the unconscious, devious and difficult to hear, cannot be articulated in its own voice. It relies on the discourses of consciousness through which it speaks. It is thus expressed most readily as interruption, eruption, silencing, betraying, or rendering conscious discourse ambiguous. It speaks only as interference, submerged in and subverting the intentions of conscious speech;

– consequently, psychoanalysis is indeed 'the talking cure'. Its only techniques are linguistic or literary (listening, deciphering), its object is nothing but discourse, its questions are directed to the location of enunciation – who speaks in and as the subject? And the processes of 'cure', where this occurs, are the result of the position-ing of symptoms, and indeed the subject's desire, within discourse. Psychoanalysis has no aim, object, procedures, or techniques other than those given by language.

5

Sexual relations

For Freud, adult sexuality extends and reorganizes infantile sexual drives. There is a continuity in so far as the adult's choice of love object is based on unresolved attachments to infantile object-cathexes; there is a discontinuity in so far as adult sexuality is genital in orientation and is generally (normatively) directed to a love-object of the opposite sex, beyond the confines of the family. The resolution of (pre-oedipal) object-choices, and the (oedipal) prohibitions against incest, ensure that adult sexual and love relations can never be entirely satisfying, for the beloved is always a displacement of and substitute for the primal, maternal lost object. As Freud suggests,

> Psychoanalysis has shown us that when the original object of wishful impulses has been lost as a result of repression, it is frequently represented by an endless series of substitute objects none of which, however, bring full satisfaction. This may explain the inconstancy in object-choice, the 'craving for stimulation' which is so often a feature of the love of adults. (Freud 1911a: 188–9)

Freud's analysis of love relations is among the most significant and neglected themes in psychoanalysis. Freud's three papers published together as 'Contributions to the Psychology of Love' (1911a) and his metapsychological paper, 'On Narcissism. An Introduction' (1914a) form the nucleus of an analysis of relations between the sexes that is predicated on the oedipal resolution, the distinction between the sexes, and the social/libidinal positions henceforth opened or closed to each of them.

Lacan has also devoted some of his most difficult papers to the question of relations (or rather, the *absence* of relations) between the sexes ('The Signification of the Phallus' (1977a), see also Mitchell and Rose (1982), in which this paper is translated as 'The Meaning of the Phallus' and the notorious Seminar XX, *Encore*, which is partially translated. These are among the most fascinating and problematic of Lacan's works; they provide a clear indication of his notions of femininity and female sexuality. Because Lacan's work relies heavily on an assumed familiarity with Freud's texts, it is difficult if not impossible to understand his position without some understanding of Freud's texts. I will therefore move freely between Freud's and Lacan's texts, starting with the latter's distinction between the penis and the phallus.

The penis and the phallus

The processes by which the phallus, a signifier, becomes associated with the penis, an organ, involves the procedures by which women are systematically excluded from positive self-definition and a potential autonomy. The relations each sex has to the phallus *qua* signifier map the position(s) each occupies as a feminine or masculine subject in the patriarchal symbolic order. Moreover, it defines the structure of romantic relations between them.

The misappropriation of the penis by the phallus is delineated step-by-step in the relations between need, demand, and desire outlined earlier. The penis is removed from its merely anatomical and functional role within ('natural') need, (where its organic role for the little boy lies in urination in the first instance, and insemination, in the second), to the role of object, the *objet a*, in a circuit of demand addressed to the (m)other. It is then capable of taking on the symbolic role of signifier at the level of desire, an object of unconscious phantasy.

As the successive 'object' of need, demand, and desire, the phallus is the valorized signifier around which both men and women define themselves as complementary or even supplementary subjects.[1] Because the penis and the phallus are (albeit illusorily) identified, women are regarded as castrated. By its presence or absence, the penis becomes the defining characteristic of both sexes. Lacan himself concedes that this equation is illusory or misrecognized, but claims that nevertheless the equation is constitutive of human desire, and of the symbolic order.

> Castration may derive support from privation, that is to say, from the apprehension in the Real of the absence of the penis in women – but even this implies a symbolisation of the object, since the Real is full and 'lacks' nothing. In so far as one finds castration in the genesis of the neuroses, it is never Real but symbolic and aimed at an imaginary object. (Lacan, Seminar March–April 1957: 851–2)

The phallus functions to enable the penis to define all (socially recognized) forms of human sexuality. The *differences* between genitals becomes expressed in terms of the presence or absence of a single (male) term.[2] The Real, where the vagina, clitoris, or vulva have the same ontological status and functional utility as the penis and testicles, must be displaced and recoded if women's bodies are to be categorized as *necessarily* incomplete. The narcissistic imaginary order mediates between the Real, in which there is no lack, and the symbolic, where women represent *for men* a lack men have disavowed. It is during the identificatory blurring of self and other that (from the boy's point of view, at least), the penis becomes regarded as a 'detachable' organ, along the lines of the fantasy of the body in bits-and-pieces. The detachable penis, the penis that the mother once had, prefigures the function of the phallus. It produces the penis as an object of signification, rather than a biological organ. It represents what some 'possess' and others have lost, becoming the term through which the child comes to recognize sexual difference.

The imaginary object – the detachable penis – becomes an element in the symbolic circuit of exchange when it comes to stand as the link or bridge between the two sexes, a form of linguistic *copula*. It becomes a signifier within a signifying system, and cannot thus be possessed or owned by anyone.

The phallus is both the signifier of the differences between the sexes and the signifier which effaces lack and thus difference. It is the term with respect to which the two sexes are defined as different, and the term which functions to bring them together, the term of their union: 'It is a copula, a hyphen – in the evanescence of its erection – the signifier par excellence of impossible identity' (Leclaire, quoted in Lemaire, 1977: 86). For both sexes, though in quite different ways, the phallus serves as a means of access to the 'domain of the Other'. The Other is understood here in two senses: as a socio-symbolic network regulated according to language-like rules; and as a psychical structure, representative of this social Other, internalized in the form of the unconscious. According to Lacan, the signifier orders and organizes the radically heteronomous drives and impulses from the raw data of the unconscious. He follows Freud here in seeing the unconscious as a consequence of primal repression, where the phallus is the preserved infantile nucleus of the unconscious, a residue of the child's primal repression of its maternal desire.

If the penis assumes the function of the phallus this is because female sexuality is considered a mutilation or castration. Because of its erectile form and 'preference' for penetration, the phallus serves to 'fill' the lack. This function can only be 'performed' in so far as the phallus can also be regarded, in addition to being the sign of sexual difference, as the signifier of the object of the other's desire. As a signifier, the phallus works its effects on the subject only through the mediation of the other.

Even in Lacan's terms, the penis can only ever approximate the function of the phallus. 'Having' a penis, i.e. being a man, is no guarantee of warding off lack. On the contrary, rendering them equivalent has problems of its own, manifested in anxieties about sexual performance (impotence fears) as well as a sometimes desperate search for the other through whom the man can have his position as the possessor of the valued/desired organ confirmed. Without circulation, without the mediation of the other and the Other, no one has access to it. As a signifier, no one has a privileged or unique relation to it, for it exists only by virtue of the entire signifying chain and an intersubjective, multi-subjective, symbolically regulated social order. It functions only through the Other and the other, and this makes clear its divergence from the male biological organ.

The fetishist's relation to the phallus makes clear the socio-linguistic/symbolic investment in the phallus. The fetishist demands that there be such a thing as the maternal phallus. By this demand, he falsifies or disavows his perception of female genitals. Disavowal is the simultaneous affirmation and denial of perception. It is a common mode of defence against undesired perceptions (e.g. the oedipal boy disavows women's castration by simply refusing to believe what he sees). The fetishist is the adult who, because of his attachment to the fetish, is 'saved' from psychosis (which is the more typical consequence of disavowal in adults). The fetishist demands that the mother have a genital organ the same as his own. His disavowal functions to ward off threats to his own organ, threats which force him to acknowledge the possibility of its loss. In place of the missing maternal phallus, he will position the fetish (shoe, raincoat, underwear, etc.). The substitutability of the fetish for the maternal phallus is not the effect of a simple coincidence in reality (there is little or no resemblance between the maternal phallus and, say, the raincoat), but is always an effect of signification in so far as the phallus is *already* a signifier. The link between the fetish and the phallus is always already a signifying relation.

The whole problem of the perversions [incidentally, fetishism is the only perversion for which there is no corresponding neurosis] consists in conceiving how the child, in his relation to the mother, a relation constituted in analysis not by his vital dependence on her but by his dependence on her love, that is to say, by the desire for her desire, identifies himself with the imaginary object of this desire in so far as the mother herself symbolizes it in the phallus.

The phallocentrism produced by this dialectic is all that need concern us here. It is, of course, entirely conditioned by the intrusion of the signifier in man's psyche and is strictly impossible to deduce from any pre-established harmony of this psyche with the nature that it expresses. (Lacan 1977a: 197–8)

The paternal metaphor is the threshold permitting access to the symbolic. It does not presume a Real castration but an acknowledgement by the boy of his willingness to give up his most powerful desires to accept the Law. His 'reward' is the preservation of the penis as a narcissistic organ, and its (provisional) elevation to the position of object of desire for the other. Through the (castrated) other's desire, the penis approximates (even if only on loan, as it were) the phallus. By means of the desire of the other, the male comes to be affirmed as possessing or *having* the phallus.

Women, the mother in particular, must therefore be construed as *not having*, that is, as *lacking* the phallus in order for men to be regarded as having it. Women desire the penis as castrated subjects; men can offer them the sexual organ, object of desire, as a means of secondary access to phallic status. The (imaginary, detachable), penis is not a *representation* or sign of the phallus. For one thing, this would relegate the phallic signifier to the barred position of signified; for another, it would create two parallel orders – organic and symbolic – that are only externally, not constitutively, connected. The signifier is active in giving meaning and value to the organ, i.e., in constituting it as an organ with particular attributes and values. The penis, in other words, does not have the sole right of alignment with the phallus. Not only does the penis act as if it were the 'meaning of the phallus', a series of substitute objects are also capable of taking on this function; a baby (in the equation of penis = baby. Cf. Freud 1917a: 128–9, 132–3); the whole of a woman's body (in narcissism, 1914a); and parts of her body (in hysteria, 1900: 387, 390). The penis, as imaginary object is *already* bound up with signification. It is itself already a signifier, and as such, can function as a *metonymic displacement* of the phallus.

If we take the case of Little Harry,[3] cited by Lacan in his detailed discussion of fetishism (Lacan and Granoff 1956), the boy has had ample pre-oedipal access to the mother's body, having slept in the same bed as her until he was over three (Lorand 1930: 423). He knew that she had no penis or organ similar to his own. It is also clear that the boy occupied the role of the object of her desire. He takes on the role of phallus *for her*. He disavows any knowledge of genital differences in order to stave off the threat of castration directed towards his own organ, thereby being able to continue his special relationship with the mother. His desire is the desire of the other. He functions as the phallus for her, and for himself.

Harry develops a fondness for caressing shoes, especially those belonging to women he likes. His other symptoms are also relevant to understanding the role of representation in the function of the phallus: he develops a phobia about pendulum clocks (which reminded him of the doctor's surgery when he had an operation for phimosis at the age of two); he impulsively, almost obsessively cuts locks of his own hair without knowing why (ibid.: 422); and particularly, he develops a mortal dread and fear of amputees:

> a relative came in to visit the family, a man with one leg amputated. Harry could not be induced to enter the room; the moment he had heard the voice of the man outside the door he ran screaming into the bedroom. (Lorand 1930: 422)

Harry thus both affirms and denies, both acknowledges and refuses to accept, the possibility of his own castration:

> To stress the point: if the strength of repression (of the affect) is to be founded in the *interest* of the successor of the feminine phallus, it is the denegation of its absence which will have constructed the memorial. The fetish will become the vehicle both of denying and asseverating the castration. (Lacan and Granoff 1956: 268)

Shoes, in Harry's case, or shiny noses in the case discussed by Freud (1927a), do not function as signs by virtue of their resemblance to the penis. The penis *already* functions as a signifier, an imaginary object, from the moment the boy attributes it to the mother. The fetish is thus not based on a one-to-one representation of the penis, any more than, in Freud's example, a pore of the skin can represent a vagina (1914c). The relation is not one of visual resemblance, analogy, nor even contiguity or simultaneity. The child's perception of the mother's lack, and his symbolic use of the last object seen before witnessing the mother's 'absence', including shoes, stockings, underwear, fur, etc. – (those objects the child is likely to see when looking up at his mother) does not adequately explain fetishism. The relation between the maternal phallus and the fetish is not Real. As Freud saw in his analysis of the fetishist who was attracted to shiny noses, the connection is purely verbal, a relation entirely within signification:

> Indeed, if a slipper were, strictly speaking, a displacement of the

female organ and no other elements were present to elaborate the primary data, we would consider ourselves faced with a primitive perversion completely beyond the reach of analysis. (Lacan and Granoff 1956: 268)

The penis takes on the function of the phallus only because it is a mark or trace that is able to signify, indeed, produce, the exclusion of half the population. From being a Real organ, the penis becomes an imaginary object dividing the sexes according to its presence or absence, possessed by some, desired by others; it then functions as a symbolic object (an object of exchange or union) between the sexes. Because the phallus is the term signifying both division and union, the penis is not the only 'object' that is able to serve as its metonym. In different socio-political structures, the phallus seems to function as the signifier of the presence and absence of access to power and self-definition. In spite of Lacan's otherwise universalist claims, he acknowledges at some points in his work that the chain of signifiers in which the phallus finds its context varies historically:

> the phallus is not a question of a form or of an image, or of a phantasy, but rather a signifier, the signifier of desire. In Greek antiquity, the phallus is *not represented by an organ but as an insignia*. (Lacan, quoted in Wilden 1981: 187, emphasis added)

The phallus thus distributes access to the social categories invested with various power relations. In Greece, the family insignia, which served to differentiate one class from another through the exclusion of slaves from access to the family name, functioned as the phallus. In our culture, the presence and absence of the penis serves to differentiate one sex from another, according to the interests of one of them. It can thus, if interpreted socio-politically, be seen to represent some of the ways in which subjects are positioned in different locations within a hierarchized social geography.

For Lacan, the phallus is the 'signifier of signifiers',[4] the term which defines each subject's access to the symbolic order. It is an emblem of the structure of language: the gap in language which makes the sliding of the signifier over the signified and the regulation of the polyvalence and play within language possible. This gap or lack is also the founding trace of the unconscious, constituted as such by the repressed signifier: 'It is the ultimately significative object which appears when all the veils are lifted. Everything related to it is an object of amputations and interdictions . . . '. When the veils are lifted, there is only the Medusa – woman's castrated genitals, lacking, incomplete, horrifying (for men). Salomé's dance, like strip-tease, can only seduce when at least one veil remains, alluring yet hiding the *nothing* of woman's sex.

the phallus, that is, *the image of the penis*, is negativity in its place in the specular image. It is what predestines the phallus to embody *jouissance* in the dialectic of desire.

. . . the specular image is the channel taken by the transfusion of the body's libido towards the object. But even though part of it remains preserved from this immersion, concentrating within it the most intimate aspects of auto-eroticism, its position at the 'tip' of the form predisposes it to the phantasy of decrepitude in which is completed its exclusion from the specular image and from the prototype that it constitutes for the world of objects,

Thus the erectile organ comes to symbolize the place of *jouissance* not in itself, or even in the form of an image, but as a part lacking in the desired image . . . (Lacan 1977a: 319–20, emphasis added)

The phallus and power

The phallus and penis can only be aligned if there are those who lack it. It is assumed only on the basis of division and dichotomy, represented by the lack attributed to women. The penis can only enhance one's narcissism if it is somehow distinguished from other organs and parts of the body. It enhances men's narcissism because it constitutes their corporeal unity in relation to women's incompleteness. The penis comes to represent tangibly the differences between the sexes as other organs, in our culture, do not, enabling it to function on an imaginary level to signify presence and absence or fullness and privation.

In spite of Lacan's claims, the phallus is not a 'neutral' term functioning equally for both sexes, positioning them both in the symbolic order. As the word suggests, it is a term privileging masculinity, or rather, the penis. The valorization of the penis and the relegation of female sexual organs to the castrated category are effects of a socio-political system that also enables the phallus to function as the 'signifier or signifiers', giving the child access to a (sexual) identity and speaking position within culture. Its position as a threshold signifier is symptomatic of the assumed patriarchal context in Freud's and Lacan's work.

The phallus cannot be merely a signifier like any other. In Saussure's understanding, the materiality of the signifier is irrelevant to its signifying capacities. For Saussure, only the relations between the signifier and the signified, or relations between signs confer meaning and value on any term. Yet, if the relation between signifier and signified is arbitrary, Saussure describes one relation between signifier and signified as relatively motivated, motivated, that is, by the already existing structure of language. The symbolic function of the phallus envelops the penis as the tangible sign of a privileged masculinity, thus in effect naturalizing male dominance.

In this context, it is significant that although Lacan is at least partially responsible for feminist rereadings of the Freudian concept of penis-envy in terms of the socio-symbolic meaning of the organ, he is also responsible for positing a metonymic relation between an organ and a signifier which may turn out to be just as problematic in feminist terms as Freud's biologism. The penis comes to function as the signified for the phallic signifier.

Lacan's distinction between the penis and the phallus enables Freud's biologistic account of male superiority and women's penis-envy to be explained in linguistic and symbolic, and thus historical terms. This had the major advantage of enabling the possibility of change to be articulated. Yet although Lacan's account is directed to the phallus as signifier, not to the penis as an organ, it is committed to an *a priori* privilege of the masculine that is difficult, if not impossible, to dislodge. It is unclear if Lacan does distinguish his position from Freud's as sharply as I have suggested, when one reads passages like the following:

> the fact that the penis is dominant in the shaping of the body-image is evidence of [an autonomous, non-biological imaginary anatomy]. Though this may shock the champions of the autonomy of female sexuality, such dominance *is a fact* and one moreover which *cannot be put down to cultural influences alone.* (Lacan 1953: 13, emphasis added)

Lacan has been avidly defended by a number of feminists for his use of the phallic signifier in place of the male sexual organ. Ellie Ragland-Sullivan, for example, argues that:

> the phallic signifier is intrinsically neutral, meaningless in its own right, and only takes its power from association catalyzed in the Oedipal drama . . . Lacan is describing first causes, not approving them. (Ragland-Sullivan 1982: 10)

Her defence of Lacan is strongly reminiscent of Juliet Mitchell's justification of Freud's phallocentrism a decade earlier in *Psychoanalysis and Feminism*. Mitchell's defence of Freud consisted in claiming that psychoanalysis merely provides a description of patriarchal power relations. It explains the transmission and reproduction of sex roles and their different social values. Both claim the structural neutrality of oedipal or phallic law in positioning the two sexes as subjects:

> Sexual difference can only be the consequence of a division; *without this division it would cease to exist*. But it must exist because no human being can become a subject outside the division into two sexes. One must take up a position as either a man or a woman. Such a position is by no means identical with one's biological sexual characteristics, nor is it a position of which one can be very confident . . . (Mitchell, in Mitchell and Rose 1982: 6, emphasis added)

Mitchell's coeditor, Jacqueline Rose, acknowledges that the phallic signifier should remain arbitrary and purely conventional in its relations to the penis and the attributes of masculinity. She asks 'why that necessary symbolisation and the privileged status of the phallus appear as interdependent in the structuring and securing (never secure) of human subjectivity?' (ibid.: 56). This is a crucial question. It locates the key differences between Lacan's feminist defenders and critics. Given that his work *does* provide a description of our culture in its past and present forms, the question remains as to how relevant and useful or constricting and pre-committing his understanding is for conceptualizing a non-patriarchal future. Contrary to Mitchell, Ragland-Sullivan and others, I will claim that the phallic signifier is *not* a neutral 'third' term against which both sexes are analogously or symmetrically positioned. The relation between the penis and phallus is not arbitrary, but socially and politically motivated. The two sexes come to occupy the positive and negative positions not for arbitrary reasons, or with arbitrary effects. It is motivated by the already existing structure of patriarchal power, and its effects guarantee the reproduction of this particular form of social organization and no other. They are distinguished *not* on the basis of (Saussurian 'pure') difference, but in terms of dichotomous opposition or distinction; not, that is, as contraries ('A' and 'B'), but as contradictories ('A' and 'not-A'). In relations governed by pure difference, *each* term is defined by all the others; there can be no privileged term which somehow dispenses with its (constitutive) structuring and value in relations to other terms. Distinctions, binary oppositions, are relations based on one rather than many terms, the one term generating a non-reciprocal definition of the other as its negative. The presence and absence of *one* term defines *both* positions in the dichotomy.[5] Mitchell believes that the subject must occupy a symbolic position as either male or female. Yet it is surely arbitrary, in the sense of social or conventional, that the continuum of differences between gradations of sexual difference along a continuum is divided into categories only according to the presence or absence of the one, male, organ.

Lacan, as usual, is ambiguous. If he blurs the boundary between the biological and the symbolic, he also helps to undo the certainty that many men have about their phallic position:

> It can be said that this signifier is chosen because it is the most tangible element in the real of sexual copulation and also the most symbolic in the literal (typographical) sense of the term, since it is equivalent there to the (logical) copula. (Lacan 1977a: 287)

As the logical or grammatical copula, it serves to connect two terms together while disappearing or evacuating itself of any identity of its own. It functions to unite (and disappear) or to separate and divide. This fundamental ambiguity or duplicity in the term will provide a vulnerable, contradictory point within male relations and sexual domination. As signifier, the phallus is not an object to be acquired or an identity to be achieved. It is only through the desire of the other that one's own position – as either being or having – the phallus is possible.

To summarize in point form:

1 the phallus is the crucial signifier in the distribution of power, authority and a speaking position, a kind of mark or badge of a social position;

2 the phallus is the signifier of lack marking castration. As such, it also signifies presence or possession, for only in opposition to the absence of the term does its presence have any meaning or value. It thus signifies what men (think they) *have* and what women (are considered to) *lack*;

3 the phallus is the 'signifier of signifiers', the representative of signification and language. By means of the phallus, the subject comes to occupy the position of 'I' in discourse; by means of its signification as lack, the subject can use language in place of a direct or unmediated relation to the Real, a relation that it must relinquish;

4 as a signifier, the phallus has no given content or signified; it is 'filled in' only in concrete contexts, in momentary alignments with other signifiers. For this reason, it is capable of enveloping many objects or bodily organs – the child, the woman's body, the penis,

the hysterogenic zone have all functioned as phallic for subjects Freud analysed;

5   the phallus designates the object of desire. It is the heir to the role of the *objet a*. It signifies the desire of the other, which is always organized with reference to the Other;

6   the phallus is the condition of symbolic exchange relations which Levi-Strauss (1961) saw as the condition of culture. The phallus is both the object circulated in ritually inscribed networks of social exchange; and in the rules which govern the direction and flow of the object;[6]

7   the phallus represents the name-of-the-father, through which the subject is positioned in culture;

8   the phallus is the signifier which established the subject's unconscious, an internalized locus of the Other and the repository of repressed desire.

It is thus simultaneously and indissolubly the mark of sexual difference (and identity), the signifier of the speaking position in language, and the order governing exchange relations.

Anaclisis, narcissism, and romantic love

Freud divides adult love relations into two broad categories, those modelled on 'anaclitic' attachments, and those modelled on narcissistic infantile object-cathexes. The anaclitic or attachment type includes those who love 'persons who are concerned with the child's feeding, care and protection . . . in the first instance, his mother or a substitute for her' (1914a: 87). The narcissistic type consist in those who are 'plainly seeking *themselves* as a love object' (1914a: 88).

Although each position is available to either sex, Freud suggests that there is a tendency for men to occupy the more masculine, anaclitic position, and for women to occupy the more feminine, narcissistic position. Both types, however, find a common origin in the *infantile* phase of primary narcissism, the phase of imaginary identifications based on the mirror double or (m)other.

> We say that a human being has originally two sexual objects – himself and the woman who nurses him – and in doing so we are postulating a primary narcissism in everyone, which may in some cases manifest itself in a dominating fashion in his object-choice. (Freud 1914a: 88)

Anaclisis is an active, masculine form of love, modelled on loving another who resembles the subject's infantile nurturers; the feminine form involves the passive aim of being loved. These two poles represent complementary desires which, ideally, enable the heterosexual couple to form a satisfying partnership.

Freud argues that the anaclitic lover tends to over-evaluate the love-object. This type conforms most readily to the stereotyped image of romantic love, a love based on putting the love-object on a pedestal and abjecting the self. What is apparent in the dynamic relation between anaclitic and narcissistic lovers is the elevation of the latter to a superior, adored, idealized position.

Freud, however, is correct in his cynical assessment of the lover's state of adoration: anaclisis is not so much based on a valorization of *her* unique charms and attributes as much as in *his* position as lover. He suggests that this state is 'derived from the child's original narcissism and thus corresponds to a transference of that narcissism to the sexual object' (1914a: 88). The lover transfers narcissistic self-regard onto the love object and is thus able to love himself, as it were, in loving the other.

While claiming to love the woman desperately, the anaclitic lover strives for a recognition of his own active position. His own esteemed ego is complemented and its value proven if the love object attains perfection in his eyes. Freud suggests that this structure of desire lies behind the common rescue fantasies typical of male sexuality (1911a: 168ff). The lover repeats the structure of his infantile narcissistic relations with the mother, where he is affirmed as the object of her desire, the phallus for her. He is positioned here, and in adult relations, as the subject who has what the (m)other lacks. His position as phallic is conditioned on women's valorized, 'superior' position coupled with their real social powerlessness (this repeats the characteristics of the phallic mother). In short, he displaces his infantile narcissism onto an extraneous love object, and, by projecting her as an extension of himself, is able to receive his narcissistic investment back.

Narcissism, by contrast, is a secondary, defensive reassertion of the girl's pre-oedipal narcissism, a compensation for her oedipal castration. Women compensate for their 'phallic loss' by a number of pathways: 'normal' femininity (i.e. passivity) and motherhood; the masculinity complex; or a reactivated (secondary) narcissism. Here the woman, in recognizing her castration, attempts to make her whole body take on the role of object of (the other's) desire (see also 1931: 132). She strives to affirm her position as desirable for the other, as a phallus for the other. This aim is structurally quite different from that of the boy. His position as the subject of desire is confirmed, while her position as the object of desire is affirmed. This is the difference between *being* and *having* the phallus, a non-symmetrical hierarchy between a subject (who 'has' the phallus, has the object of desire) and an object (who 'is' the phallus, the desired object).

The narcissistic woman is described as vain, shallow, skilled in artifice, but above all, she is bound up with the desire to be loved. What threatens her most is the loss of love. She becomes especially dependent on men who may withhold or withdraw their love. The strength or degree of the other's love for her is the measure of her own value and worth. Her aim is thus to catch, and keep, one or many lovers as a testimony of her value.

Freud describes melancholia as a state of psychological impoverishment without the prospect of love (1917c). The narcissistic woman's ego is melancholic in the absence of an other to love her. Her love-relations involve an identification with and incorporation of the other (as alter-ego or ego-ideal). She feels a sense of the irreplaceability of the other, his central importance to her existence. Without this (or some other) love, she feels worthless, a mere fragment of a person. In spite of her aura of power, aloofness, and confidence, she is in desperate need of a subject to affirm her.

Although the narcissistic woman's amorous relations with men do not involve the overvaluation Freud considered necessary for 'proper' object-love, there is one love relation in which this overvaluation does occur – in her relations with her child:

> Even for narcissistic women, whose attitudes towards men remain cool, there is a road which leads to complete object-love. In the child which they bear, a part of their own body confronts them like an extraneous object to which, starting out of their narcissism, they can give complete object-love. (1914a: 89–90)

This form of object-choice enables the woman to effect a 'proper' object-choice, and yet to maintain her own central narcissistic position as the love-object of another.[7] In loving her child, she is both loving herself (a biological/specular extension of herself) and another who is like her. She extends her self-love through maternal love.

In the 'Contributions to the Psychology of Love' (1911a), Freud outlines some of the effects of the boy's resolution of the oedipus complex on his later love relations. The requirements of symbolic functioning are contradictory: on the one hand, the boy's sexuality is virile, active, predatory; yet, on the other hand, it must be controlled, repressed, sublimated, and redirected. This split attitude may effect the man's choice of love-object. For example, Freud suggests that men may feel split between feelings of tenderness, respect, affection, and sexual 'purity'; and feelings of a highly sexual yet debasing kind. Affection and sexual desire seem to inhabit different spheres, often being resolved only by splitting his relations between two kinds of women – one noble, honourable, and pure (the virgin figure), the other a sexual profligate (the prostitute figure). He treats the first with asexual admiration, while he is sexually attracted to, yet morally or socially contemptuous of, the second. Here the male lover attempts to preserve the contradictory role of the mother (as pure and as seducer), while removing its contradictions by embodying its elements in separate 'types' of women, either virgin or whore, subject or object, asexual or only sexual, with no possible mediation.

The woman who occupies either position confirms his primacy. In taking on the virginal role, the woman acts as an externalized ego-ideal, a perfected counterpart which the man himself can only hope to emulate. He exalts her in exactly the same way as he treats his own worthy ideals and aspirations. When the woman takes on the prostitute role, the man can debase her and give vent to his desire to humiliate her. Such impulses would be inappropriate with the virginal figure. He can fully indulge his sexual desires because he believes that he is in no danger of being judged by her. He can treat her as if she were not a subject at all but a physical object. After all, he has paid for her (temporary) allegiance. With her, he can openly admit and enact socially forbidden desires and impulses, hiding and/or exercising his potency independent of her judgement (Freud 1911a: 185). At the origin of the hostility and contempt for women the man thus feels for his sexual partner is his ambivalent pre-oedipal relation to his mother. She is *both* virginal, pure, noble, sexless (as a consequence of his repression of his own sexual wishes about her), *and* a whore, the result of his realization that, long before his birth, the mother has already been unfaithful to him (with the father). If she is a sexual being, she has betrayed him by being desired by others, like his fantasy of the prostitute.

Freud's description of anaclitic and narcissistic types of love-object seems, on a superficial reading, to confirm the stereotyped image of romantic love: the woman *seems* to be in the powerful position. She is distant, aloof, self-preoccupied, on a pedestal, regarded as a queen or goddess whose every wish is her lover's command. The man *seems* to be her willing slave, happy to satisfy her needs in order to remain in some relation with her. However, as Freud astutely observes, these appearances in fact belie the real power relations invested in romantic myths. He observes that the anaclitic lover directs all his ardour and passion to a woman whose unique identity, 'personality', beauty, are his avowed objects. However, her identity is surprisingly irrelevant to his passion. The anaclitic lover makes this kind of passionate commitment not once, to a rare, exceptional woman – as he professes – but to a large number of women with whom he forms a number of *serial* romantic liaisons:

> passionate attachments of this sort are repeated with the same peculiarity – *each an exact replica of the others* – again and again in the lives of men of this type; in fact, owing to external events such as changes in residence and environment, the love-objects may replace one another so frequently that a *long series* of them is formed. (Freud 1911a: 185, emphasis added)

By implication, it is not any particular woman whose unique identity is the privileged object of his desire. It is the loving attitude itself he desires. He desires to be in love, and to be active in his idealization of the other; his passion is to be out of control of his passion. He is attracted to active forms of loving, and to his ability to define the position and value of the love-object.

He strives to affirm his *narcissistic* position by loving the woman and 'producing' her as an ideal for himself whom he can love as he loves himself. His centrality to her position duplicates his pre-oedipal position in relation to the phallic mother – the mother who both has and lacks the phallus. Freud confirms that this type of love relation is not a consequence of the boy's oedipus complex, but a function of his earlier pre-oedipal relation to the mother: his 'conditions for loving and . . . behaviour in love – do in fact arise from the psychical constellation connected to the mother' (1914a: 169), even if the pre-oedipal boy's perception of the mother is bound up with an understanding of the mother's relation to the father: 'It is at once clear that for the child who is growing up in the family circle the fact of the mother belonging to the father becomes an inseparable part of the mother's essence' (ibid.: 169). Paradoxically, the anaclitic lover, who 'clings to' the other is in fact fundamentally narcissistic, loving the other in order to love himself, or rather his own processes of loving. He transfers his own (infantile) narcissism onto the beloved, who is then able to reflect the ego's magnitude and value, without herself being the centre of focus. He affirms his own position of mastery, control, activity – the phallic position – rather than her value as loved object. His anaclisis is, in this sense, self-directed: its effects are narcissistic.

In the case of the narcissistic woman, there is a complementary paradox. Given Freud's description of the women's aloof, contented, and inaccessible self-containment, and given Freud's claim that another's narcissism exerts a powerful appeal for us (see 1914a: 89), she *appears* to be autonomous and independent of her lover, occupying an 'unassailable libidinal position' as Freud describes it (ibid.). The self-image of this woman is affirmed as a positive and resistant femininity which refuses phallocentic circulation, as Kofman suggests in *The Enigma of Woman* (1985). Yet the woman's narcissistic relation is far more dependent and subordinate than it seems. Her identity as narcissistic is in fact dependent on her being desired by the other. Such women will usually not dare do anything to lower the lover's high estimation of them. Their position is not thus the active position of self-definition but a passivity, an inability to speak or act in their own voices; it is the passive position of *semblance* and *seduction*. The woman's passivity is confused with a coolness that makes her attractive to as well as frustrating for men. She always remains one step beyond her lover's grasp, always slightly out of reach, a lack sustaining his desire. His desire is kept alive because he never truly 'has' her. Ultimately what she values is his desire for her. It enables her to maintain her apparent independence. She can feel confident in so far as she is wanted. Ironically, her (secondary) narcissism is fundamentally other-directed, based on the other's evaluation of her. Her narcissistic position is in fact anaclitic!

Lacan and romantic love

Lacan argues that both sexes are constituted as sexually different, as sexed subjects, only with reference to the phallic signifier. Masculine and feminine positions are a function, not of biology but of the very structure of language. In French as in English, the verb is modified by its conjugation with either *being* (*être*) or *having* (*avoir*). The two sexes are positioned as such in the mode of being (for the feminine), and having (for the masculine), the phallus:

> But one may, simply by reference to the function of the phallus, indicate the structures that will govern the relations between the sexes.
>
> Let us say that these relations will turn around a 'to be' and a 'to have', which, by referring to a signifier, the phallus, have the opposed effect, on the one hand, of giving reality to the subject in this signifier, and, on the other, of derealizing the relations to be signified. (Lacan 1977a: 289)

Through the phallus, each sex is positioned as a speaking being, 'giving reality to the subject'; through the phallus, the *reality* of anatomical sex becomes bound up with the meanings and values that a culture gives to anatomy, 'derealizing the relations to be signified'. Yet if, as has been suggested, the man can be affirmed as phallic only through the other who desires (and therefore lacks) what he has, the processes positioning the woman as a female subject with respect to the phallus are more problematic and her relation to the desire of the other more tenuous.

Her castration complex functions to ensure that she accepts her castrated condition as a *fait accompli*. She 'resolves' her oedipal entanglements by accepting that she does not *have* the phallus. However, as a recompense for her turning from the mother to the father as her primary love-object, she acquires a number of reactive strategies and devices for gaining pleasure even if she has had to relinquish the active pre-oedipal position. The characteristics of femininity Freud outlines (1933: 132) – seductive, coquettish behaviour, narcissism, vanity, jealousy, and a weaker sense of justice – are a consequence of her acceptance of her lack (of the phallus). They are strategies developed to ensure that, even if she doesn't *have* the phallus, she may *become* the phallus, the object of desire for another.

She retains her position as the object of the other's desire only through artifice, appearance, or dissimulation. Illusion, travesty, make-up, the veil, become the techniques she relies upon to both cover over and make visible her 'essential assets'. They are her means of seducing or enticing the other, of becoming a love-object for him. While concealing her 'deficiency' by these means, she also secures a mode of access to the phallic. Ironically, in this aim of becoming the object of the other's desire, she becomes the site of a rupture, phallic and castrated, idealized and debased, devoted to the masquerade (an excess) and a deficiency:

> Paradoxical as this formulation may seem, I am saying that it is in order to be the phallus, that is to say, the signifier of the desire of the Other, that a woman will reject an essential part of femininity, namely all her attributes in the masquerade. (ibid.: 290)

The woman can be the phallus only through semblance, masquerade, or appearance, but this ensures that she is also *not* the phallus. Paradoxically, to be affirmed as the phallus is to be annihilated as woman. In being the phallus that each man has, the woman is reduced to being little more than a sexual receptacle for him, interchangeable with any other. It is only through the mediation of the other, through whom she has access to the Other, that she establishes a relation to the phallus and thus the socio-symbolic order.

Lacan suggests that love consists in a series of (non-symmetrical) demands for the proof of the other's commitment. The proofs sought from the other are impossible, imaginary tests of love. They are bound up with the subject's status as the object of the other's desire; but, more strictly, with the demand that the subject be the *cause* of the other's desire. While affirming the degree of the other's love, the value of the ego itself is affirmed: 'for both partners in the relation, both the subject and the Other, it is not enough to be the subject of need, or the objects of love, but that they must stand for the cause of desire' (ibid.: 287). Demand functions in the register of *the impossible*, for it is basically a demand to annihilate the distinction between self and other, the demand that the 'lack' constituting the ego be filled by the other. In adult life, genital sexual relations are attempts to satisfy this impossible demand, the demand to be/to have the phallus for and through the other.

The phallus functions only intersubjectively, for it is only by means of the other that one's possession of or identity with the phallus can be confirmed. To have or to be the phallus entails having a place within a circuit in which the other's desire plays a crucial part. Ideally if not in practice, the two sexes complement each other: through a man, a woman can become the phallus (his object of desire); through sexual relations with a woman, a man be affirmed as having a phallus. However, this ideal, like demand itself, is impossible. The demands of each make the satisfaction both seek impossible.

The phallus is heir to the role of *objet a*. The chain of substitution of one partial-object for another renders the man's penis and the whole of the woman's body psychically equivalent. The woman's body is the object of the man's desire in the same way that a part of his body, the penis, is the object of her's. It is for this reason that the sexual relation between the man and the woman is so fraught with the 'ghosts' or memories of a never-really remembered, pre-oedipal past, a dim pre-historic horizon for all love relations.

The narcissistic woman strives to make her body into the phallus. She devotes loving time and energy to the image she has for others, her representation in the world. She paints/shaves/plucks/dyes/diets/exercises her body, and clearly derives pleasure from compliments about her looks. Her whole body becomes the phallus to compensate for a genital 'deficiency', which she is able to disavow through her narcissism. The art of illusion and semblance become her greatest assets. She can utilize these techniques to mask, or cover over this 'secret' insufficiency:

> This is brought about by the intervention of a 'to seem' that replaces the 'to have' in order to protect it on the one side [i.e. the man's] and to mask its lack on the other [i.e. the woman's], and which has the effect if projecting in their entirety the ideal or

typical manifestations of the behaviour of each sex, including the
act of copulation into the comedy. (ibid.: 289)

It is only in so far as she is the object of the other's desire that she
can be the phallus. All her artifice is directed to this end. It projects
her in a series of images which more or less approximate the ideal,
prescribed behaviour of femininity. Her modes of seduction
through illusion, however, divide her once again between a (perfect)
ideal and an imperfect 'reality'. In a sense, she never receives the
affirmation of her subjectivity she desires. At best, the man's desire
for her affirms her as a sexual being but not as a unique, specific
subject. She is not a subject who happens to be in some relation to
the phallus; she *is* the phallus for him only in the 'comedy' of
copulation, an object of his passion, love, or gratification.

The man too, for his part, participates in this play of semblance.
He too must confirm having the phallus through the desire of an
other. He must appropriate the woman as a love-object, make her
his own, for only then is the alignment between penis and phallus
confirmed. The masquerade or veil is typically 'feminine' in either
men or women, Lacan claims, because it operates to deny or cover
over lack.

She strives to be affirmed as a unique, desirable, special subject,
an individual distinct from all other women; yet romantic love
relations involve, instead, 'putting her on a pedestal' (the projection
of the man's narcissistic self-conception) and/or a reduction to the
position of sexual object (receptacle of active masculine desire).
What is more clearly affirmed is not her subjectivity but her ability
to be reduced to desired object, which she shares in common with
all women in patriarchy. She is a sexual receptacle, property,
object, lacking, wanting what men have. In this sense she is
interchangeable with any other woman. In the sexual act, she finds
her demand for affirmation frustrated; she is homogenized to the
category of passive object. Yet, although sexual relations are the
'culmination' of romantic impulses and their most intimate form of
expression, they do not provide the gratification of her demand for
recognition and the other's desire.

The man also finds his expressions of romantic love frustrated.
He desires his 'possession' of the phallus be affirmed through the
woman's desire for his penis, which is (symbolically) detachable
from him and capable of being 'given' to her. She desires access to
the phallus he 'owns'. Ironically, sexual relations problematize the
very link between penis and phallus that he strives to affirm. Sexual
intercourse is both the affirmation of his possession of the phallus
and a reminder of the possibility of castration. For a moment at

least, he fills the woman's 'lack' and at that moment becomes the site of lack himself:

> The man is afraid of being weakened by the woman, infected with her femininity and of then showing himself incapable. The effect which coitus has of discharging tensions and causing flaccidity may be the prototype of what the man fears: and the realisation of the influence which the woman gains over him through sexual intercourse, the considerations she thereby forces from him justify the extension of this fear. Psychoanalysis believes that it has discovered a large part of what underlies the narcissistic rejection of women by men, which is so mixed up with despising them, in drawing attention to the castration complex and its influences on the opinion in which women are held. (Freud 1911a: 198–9)

In the process of 'taking' the woman, the man is reminded of her lack. He is thus reminded of the possibility of his own, which is reinforced by the fact that he loses erectile power after orgasm. Like the woman, whose unique subjectivity is submerged in her sexual status as object, the man betrays the subjectivity lying beneath his position as the 'possessor' of the phallus. He is only a 'place' within the circuit of exchange; at this moment he has 'exchanged' it by receiving another term in reciprocation. For a moment at least, she has what he 'lacks'. This residue of the castration threat lies behind the paranoid fantasy of the *vagina dentata*, the sexually insatiable woman who exhausts men and depletes them of their sexual 'resources'.

The man proclaims his love for the woman, but when she takes him as her sexual object his desire is reduced to the sexual performance, and thus the phallus is reduced to the penis. In this sense, he cannot satisfy the woman's desire. The woman desires the phallus, but instead she 'receives' the penis. Moreover, in focusing his relation to the phallus on virile sexual performance, he becomes vulnerable to anxiety, the loss of self-esteem and a fear of impotence. His relation to virile activity is over-invested.

In orgasm, the man loses his place in the woman's desire. His single orgasm neither exhausts nor even approaches the multi-orgasmic, anorgasmic, or supraorgasmic pleasures of which she is capable (see Irigaray 1985b: chapter 2). In her sexual relations with him, she loses her place as desirable subject in order to become a sexual object. The aims of neither are satisfied.

This is because love relations involve an unresolved tension between demand and desire. When the woman functions in the register of demand, it is to the man, his attentions, affections, and his capacity to reflect her and give her identity, that her demands are addressed. But when she functions in the register of desire, she desires (to be) the phallus. This entails that she is treated as a sexual object by the other, undermining her demand for recognition as a subject. Women are left with a disjunctive choice: either demand or desire, either narcissistic affirmation of the ego or affirmation as a sexual being, either love or sex. In an impossible attempt to satisfy both wishes, she vacillates between the penis *qua* phallus, and the penis *qua* sexual organ.

Given her 'preference' for passive aims and the strength of her demand for affirmation through the other, love and affection may serve in place of the satisfaction of her desires. This is perhaps why Lacan can with some justification claim: 'one can observe that a lack of satisfaction proper to the sexual need, in other words, frigidity is relatively well tolerated in women . . .' (Lacan 1977a: 290). This may also explain why the woman may tolerate a lack of the satisfaction of desire in her relations with men. She can readily substitute the body of the child, the phallus he 'gives' her, for *his* phallus. Indeed, this is as close to 'having' the phallus as woman is able to come.

In the case of men, by contrast, there is a 'specific depreciation of love' and a concomitant elevation of (sexual) desire. Yet the woman can be his object of desire in so far as she 'veils' the 'mysteries' for which he searches, only, that is, in so far as her 'lack' is veiled or hidden. He desires conquest of these mysteries initiating a cycle of desire and frustration: if his conquest is successful, its mystery vanishes and the object loses its fascination. This may lead to frustration or disappointment and a sense of betrayal for not living up to his image of her. The nearer satisfaction comes, the more impossible is its attainment. The imaginary vacillation between a yearning for, and fear of, incorporation by the other provides the structural framework within which his phantasies and practices are developed. He is enticed by his own narcissistic fantasies of wholeness and perfection: he is trapped by his belief that there is no difference between the veil and what lies behind it:

> If, in effect the man finds satisfaction for his demand for love in the relation with the woman, in as much as the signifier of the phallus constitutes her as giving in love what she does not have – conversely, his own desire for the phallus will make its signifier emerge in its persistent divergence towards 'another woman' who may signify the phallus in various ways, either as virgin or as prostitute. There results from this a centrifugal tendency of the genital drive in love life, which makes impotence much more

difficult to bear for him, while the *Verdrangung* [repression] inherent in desire is more important. (ibid.: 290)

His 'exploration', 'conquest', and 'appropriation' of her enigma forces him to confront the question of castration. This is why, even if the man distinguished two types of women, one, an alter-ego he respects but who holds no mystery for him; the other, a phallus, object of fascination and desire, the latter collapses into the former after a period of close familiarity. His sexual partner becomes more an object of affection than of desire after sustained intimacy. Then his desire diverges to another woman, and the cycle starts again.

From being an object of desire, the woman becomes the other of demand. Her demands – for attention, love, fidelity, etc. – reduce her from the status of *being* the phallus, the object of desire, to becoming the *other*, subject of demand. Men, by contrast, submerge or leave unspoken their corresponding demands in the expression of their desires. They are made visible only when there is some doubt about her having satisfied them. His demand for recognition of having the phallus is thus always directed towards the woman he does not have. As Freud recognized, the 'two sexes love a phase apart'.

'There is no sexual relation'

For Lacan, love is an entanglement, a knot, of imaginary gratifications and symbolic desires. It is always structured with reference to the phallus, which, in a sense is the third term coming between two lovers. The subject demands a wholeness, unity, and completion which it imagines the other can bestow on it. The symbolic, on the other hand, requires a subject irrevocably split, divided by language, governed by the phallus and the Other. Love relations aspire to a union or unity that is strictly impossible. The two can never become *One*. The desire for the One is, for Lacan, the desire of the Other, the Other beyond the other. The Other, in this context (and in its therapeutic analogue, the transference relation) is the 'subject-supposed-to-know'. Love is an investment in the other as the subject supposed to know.

In other words, the Other always intervenes between the subject and the other. There is no direct, unmediated relation between the sexes. The obstacle to love, so central to chivalric forms of love, is not external. It is the internal condition of human subjectivity and sexuality, constituted as they are by a rift governed by the Other.

Courtly love is a masculine way of refusing to recognize this fundamental rupture. It is a (spurious) attempt to put the Other in place of the other. Lacan devotes much of his biting irony to the self-deceptions of the male lover and to the romantic ensnarements in which the man rationalizes his obsession with his amorous counterpart.

In 'God and the Jouissance of ~~The~~ Woman' (in Mitchell and Rose 1982), Lacan elaborates woman's status for man in love, while subverting the man's expressed intent in courtly ideals. He focuses on the male ideal of One-ness or union with his sexual partner, asserting that woman is *not-all* (which he represents pseudo-algebraically as ExΦx. – to be read as 'Not all subjects are phallic', or its logical equivalent, 'there is a subject who is not phallic'). This does not mean that women are *not-all* and men are *all*. Rather, men *have* the phallus only if some subjects (i.e. women) do not have it, because the phallus is predicated on the division of some from all. They define the others as *not-all*. No-one is *all*. Yet women are distinguished from men by being *not-all* (men, presumably must be not *not-all*).

Like the phallus, the formulation of woman as *not-all* is Lacan's way of simultaneously including and excluding women. This negative definition does not tell us what woman *is*; it is a device for revealing the masculine myths and phantasies invested in representing woman as *all*. She is defined as *not-all* partly through a reversal of her mythical status for the man, especially the myth of unity that posits love as a form of self-completion. This demand for One-ness is the demand behind the profession of desire for the woman in romantic love, for a 'cure' from the analyst in the therapeutic relation, and for God in religious faith.

Lacan makes it clear that this demand for One is a demand for an impossible harmony and complementarity between the sexes. It is impossible, he asserts, because the relation to the other is always mediated by the Other. Lacan suggests that the man attempts to put his amorous relations in place of his relation to the Other. God, perhaps man's most sustained atempt to come to grips with the Other, always intervenes between man and his other, creating a sort of 'philosophical *ménage-a-trois*' (Mitchell and Rose 1982: 141). 'The good old God of all times', as Lacan calls him, is a reification of the Other. This Other is the condition of sexual difference and love, but also dooms any project that seeks the One through love.

Lacan describes courtly love as a love of the impossible, a love of the obstacle which forever thwarts love. Romantic love is not a form of homage to the woman, but to the Other. For the man, the woman is a means to this greater end. Courtly love is his attempt to equate the penis with the phallus and preserve a direct relation to the Other: 'For the man whose lady was, in the most servile sense of the term, his female subject, courtly love is the only way of coming off elegantly from the absence of sexual relation' (Mitchell and Rose 1982: 141). Against this God, this Other, Lacan counterposes a resistant and residual *jouissance* of the woman, an ecstasy that man has (mis)taken for divinity. Woman experiences a *jouissance beyond the phallus*. But if this enigmatic *jouissance* is attributed to woman as her mark of resistance to the Other, at the same time, this *jouissance* is, by that fact, strictly outside of articulation and is thus *unknowable*. Lacan accords women the possibility of refusing a pleasure and desire that is not theirs, but not of claiming one that *is* theirs. In attributing a non-phallic sexual pleasure to women, Lacan exceeds the narrow constraints of Freud's understanding of female sexuality as necessarily bound to male sexuality. Yet in claiming that this *jouissance* is also beyond discourse and knowledge, ineffable, he back-handedly repositions women in a dependent position. This is a pleasure, a series of sensations and experiences about which nothing more can be said than that they are *non*-phallic.

In this way he takes back the potential autonomy he granted women. It is significant that Lacan uses Bernini's statue of St Teresa to illustrate this enigmatic pleasure of women. No less than Freud, Lacan also discovers in women's pleasure a fundamental passivity. His use of St Teresa, of course, enables him to establish the connections between 'good old God' and sexual pleasure:

> You have only to go and look at Bernini's statue in Rome to understand immediately that she's coming, there's no doubt about it. And what is her *jouissance*, her coming from? It is clear that the essential testimony of the mystics is that they are experiencing it but know nothing about it. (Lacan in Mitchell and Rose 1982: 147)

If phallic *jouissance* is 'the jouissance of the idiot', (ibid.: 152), what is a *jouissance* 'beyond the phallus'? Women can't know and won't say. It is not clear from Lacan's discussion whether it is because this *jouissance* is in itself unknowable; or simply that women can't know it. Ironically, it is now Lacan who acts as the courtly lover. Through women, he can obtain an answer to the question that most perplexed Freud, *Was will das Weib?*, (what does woman want?). Her enigmatic nature is the means by which material about the Other can be obtained. Women are not so much the direct objects of this knowledge as a means of men's access to the Other: 'By her being in the sexual relation radically Other, in relation to what can be said of the unconscious, the woman is that which relates to this Other' (Lacan 1977a: 151).

Not believing in women (see Lacan 1977a: 168–9), he nevertheless pays homage to them, woos them, courts them. He rallies against the myth of the Eternal Feminine – *The* Woman – arguing that Woman does not exist, Woman exists only 'under erasure' (a quite different point from claiming that *women* don't exist). Femininity, as much as masculinity, is the product of a signifying chain. Yet Lacan also seems to want to retain some of the allure and the mystery of the Eternal Feminine, some romance about her unspeakable pleasure. Women remain for him the mode of access to the other side of the Other.

The sexual relation is thus not a relation between two subjects, but rather between *five* beings – the Other, the subject, the other, the phantasm of the other desired by the subject, and the phantasm of the subject desired by the other:

> what makes man desire, what is the cause of their desire, is cut out, restricted and logically articulated: it is this 'objet-a' which fascinates them . . . it is this 'objet-a' which allows them what Freud opposed to narcissistic love with object-love – except that what is involved is not the partner, the sexed other, but a phantom. (Lacan, quoted in Benvenuto and Kennedy 1986: 187)

While men develop courtly or romantic love in a refusal to accept the split in their subjectivity, women attempt to preserve a sense of wholeness or completion through frigidity. Frigidity is the counterpart of men's romantic passions! Lacan claims that frigidity involves 'the whole structure which determines neurosis, even if it appears outside the web of symptoms' (Mitchell and Rose: 1982 93). Her unconscious is largely determined by the effects of castration. On his reading, frigidity is not the renunciation of sexuality, nor is it refusal of phallic sexuality. On the contrary, it is an effect of the split between conscious and unconscious within desire itself. Frigidity, the (passive) feminine counterpart to male romanticism, amounts to the woman's saving herself for the Other. It is the preservation of a relation to a *dead* lover to whom she can be eternally faithful, not the abandonment of a sexual relation altogether (ibid.: 146).

Lacan and femininity

If I have avoided directly presenting critical feminist responses to Lacan's account of human subjectivity, sexuality, and particularly femininity this is because it is important to be as clear as possible about what it is one is criticizing. This is not to claim an objectivity to which a later evaluation could be attached; quite the opposite – all readings are *interpretive* through and through, no one interpretation being privileged as the true or correct one. Interpretations come from particular perspectives and represent particular values. Nor is it to advocate an interpretive relativism which attributes equal value to all interpretations. Readings are always motivated, interested, and represent strategies of textual expedience and selection that are often beyond conscious awareness. I have attempted to present as sympathetic and coherent an account of Lacan's work as possible, in order to show both what is of value for feminists (also, incidentally, explaining why there is a consistent feminist fascination with psychoanalysis), and to indicate what are its problems.

The existence of a huge body of feminist texts contesting the value of Freudian and Lacanian theory for feminism shows its controversial status and the polarizations within feminism that it has effected. Perhaps (with the exception of Marxism) no other patriarchal theory has generated as much debate as the status of psychoanalysis. While the final chapter will be devoted more directly to a discussion of the relations between psychoanalytic and feminist theory, I will conclude this chapter with a brief outline of some feminist criticisms and defences of Lacan's account of femininity and the role of the phallus.

Lacan's work seems to demand an either/or response in feminist terms. Given its difficulty, sophistication, and obscurity, undertaking to read his work with the aim of, as it were, independently evaluating it seems impossible. If one is to comprehend even some of his work in its depth this is to be already committed to supporting it. As Lacan himself said in describing his work: 'I prefer there to be only one way in, and for that to be difficult . . .' (Lacan 1970). This ensures that the 'way into' his texts is *his* way. It is only by a willing, if provisional, suspension of logical judgements and a belief in the underlying coherence of his work that there is any possibility of understanding it.

Consequently, feminist relations to psychoanalysis, with a few significant exceptions, fall into two broad categories: those committed to Lacan's work, and ultimately, to his underlying framework, seeing it as a means of describing and explaining patriarchal power relations; and those who reject it from a pre- or non-psychoanalytic position. In the first category can be included Mitchell, Ragland-Sullivan, Julia Kristeva, Monique Plaza, and Catherine Clément, while feminists such as Spender, Greer, and others seem to illustrate the second. This latter position seems to me less significant and relevant to the concerns of this book than those 'miscellaneous' feminists who occupy neither category. Here can be included Irigaray, Gallop, Rose, and Kofman, all of whom seem to have an impressive familiarity with Lacan's work while maintaining a critical distance from it – either by developing (internal) critiques of his position or using it to develop other arguments and positions which may or may not be compatible with his framework.

Mitchell may be taken as representative of defences of Lacan developed by other feminists of the first category. Her vindication of him takes several forms: first, she claims that feminists have not adequately understood his (or Freud's) position; second, she claims that he provides an accurate description of patriarchal power relations (a necessary condition for feminist transformations of culture); and third, she claims that feminists stand corrected by the psychoanalytic explanation of patriarchy in so far as it is not simply relations between men and women, but the relations both have to the phallus that explain the transmission of patriarchal values:

> Freud, and Lacan after him, are both accused of producing phallocentric theories – of taking man as the norm and woman as what is different therefrom – To both Freud and Lacan, their task is not to produce justice [unlike Ernest Jones, in his claim that women are equal to but different from men] but to explain this difference which uses them, not the man but the phallus to which the man lays claim as its key term. (Mitchell, in Mitchell and Rose 1982: 8)

Mitchell, Ragland-Sullivan, and others in this category defend Lacan against the charge of phallocentrism in an argument which can be reconstructed in the following terms: subjectivity and sexuality are socially produced, not the effects of nature or development. The mirror stage initiates a process which culminates in the oedipus complex or paternal metaphor. Together they explain the psychological dimensions of the social construction of subjectivity. Independent of these cultural givens, the child has neither a stable identity nor a determinate sexuality. This process of social construction is predicated on the *necessary* renunciation and sacrifice of the child's access to the maternal body and the child's submission to the Law of the Father. The paternal figure serves to separate the child from an all-encompassing, engulfing, and potentially lethal relation with the mother. The father intervenes into this imaginary dyad and represents the Law. The Father embodies the power of the phallus and the threat of castration. Accepting his authority and phallic status is the precondition of the child's having a place within the socio-symbolic order, a name, and a speaking position. The phallus is the pivotal term around which the social production of both sexes is oriented. On Mitchell's reading, it is a 'neutral signifier' equally affecting both sexes, introducing to both the concept of loss or lack (actual in the girl, and only possible in the boy) and law. The phallus subjects both sexes to the symbolic; it is the neutral term in relation to which the subject is positioned as masculine or feminine in the socio-cultural and linguistic order.

Mitchell's position in her introduction to *Feminine Sexuality* (1982) remains fundamentally the same as her position in *Psychoanalysis and Feminism* (1974). But she is by no means the only feminist defender of Lacan. Besides Stephen Heath, Fredric Jameson, and other male notables, we find analysts with feminist credentials, such as Michèle Montrelay or Jacqueline Rousseau-Dujardin, and academics like Ellie Ragland-Sullivan and Jacqueline Rose defending Lacan against the claim that he privileges masculinity and participates in, and perhaps develops, Freud's phallocentrism. For example,

> I find no a priori Lacanian support for phallocentrism – any more than for Lacanian-supported feminism. Lacan discovered the phallic signifier, its effects and the resulting structure of substitutive Desire. These intrinsically neutral elements give rise to ideologies of the masculine and feminine that cluster around the male-female difference and dramatize themselves in a parade. (Ragland-Sullivan 1986: 298)

Lacan is defended in terms of ridding Freud of biologism and naturalism, and thus providing the necessary ingredients of a social account of how masculinity and femininity are produced as the effects of discourse. It is on these grounds that feminist critics of Lacan, particularly Irigaray, are questioned and Lacan defended. If Lacan is criticized for his conception of woman as lack, as other, as Other, as castrated, these feminists will defend him by arguing that he is merely describing but not advocating patriarchal forms of social production. They claim that he is attacked on naturalistic or essentialist grounds (as if his critics use a natural or essential femininity which has somehow been alienated or ignored by his account). Ragland-Sullivan can serve here to represent a number of others:

> Irigaray . . . reads him [Lacan] substantively rather than structurally and thus sees him as prescriptive instead of descriptive and analytic. By equating Lacan's phallic signifier with patriarchy, she substantivizes the concept biologically so that Phallus = penis = male. Her views therefore imply that males and

females have natural psychic attributes in keeping with gender. By failing to accept the structural effect and symbolic nature of the Lacanian phallic signifier – neutral in its own right – Irigaray's assessment of Lacan as a phallocrat is wrong. (ibid.: 273)

Ragland-Sullivan argues from the premise that Irigaray equates the phallus with patriarchy to the conclusion that this entails her assumption of a natural set of male and female attributes. Clearly Ragland-Sullivan presumes that the phallus can be seen as a patriarchally privileged term *only* on biologistic grounds. Rose also levels the charge of essentialism at Irigaray and Cixous, even if she does not mention them by name:

If the status of the phallus is to be challenged, it cannot, therefore, be directly from the feminine body but must be by means of a different symbolic term (in which case the relation to the body is immediately thrown into crisis), or else by an entirely different logic altogether (in which case one is no longer in the order of symbolisation at all). (Mitchell and Rose 1982: 56)

This criticism is considerably weakened if it can be shown that the feminists criticized, Irigaray in particular, rarely if ever rely on a natural or biologically given body. It presumes that the body can *only* be a biological and thus immutable object. Irigaray and other 'feminists of difference', do not refer to the female body in biological terms, but only in so far as it is enveloped, produced and made meaningful by language. Irigaray develops an *internal* critique of Lacan, one versed in the details of his work, and reliant on his own techniques. This is why she refers to the *morphology* not the anatomy of the female body. Her work, as I argue in the next chapter, poses precisely the kind of symbolic and representational challenge Rose affirms as politically necessary, but which Rose herself does not undertake. Irigaray does not oppose the phallus to a 'raw' or 'pure' female body; on the contrary, she demonstrates that the female body is the site for patriarchal power relations and, at the same time, for symbolic and representational resistances. In simplifying Irigaray's challenge to Lacan, they open up the possibility of a more serious and far-reaching challenge to this work on the level of imaginary and symbolic, not real, relations.

Lacan's defenders are correct, it seems to me, on two counts: he *does* shift the ground of our understanding of patriarchal power relations and their social reproduction. It is not men *per se* who cause women's oppression, but rather the socio-economic and linguistic structure, i.e. the Other. Yet in his formulation of this structure as an inevitable law, patriarchal dominance is not so much challenged as displaced, from biology to the equally unchangeable, socio-linguistic law of the father. Second, Lacan does provide some crucial elements for a description and explanation of the psychic components of women's oppression, although he himself does not acknowledge the structure of patriarchal oppression.

Yet there are also many respects in which his understanding of femininity must be inaccurate or inappropriate. His work clearly exhibits a number of assumptions that are entirely problematic in feminist terms, to which these female defenders are apparently blind. His account can only be descriptively accurate if it takes into account the historical, changeable nature of patriarchy and its key signifier, the phallus. The Law of the Father cannot be the universal condition of culture: it remains the form of specific cultures. Without this historical qualification Lacan's work has the same air of inevitability as biologistic accounts.

As Lacan recognized, the symbolic order is not simply an abstract or external system of signification whose phallic status is *purely* discursive. The symbolic is the field within which our lives and social experiences are located. Unless the symbolic order is conceived as a system where the father and the penis are not the only possible signifiers of social power and linguistic norms (even if they are the dominant ones here, today), feminism is no better off with Lacan than without him.

His work is a necessary counterbalance to the naturalisms, humanisms, essentialisms, etc. so common in theories of human subjectivity. His sharp distance from ego-psychology and object-relations accounts of psychoanalysis makes Freud's work more palatable and useful to feminism. His intermingling of language-like processes with Freud's notion of sexuality and the unconscious have been useful to feminists in a wide variety of disciplines in which questions of subjectivity, desire, discursive disruption, reading, and interpretation are usually ignored. His account of masculine desire provides, for example, one of the more astute male self-critical observations, undermining men's pretensions to an identity with the phallus. Yet the very real problems, and strategic evasions, and ambiguities in his work, particularly concerning women, female desire, and sexuality, must also be recognized instead of covered over or rationalized away.

Women must take on the effects of castration, according to Lacan's defenders, because the universal problem of the child's identity is its ability to separate itself from the mother: 'the link between the mother and infant prior to castration and . . . the

145

painful effect of individuating is the reason that women are identified with loss' (Ragland-Sullivan 1986: 288). None of them explains why a universal maternal nurturance is assumed. Given the mother's (up-to-now) indispensable role in bearing children, the presumption that she, or some woman, nurtures the child is social, not given. It seems that Lacan's defenders, rather than his critics, base their positions on biologistic presuppositions. By contrast, Irigaray and other more critically minded feminists seek a positive representation of the two sexes, and not simply the inclusion of women in so far as they are mothers.

If Lacan begs women to tell him in what their pleasure consists,[14] he is not prepared to hear what they have to say. The absence of an answer from women is clearly itself an answer – that this is a problem for men who want to know, to master, to name, that which is not theirs. Women, for Irigaray, are the sex 'which is not one': not one (like the phallus), but not none either! Woman is not one for she doesn't conform to the logic of singular identity, sexuality, and desire: the sex which is more (*encore*) than one, in excess of the one (organ) demanded from women's bodies to render them definable in men's terms. If Lacan's interrogation is directed to a man's stone representation of a woman, i.e., to Bernini's representation of St Teresa, it is not surprising 'she' has nothing to say! But if Lacan had looked at her own words (she was a prolific diarist and writer), he may have heard something quite different – the 'corporeal' language of hysteria, not the *jouissant* experience of unspeakable intensity (see Irigaray, 'Cosi Fan Tutti' in 1985b)

If he has succeeded in describing women's containment in men's fantasies, Lacan has not left any room for the representation of women in other, more autonomous, terms. If he places this pleasure beyond the phallus and thus beyond the symbolic and representation, this is because the symbolic, linguistic structure he describes is restricted to those dominant discourses and systems which accord women no place of their own. There are, there must be, other discourses and forms of possible representation capable of speaking of/as women differently.

6

Lacan and feminism

Lacan continues to be one of the most controversial figures within contemporary feminist theory. Many feminists use his work on human subjectivity to challenge phallocentric knowledges; others are extremely hostile to it, seeing it as elitist, male-dominated, and itself phallocentric. These contradictory evaluations of his work seem irresolveable; in some cases they are maintained within one and the same person. Like Freud's work, Lacan's *is* contradictory (sometimes intentionally and sometimes not). His is a self-consciously paradoxical, oxymoronic style; there is nothing he seems to enjoy as much as punning, playing with language, wrenching the maximum resonance from each term. The relations between his version of psychoanalysis and feminism remain ambivalent. It is never entirely clear whether he is simply a more subtle misogynist than Freud, or whether his reading of Freud constitutes a 'feminist' breakthrough. The utility of psychoanalysis for feminist endeavours remains unclear. It is a risky and double-edged 'tool', for as a conceptual system it is liable to explode in one's face as readily as it may combat theoretical misogynies of various kinds.

I will focus on some of the relations between Lacanian psycho-analysis and contemporary French feminisms in this chapter. As the two most influential and well-known French feminists working within psychoanalysis, and as feminists diametrically opposed in the kinds of commitment they make to Lacan, I will focus on the work of Julia Kristeva and Luce Irigaray.

Before proceeding, I would like to make clear some of the reasons why Lacan's work has held so much appeal for otherwise quite divergent feminist positions – why, that is, his work *can* be defended (at least up to a point) by feminists. Below is an outline of some elements of his work that are significant in relation to Kristeva's and Irigaray's projects.

a. Central to both is Lacan's critique of the Cartesian *cogito*, the pre-given, indubitable, unified subject. Lacan denounces the illusory mastery, unity, and self-knowledge that the subject, as a self-consciousness, accords itself. For him, consciousness is continually betrayed by the evasion typical of the unconscious. The subject, considered as natural individual, is problematized by Lacan. He proposes a theory of the socio-linguistic genesis of subjectivity which enables male and female subjects to be seen as social and historical effects, rather than pre-ordained biological givens.

b. Lacan's work also helped to introduce questions about sexuality[1] to legitimized academic and political discourses. Although there may be a number of serious problems with Lacan's understanding of sexuality (as mentioned in chapter 5), his work does make it clear that patriarchal subjects acquire a social and speaking position only by confronting the question of castration and a sexual difference conceived in terms of the presence and absence of the male sexual organ (the oedipus complex/name-of-the-father). Lacan inserts the question of sexuality into the centre of all models of social and psychical functioning.[2] To be a subject or 'I' at all, the subject must take up a sexualised position, identifying with the attributes socially designated as appropriate for men or women.

c. His work has been instrumental in demonstrating the centrality of systems of meaning or signification to subjectivity and the social order. The discursive/linguistic order constitutes human socio-cultural and sexual activity as such.

In place of a Cartesian *res cogitans*, a thinking being, Lacan posits the speaking subject, a subject defined by and in language. This subject is not simply a speaking being, a being who happens by chance to speak, but a being constituted as such by being *spoken through* by language itself. It cannot be conceived as the source or master of discourse, but is the locus or site of the articulation (*énonciation*) of representations, inscriptions, meanings, and significances.

These three key areas in Lacan's work – the interlocking domains of subjectivity, sexuality, and language – define broad interests shared by many French feminists. His decentring of the rational, conscious subject (identified with the ego), his undermining of common assumptions about the intentionality or purposiveness of the speaking subject's 'rational' discourses, and his problematizations of the idea of a 'natural' sexuality, have helped to free feminist theory of the constraints of a largely metaphysical and implicitly masculine, notion of subjectivity – humanism. He has thus raised the possibility of understanding subjectivity in terms other than those dictated by patriarchal common-sense.

Kristeva and Irigaray share Lacan's broad anti-humanism, his commitment to the primacy of language in psychical life and his understanding of the necessarily *sexualized* position assumed by the subject in the symbolic. They share a familiarity with Freud's work, with the texts of a history of (largely) idealist philosophies, as well as a background in Lacan's seminars. Both are practising psycho-analysts. Both are committed to developing analyses of the production of sexed subjectivity. Both focus on the relation obscured in Freud's and Lacan's work – the mother-child relation (for Kristeva), and the mother-daughter relation (for Irigaray). In articulating the mother-child relation as a site for both the transmission and the subversion of patriarchal values, both affirm the archaic force of the pre-oedipal, which although repressed is thus also permanently preserved. Both affirm the fluid, polymorphous perverse status of libidinal drives and both evoke a series of sites of bodily pleasure capable of resisting the demands of the symbolic order.

In spite of their adherences to a Lacanian framework, both remain at a critical distance from his position, though in very distinctive ways. Kristeva presents a series of internal adjustments or modifications to his position while remaining within his overall conceptual frame. As a literary theorist and semiologist, her major interests are directed towards transgressive discourses, the texts of the avant-garde, which destabilize the unified or 'thetic' subject. She directs her researches towards understanding the mutual interplay between a discursive realm and the domain of psycho-sexual, i.e., individual development. Irigaray, by contrast, poses questions about the outside, the absences, and silences of psychoanalysis, its repressions, disavowals, intolerable impulses, and wishes. While also concerned with the relations between subjectivity and discourse, Irigaray is more interested in elaborating a theory of enunciation, a theory of discursive production which makes explicit the positions of woman as a speaking subject. Her project is committed to making explicit the sexualization of all discourses. Ultimately this may mean that, whatever the similarities of their reliances on Lacan, Kristeva's and Irigaray's projects are incompatible in aim, and contradictory in methods and underlying political commitments. This will form the basis of discussion for this chapter.

Dutiful daughters

The dutiful daughter is the one who submits to the Father's Law. Her submission may take various forms: a submission to the oedipalization of desire, to the patriarchal denigration of her corporeality and pleasure, to a femininity defined as passive, castrated, superficial, seductive, narcissistic; or even a submission through what appears to be resistance to the oedipal law, i.e., the so-called 'masculinity complex'.[3] The dutiful daughter must occupy one of the (three) positions Freud outlined as the girl's 'resolution' of her oedipus complex: 'normal' castrated passivity, frigidity, or the masculinity complex (Freud 1933: 126–7). In a rather surprising move, Jane Gallop accuses Irigaray of playing the dutiful daughter to the Symbolic Father(s), Freud and Lacan, when it may have been more appropriate to see Kristeva in this role. In the second half of this chapter, I will argue that Irigaray attempts to create a position for women beyond Freud's circumscribed alternatives in her project of outlining an (impossible) genealogy of women. Unlike Kristeva, Irigaray refuses the Father's Name, risking, it could be argued, a psychosis, but subverting the preordained space within which women are confined in the (masculine, phallocentric) symbolic order.

The semiotic and symbolic

Kristeva's general model of signifying practice is derived from Lacan's integration of Freudian psychoanalysis and structural semiology. Her conception of the semiotic and the symbolic functions operating in psychical, textual, and social life[4] seems to be based on the distinction Freud developed between pre-oedipal and oedipal sexual drives. The semiotic and the symbolic are two modalities of all signifying processes (Kristeva 1984a: 22–3) whose interaction is the essential even if unrecognized condition of sociality, textuality, and subjectivity.

The 'semiotic' must be understood in its etymological rather than in its Saussurian sense: 'distinctive mark, trace, index, precursory sign, proof, engraved or written sign, imprint, trace (sic), figuration' (ibid.: 24). It can be correlated with the anarchic pre-oedipal component-drives, and polymorphous erotogenic zones, orifices, and organs. In the terminology of metapsychology, it consists in the facilitations and neural pathways traversed by pre-oedipal wishes – that is, the psychical primary processes (ibid.: 24). The semiotic is the order of the sexual drives and their articulation (1976: 66; and

1984: 43). It provides the *matter*, the impetus, and the subversive potential of all signification. It is the 'raw material' of signification, the corporeal, libidinal matter that must be harnessed and appropriately channelled for social cohesion and regulation.

Yet, in their 'raw', a-symbolic operations, these infantile drives do not have the stability of copulative heterosexuality, or definitively separated, privileged, or hierarchized (phallic) organs and pleasures. They are indeterminate, capable of many (even contradictory) aims, sources, and objects. In agreement with Freud, Kristeva describes the semiotic as 'feminine', a phase dominated by the space of the mother's body.

She defines this space, following Plato's *Timaeus*, as the semiotic *chora*. It is a space or receptacle, an undecidably enveloped and enveloping locus from which the subject is both produced and threatened with annihilation. The *chora* defines and structures the limits of the child's body and its ego or identity as a subject. It is the space of the subversion of the subject, the space in which the *death drive*, i.e., the compulsion to repeat, emerges and threatens to engulf the subject, to reduce it to the inertia of non-existence (Freud 1919b).

The space of the maternal *chora* is the *pre-imaginary* space from and in which the drives emanate and circulate. Their differentiation into component-drives, and the emerging distinction between self and other (Lacan's imaginary order) – also contribute to Kristeva's concept of the semiotic. Like Lacan's imaginary and Freud's pre-oedipal, she remains committed to their assumption that, even though this is a 'feminine' phase dominated by the mother, the mother is always considered *phallic*. 'She' is thus the consequence of a *masculine* fantasy of maternity, rather than women's lived experience of maternity.

> As the addressee of every demand, the mother occupies the place of alterity. Her replete body, the receptacle and guarantor of demands, takes the place of all narcissistic, hence imaginary, effects and gratifications; she is, in other words, the phallus. (Kristeva 1984a: 47)

If the semiotic is pre-oedipal, based on primary processes and is maternally oriented, by contrast, the symbolic, Kristeva's second energetic organization within representation and the social, is an oedipalized system, regulated by secondary processes and the Law of the Father. Kristeva regards the symbolic as the condition of ordered, regulated, and rule-governed signification. It consists in the procedures which establish unities, whether at the level of the individual psychical experience, signifying and representational practices, or social institutions and rules (including the state and its apparatuses) (1976). It is the domain of positions and propositions.

She relies largely on Lacan's model of the symbolic. For her, the symbolic is the stability which ensures a cohesive, unified speaking subject and a coherent, meaningful text. The symbolic is based on the 'repression' or subsumption of the chaotic semiotic fluxes, and their utilization under regulated conditions so that they are capable of functioning as ordered, meaningful signifying elements:

> We shall call *symbolic* the logical and syntactic functioning of language and everything which, in translinguistic practices is assimilable to the system of language proper. The term *semiotic*, on the other hand, will be used to mean: in the first place, what can be hypothetically posited as preceding the imposition of language, in other words, the already given arrangement of the drives in the form of facilitations or pathways, and secondly the return of these facilitations in the form of rhythms, intonations and lexical, syntactic and rhetorical transformations. If the *symbolic* established the limits and unity of a signifying practice, the *semiotic* registers in that practice the effect of that which cannot be pinned down as sign, whether signifier or signified. (Kristeva 1976: 68)

The semiotic is thus the rhythmic, energetic, dispersed bodily series of forces which strive to proliferate pleasures, sounds, colours, or movements experienced in the child's body. It is the repressed condition of symbolically regulated, grammatical, and syntactically governed language.

Like the repressed, the semiotic can return in/as irruptions within the symbolic. It manifests itself as an interruption, a dissonance, a rhythm unsubsumable in the text's rational logic or controlled narrative. The semiotic is thus both the precondition of symbolic functioning and its uncontrollable excess. It is used by discourses but cannot be articulated by them. It is for this reason that Kristeva seems fascinated with the avant-garde text, the 'texts' of Mallarmé, Lautréamont, Artaud, Joyce, Schoenberg, Cage, Stockhausen, and even Giotto and Bellini. These 'texts', whether they are written, dramatic, musical, visual, or auditory are disturbing precisely because they provide a more direct expression of the semiotic than is usually possible in more conventional symbolic representational systems.

The symbolic is an order superimposed on the semiotic. It leads to the acquisition of a stable speaking, desiring position and the regulation and systematization of vocalization and libidinal impulses, as required by discursive production and social order.

The symbolic harnesses libidinal flows, regulating and 'digitalizing' them (see Wilden 1972: 168–70) to form signifying elements, discourses, and practices (see Kristeva 1984: 47).

The symbolic control of the various semiotic processes is thus, at best, tenuous and liable to breakdown or lapse at certain historically, linguistically, and psychically significant moments. It results in an upheaval in the norms of the smooth, understandable, (in Barthes' term) 'readerly' text. The semiotic overflows its symbolic boundaries in those privileged 'moments' Kristeva specifies in her triad of subversive forces: 'madness, holiness and poetry' (1976: 64). These semiotic eruptions represent transgressive breaches of symbolic coherence or, put in other terms, the symbolization or representation of hitherto unspeakable or unintelligible phenomena, instances on the borders of the meaningful which reveal the coercive forces vested in the domination of the symbolic over the semiotic.

In short, the symbolic/oedipal/social mode owes a debt of existence to an unspeakable and unrepresentable semiotic/maternal/feminine. The symbolic cannot even acknowledge, let alone repay, the debt that the oedipal and the conscious owe to the pre-oedipal and the unconscious. This debt is the social equivalent of the debt the subject owes to a female corporeality which remains unrecognized in its autonomy.

This basic distinction between two kinds of psychical or libidinal circulation and significatory structure underlies even the most recent of Kristeva's works. Her orientation has changed markedly[5] and her more recent texts no longer seem oriented to the socialist revolution or to Marxism, at least not in recognizable forms. She now seems more interested in the details of the coupling of psychoanalysis and semiotics in the analysis of the transgressive features of texts and the borderline states of the subject.

Kristeva remains motivated by psychoanalytic concerns, those dealing with the individual's wishes, desires, passions. These are not considered in isolation from a more historical and social analysis (although there is some tension between these components). Her fascinating analysis of abjection in *Powers of Horror. An Essay in Abjection* (1982a) and her recent speculations in *Tales of Love* (1987), are modifications, elaborations, and specifications of features (under)developed in her earlier works. They are elaborations of the holiness, madness, and poetry at the centre of our cultural values and practices – a madness based on the subject's inability to accept its own corporeal limits (abjection), a holiness unable to tolerate the ambiguity of amorous devotion (ecstasy), and a poetry unable to accept its own constitutive sonorous materiality.

These threaten to break down symbolic norms. They are elaborations of a psychical primary narcissism Lacan singles out as constructive of the ego, overlaid with Kristeva's own account of textual/symbolic functioning.

On Kristeva's model, all texts and all cultural products are the results of a dialectical process: the interaction between two mutually modifying historical forces. One is the setting in place, the establishment of a regulated system, or 'unity' – the symbolic (see 1976). Underlying and subverting this 'setting in place' is a movement of 'cutting through' or traversing, breaking down unities. In times of 'rupture, renovation and revolution' (1976: 69), which she identifies with the symptomatic eruptions of the avant-garde, the symbolic is no longer capable of directing the semiotic energies into already coded social outlets. Its subversive, dispersing energies transgress the boundaries or tolerable limits of the symbolic. Yet their disruptive energies cannot be sustained in a self-contained or a-symbolic semiotic. Sooner or later, depending on the extent of threat it poses, the semiotic is recodified, reconstituted into a new symbolic system which has incorporated and absorbed its subversive potential. The symbolic, like the 'return' of the repressed, challenges the borders of the symbolic through the work of the avant-garde, which poses a new transgression and a new recodification of the symbolic, and so on. These are struggles between powers and resistances on the margins of the symbolic, on the border between the paternal order and a (potentially psychotic) maternal imaginary. The materiality needed for various signifying systems must be denied or disavowed by these practices in order for them to function as such. The avant-garde text thus draws attention to its own repressed conditions (a repressed 'femininity'), and therefore poses a profound threat to the conventions governing it. It gestures towards its own repressed conditions in ways normally unavailable to more convention-bound significations.

Semanalysis and psychoanalysis

'Semanalysis' is the name Kristeva gave to her methodology in her earlier works. It does not refer to the study of signification (which is the realm of semiotics), but to the study of the processes which break down or subvert the production of meaning. It is a mode of analysis of the role of the speaking subject in signification; the speaking being's identity and boundaries are imperilled by the breakdown of symbolic organization. Semanalysis is the study of the simultaneous production and subversion of subjectivity in discourse.

As the name indicates, 'semanalysis' has its genealogy in semiotics and psychoanalysis. It is the study of the subversion of the subject and signification within signification itself. It is an attempt to bring to the notice of linguists, semiologists, and those concerned with questions of representation, long-neglected questions of subjectivity and thus of social and psychical functioning usually considered outside their jurisdiction. She also attempts to bring questions of textuality and signification to those realms – particularly social/political theory and psychoanalytic or psychological theory – which have hitherto neglected them.

Her adherence to a Saussurian and a Lacanian framework is not unqualified. She remains critical of both (in so far as each has ignored the other), modifying, questioning, and rejecting some of their details even if she remains committed to their frameworks overall. Lacanian psychoanalysis remains, for all of her own researches, the fundamental methodological and conceptual grid she relies on. Her elaborations may depart from Lacan's, particularly in their temporalizations, but her allegiances remain clear.[6]

Her earliest works are based on Lacan's notions of the mirror stage and the castration complex. For her, these two moments provide the necessary conditions for the subject's acquisition of a speaking position. They are two 'thetic' phases in the processes of signification:

> the mirror-stage produces the 'spatial intuition' which is found at the heart of the functioning of signification – in signs and in sentences. From that point on, in order to capture his image unified in a mirror, the child must remain separate from it, his body agitated by the semiotic motility . . . which fragments him more than unifies him in a representation . . . Captation of the image and the drive investment in this image, which institute primary narcissism, permit the constitution of objects detached from the semiotic *chora* . . .
> . . . The sign can be conceived as the voice that is projected from the agitated body (from the semiotic *chora*) onto the facing *imago* or onto the object, which simultaneously detach from the surrounding continuity. (1984a: 46–7)

The mirror stage provides the conditions for the child's detachment from its lived experience. This is necessary if signification is to be possible or desirable for the child. If it lives only in/as the immediacy of the *chora* no experience can be represented by a sign or by anything other than itself. Any sign or representation would function simply as another pure presence, another immediately lived experience and not a delegate or representative of another (absent) experience. This detachment from the immediacy of need brings with it the possibility of substitution, and thus of symbolization. For Kristeva, this sets down the conditions of differentiation, signification, and the principle of substitution (and thus presence and absence), making a signifier present in the absence of a desired object.

Castration provides a second order threshold or condition for the constitution of the speaking subject. If the mirror stage detaches the child from its lived experiences of fragmentation, the specular image provides it with a representation or substitute that is based on wholeness and unity. Castration severs the child from the (specular) image of wholeness, separating it from too close an identification with the image of the (phallic) mother, the image through which the child attempts to displace its experiences of fragmentation.

> The discovery of castration . . . detaches the subject from his dependence on the mother, and the perception of a symbolic function – *the* symbolic function . . . Thus ends the formation of the thetic phase, which posits the gap between the signifier and the signified as an opening up towards every desire but also every act, including the very jouissance that exceeds them. (ibid.: 47)

The constitution of the ego in the mirror phase, in short, is the precondition of the semiotic, the (material) order of the signifier; the severing of the subject from the maternal, castration, is the precondition of the symbolic, and of the constitution of the domain of the (conceptual) signified.

Her adherence to a Lacanian perspective is not only at the level of analogy. The speaking subject is not simply the Lacanian split subject transposed into the 'medium' of language. Rather, Kristeva takes Lacan's conception of the subject, and some of his central methodological insights (e.g., about the illusory mastery of the *cogito*, the symbolic positioning of subjectivity, and the 'logic' of unconscious representations) to rework conventional views of literary and artistic production so that they are more amenable to a Lacanian perspective. In other words, she will use Lacan as a methodological grid for her general semanalytic project.[7]

Key Lacanian concepts and principles form the categories and framework Kristeva relies on in her investigation of the destabilization of signifying conventions. These adherences are too numerous to elaborate in detail here. We should simply note that the Lacanian categories of infantile development and linguistic functioning (the Real, imaginary, and symbolic; need, demand, and desire), unconscious functioning (metaphor and metonymy, the conditions of representability, dream and symptom-interpretation), psychical positioning in the symbolic (as neurotic, psychotic, narcissistic) and libidinal economy (desire, the circuits of the drive, the *objet a*, the phallus), and psychical 'identities' (phallic mother, symbolic Father, masculine hierarchized genitality, feminine passivity) are all essential elements in Kristeva's semanalytic endeavours.

Her relation to Lacan remains complicated and ambiguous: she takes his conceptual apparatus and reading techniques as starting points for developing her own methods and objects of investigation. She takes psychoanalysis as itself symptomatic of a socio-political and intellectual tradition dominant in our culture. She regards psychoanalysis as a privileged discourse, able to function as a critical and criteriological tool by which other discourses, including linguistics, can be examined. Yet she is highly critical of many of Lacan's commitments on at least the following issues.

1 Unlike Lacan, Kristeva remains insistent on the historical and social specificity of signification and subjectivity. While there may be a conceptual space in Lacan's account for the inclusion of concrete historical determinations, Lacan himself rarely includes them, preferring a more imperious, metaphysical, and universal style. For Kristeva, however, the social and historical determination of individuals and signifying practices is always essential.

> A signifying economy within an artistic practice . . . not only operates through the individual (biographical subject) who carries it out, but it also recasts him as historical subject – causing the signifying process that the subject undergoes to match the ideological and political expectations of his age's rising classes. . . . One cannot understand such practice without taking its socio-economic foundations into account; nor can one understand it if one chooses to reduce it solely to these foundations thereby bypassing the signifying economy of the subject involved. (Kristeva 1980: 232)

2 In contrast to Lacan, for whom the imaginary order functions in a visual register, for Kristeva, the dual narcissistic and identificatory structure of imaginary relations is synaesthetic, involving all the sensory registers without any receiving a special emphasis. If the imaginary is a visual order, it is also, she wants to claim, organized by the structure of vocalization (a sonorous register), and by touch, taste, and smell as well. These provide the conditions not only for language acquisition, but also for all signifying practices. Kristeva's analyses of music, painting, and cinema as well as the linguistic text made it clear that the preconditions of these cultural practices also provide the

preconditions of verbalization. Lacan, in short, concentrates too heavily or exclusively on verbal language at the expence of other modes of signification:

> science will no doubt establish the objective basis (biophysical and biochemical) of colour perceptions; just as contemporary linguistics, having discovered the phoneme, is seeking its corporeal, physiological and, perhaps, biological foundation. Psychoanalytic research will then make it possible, proceeding not only from the objective basis of perception and of the phases of the subject's passage through chromatic acquisition parallel to linguistic acquisition, to establish the more or less exact psychoanalytic equivalents of a particular subject's colour scale. (These phases would include the perception of such and such a colour at a given stage; the state of instinctual drive cathexes during this period; the relationship to the mirror phase, to the formation of the specular 'I'; relationship to the mother; et cetera.) (ibid.: 222; see also 1987: 40)

3 Where Lacan insists on a definitive break between the imaginary and the symbolic, which are separated by the rupture caused by castration, the intervention of the third term, and the repression of oedipal/pre-oedipal desires, Kristeva posits more of a continuity. For example, she will position 'primal repression' at the pre-mirror phase, which, in more orthodox psychoanalytic terms is usually situated at the resolution of the child's oedipus complex:

> a repression that one might call 'primal' has been effected prior to the springing forth of the ego, of its objects and representations. The latter, in turn, as they depend on another repression, the 'secondary' one, arrive only *a posteriori* on an enigmatic foundation that has already been marked off . . . (1982a: 10–11)

She will go so far as to posit a category of 'symbolic imaginary' organization prior to the oedipal structure – a contradiction in Lacanian terms (Kristeva 1987).

4 Consequently, it is not altogether surprising that Kristeva will introduce concepts, which, if they are not antithetical to Lacan's work, are not developed by him. For example, although Lacan does mention the imaginary father (the father with whom the child may identify in the mirror stage in much the same way as it identifies with the mother and its own specular image), he gives no special emphasis to the masculinity or paternity of this other. By contrast, Kristeva posits an imaginary father, distinct from Lacan's symbolic Father (or Freud's primal father) who does not embody the Law so much as represent the ideal possibilities of love for the child. She

insists that the imaginary father, rather than the phallic mother (it is not entirely clear what difference there is here!) provides the mediation or third term necessary for the child's accession to the symbolic:

> In order for [the human subject to speak and learn] . . . there must exist what I . . . name a 'father of individual prehistory': a sort of conglomeration of the two parents, of the two sexes, which is nevertheless to be considered as a father – not one severe and Oedipian, but a living and a loving father. Why father and not mother, when one knows the mother to be she who first attends to us, giving us our first kisses, our first loves? Because we are thereby permitted to pose an intra-psychic and social instance that is not the physical envelope of the mother, which exists in too great a proximity to the infant and risks provoking short-circuits leading to inhibition and psychosis. This 'imaginary father' – the zero degree of our archaic loves – plays the role of the loving third to which the 'I' in the process of constitution identifies; it permits the investing of our drives in the symbolic, the dissociating of the somatic from the psychic and consequently, the creating of a space of play, of the gift, of exchange, beyond separation and absence. (1984a: 21)

The imaginary father provides the link between the child's semiotic immersion in maternal care, and a social position, by opening the child to a world of love. She refers to the concept of the 'father of individual prehistory' Freud invokes in his study of Little Hans. Instead of Lacan's subsumption of the loving relation under maternal care, and incorporation of the phallus into the mother's unconscious, Kristeva separates (natural?) nurturance from (imaginary, and eventually symbolic) love:

> [Freud] in fact dissociates idealization (and with it the amatory relationship) from the bodily exchange with the mother and child, and he introduces the Third Party as a condition of psychic life, to the extent that it is a loving life. If love stems from narcissistic idealization, it has nothing to do with the protective wrapping over skin and sphincters that maternal care provides for the baby. (1987: 34)

5   Kristeva's work on pre-oedipal, narcissistic, and identificatory relations, maternal dependences, and corporeal pleasure provides an orientation that is underemphasized in Freud and Lacan, and which owes a debt to the work of Melanie Klein and D. W. Winnicott. Kristeva will place within the pre-oedipal, maternal phase all of the preconditions for symbolic functioning. Concepts

like her notions of abjection, amorous desire, negativity, the semiotic, the maternal *chora*, etc. testify to pre-oedipal, and in some cases, pre-mirror stage processes and relations, generally neglected in psychoanalysis, and left unelaborated by Freud and Lacan.

> What I wanted to do was two things. First, to make more detailed the archaic stages preceding the mirror stage because I think that the grasping of the image by the child is the result of a whole process. And this process can be called *imaginary*, but not in the specular sense of the word because it passes through voice, taste, skin and so on, all the senses yet doesn't necessarily mobilise sight. ('Julia Kristeva in Conversation with Rosalind Coward', 1984b: 22–3)

She will more carefully distinguish the introjection of maternal and paternal imagos than Lacan, focusing in considerably more detail on the imaginary pre-structuring of the symbolic, where Lacan, like Freud, sharply separates the pre-oedipal from the oedipal.

These differences from Lacan and Freud remain at the level of revisions, modifications, details, which, if they question psycho-analytic doctrine, leave its framework and fundamental assumptions intact and indeed beyond question. This becomes readily apparent when Kristeva relies upon Freudian and Lacanian conceptions of masculinity, femininity, sexuality, and maternity – those elements of psychoanalysis increasingly questioned by feminists. It is to this I will now turn.

Maternity or the avant-garde

Kristeva considers the semiotic as a feminine and maternally structured space. It pre-dates the imposition of (oedipal) sexual identity. It is a pre-patriarchal or proto-patriarchal phase in which the *phallic* mother is pre-eminent. This period is the precondition for and the object sacrificed by the child in establishing a position as a speaking subject within the symbolic. In Lacan's understand-ing, the imaginary mother-child relation requires the mediation of a third, external term; in Kristeva's the imaginary mother-child dyad is also considered to be crippling, but the child's relation to the imaginary father and an intra- and intersubjective third term link the child around rather than through the mother to the symbolic. The third term between mother and child provides the (intrasubjective) agency of the ego-ideal, a pre-symbolic signifier representing the mother's capacity to love someone other than the child.

Although Kristeva designates this as a feminine and maternal phase, and although she wishes to make clear an unspoken cultural debt to the maternal body, she disembodies the feminine and the maternal from women, and particularly from the female body. As she understands it, femininity is identified with a series of processes and relations that the pre-oedipal child of either sex experiences and wants before the imposition of sexual difference. It has no special or particular connection to the differences between the sexes. Admittedly, in her recent writings, Kristeva does acknowledge the specific and non-detachable alignments of sex and gender: she openly suggests that 'man's "feminine" is not woman's "feminine", and the woman's "masculine" is not the man's "masculine" ' (1987: 224). Yet she sees this not as a consequence of the social meaning of sexually specific *bodies* (i.e. Irigaray's concept of morphology), but of the 'asymmetrical bond of the two sexes with the phallus . . .' (1987: 224). She makes explicit her suspicions regarding an androgyny which professes an ideal hybrid of masculine and feminine attributes by accepting this ideal as a mode of phallic co-option of femininity: 'Absorption of the feminine by man, veiling the feminine in woman, androgeneity settles its accounts with femininity – the androgyne is a phallus disguised as a woman: not knowing the difference, he is the sliest masquerade of a liquidation of femininity . . .' (ibid.: 71).

Instead of androgyny, Kristeva presumes Freud's postulate of a fundamental bisexuality in all desiring subjects, which ensures that men too (or especially) remain in a (repressed) relation to the feminine, semiotic, pre-oedipal phase. In this sense, although it is feminine relative to the symbolic order, the semiotic has no special relation to women.

If the feminine has no particular relation to women in Kristeva's understanding, more paradoxically, the maternal itself has no particular relation to women or the female body either! On her model, maternity is a process unregulated by any subject, especially not by a female subject. The subject of maternity exists no-where. Becoming a mother is both the culmination of femininity and the abnegation and denial of any female identity:

> Within the body, growing as a graft, indomitable, there is an other. And no one is present, within that simultaneously dual and alien space, to signify what is going on. 'It happens but I'm not there.' Motherhood's impossible syllogism. (1980: 237)

Maternity effects a subject annihilation, the fading of sexual identity. It is the establishment of the grounds of *space* (and time) for the child. The chora is a nameless receptacle, an enveloping ground of identity which has no identity of its own. Pregnancy is the overtaking of woman's identity and corporeality by a foreign body, an alien intruder, who reveals the illusion of corporeal mastery that the mother may project onto the fragmentation, the 'becoming a-mother' (237) of her pregnancy:

> the maternal body is the place of a splitting, which, even though hypostatized by Christianity, nonetheless remains a constant factor of social reality. Through a body, *destined to insure reproduction of the species*, the woman-subject although under the sway of the paternal function (as symbolizing, speaking subject and like all others), [is] more of a *filter* than anyone else – a thoroughfare, a threshold where 'nature' confronts 'culture'. To imagine that there is *someone* in that filter – such is the source of religious mystifications . . . (ibid.: 238, emphasis added)

The maternal body during gestation, and the maternal *chora* during the child's infancy are conceived by Kristeva as subject-less corporeal spaces. They are not identities or roles for women (mother as womb, breast, partial objects rather than as subject). Yet they are the essential ingredients or elements required by the child's psychical movement from the imaginary to the symbolic. Kristeva suggests that the child must (retrospectively) fantasize these pre-imaginary spaces *as if* they were inhabited by a subject. This is her explanation of the child's recognition and acceptance of the mother's phallic status.

This then is a maternity which *women* as such can never inhabit. It is a maternity, a space, an energy, which, in so far as it is semiotic, cannot be spoken, *especially* not by mothers. If the semiotic is represented as feminine and maternal, it is nevertheless unable to be articulated by women:

> If it is not possible to say of a *woman* that she *is* (without running the risk of abolishing her difference), would it perhaps be different concerning the *mother*, since that is the only function of the 'other sex' to which we can definitively attribute existence. And yet, here too, we are caught in a paradox. First, we live in a civilization where the *consecrated* (religious or secular) representation of femininity is absorbed by motherhood. If, however, one looks at it more closely, this motherhood is the *fantasy* that is nurtured by the adult, man or woman, of a lost territory. (1987: 234)

This may explain why in *Tales of Love*, Kristeva focuses her analysis of maternity, not on the experience of motherhood, nor on women's representations of maternity, but on phallocentric textual images, most particularly those of the Virgin Mother presented in Christian theology. For Kristeva, Christianity provides the 'most symbolic construct in which femininity ... is focused on Maternality' (ibid.: 234). The Virgin Mary is, for her, both the tamed, symbolic representation of a femininity bonded to maternity; and, at the same time, an 'enigmatic sublimation', a precondition for all artistic production. The image of the Madonna provides, though in different ways, an image for each of the sexes; she represents a dialectical tension between symbolic and social conformity and an excessive, semiotic *jouissance*. She asks:

> What is there, in the portrayal of the Maternal in general and particularly in its Christian, virginal, one, that reduces social anguish and gratifies a male being; what is there that also satisfies a woman so that a commonality of the sexes is set up, beyond and in spite of their glaring incompatibility and permanent warfare? (ibid.: 326)

In so far as she is mother, woman remains unable to speak her femininity or her maternity. She remains locked within a mute, rhythmic, spasmic, potentially hysterical – and thus speechless – body, unable to accede to the symbolic because 'she' is too closely identified with/as the semiotic. 'She' is the unspeakable condition of the child's speech. Kristeva's position here remains surprisingly close to Lacan's conception of an unknowable feminine *jouissance*. When Lacan states that: 'the woman knows nothing of this *jouissance* ... So, as best we [male analysts] can, we designate this *jouissance vaginal* ...' (Lacan in Mitchell and Rose 1982: 146).

Kristeva seems to share in his view of a fundamentally unspeakable experience, pleasure, or corporeality. Yet, she has none of the biting humour and irony with which Lacan chastizes self-interested and largely aggressive male projections of their ideals of femininity. Moreover, Lacan seems to have more of an 'excuse' for his phallocentrism: while many of his propositions about femininity and female sexuality are developed before the emergence of a mass-movement feminism (e.g., 'The Signification of the Phallus' was first presented as a paper in 1958), Kristeva's position is developed as a self-conscious stand within contemporary feminist politics.

In spite of her overall adherence to women's castrated and secondary position, Kristeva does not claim that this maternal, semiotic contribution is incapable of *any* representation. Like the contents of the unconscious, it is capable of indirect or oblique expression or evocation. This explains the privileged position she grants to the avant-garde text in her earlier writings and the figure of the Virgin Mary in more recent texts. By transgressing the boundaries of the symbolic order, the avant-garde creates upheavals and ruptures which may enable what is usually unspoken to be articulated. Kristeva seems to accept that phallic subjects alone, only men, can re-present the unrepresented, subversive underside of the *chora* and the semiotic:

> At the intersection of sign and rhythm, of representation and light, of the symbolic and the semiotic, the artist speaks from a place where she is not, where she knows not, He delineates what, in her, is a body rejoicing. (1980: 242)

The artist, poet, avant-garde transgressor is always male. Men alone can occupy the (unstable) position of speaking subject within and transgressive of the symbolic; he is the speaker/painter/musician who subjects the symbolic to its own excesses and possibilities of subversion. Only men occupy this position because only men can acquire a guaranteed unified and stable position within the symbolic order – a consequence of the decisive repression of their oedipal desires. It is only from a position *within* the symbolic that it can be ruptured or transgressed. It is only those who actually occupy the position of speaking/representing subject who can undermine or subvert the limits of representation. If women are not positioned as speaking subjects (but as spoken-for objects), it is not surprising that they are not in any position to transgress the limits of such an order. This seems a luxury only those with a stable, guaranteed position can afford.

The position of avant-garde transgressor is not without its risks for those men who undertake it. It is fraught with psychical dangers, ranging from fetishism to psychosis. A result of the boy's unwillingness to accept his mother's 'castration', fetishism is his refusal to separate from the mother according to the father's demand. The fetish object takes over the role of the missing maternal phallus. The fetishist remains in a direct relation to the maternal space, able to draw on its resources for literary and representational production. In so far as the fetishist maintains contradictory views of the mother's castration, in affirming her castration he can take up his symbolic position; yet in denying her castration, he is able to retain his primary investments in his pre-oedipal, maternal attachments. Psychosis is a more extreme and debilitating identification with the mother. In maintaining his relation to the mother through an identification with her, the son may foreclose – that is, fail to represent – the name-of-the-father – and thus not be able to be positioned within the symbolic with a stable, ongoing position. The 'I' remains unlocated, functioning outside the symbolic.

These are the possibilities the male subject faces in transgressing his appointed position as law-abiding phallic subject:

> The modern text claims to find the repressed bearer of pleasur-able overflow in woman – the mother. But at the same time these later 19th century texts . . . either fetishize the mother as inaccessible . . . or else perform an identification with it and themselves presume the place of the mother as repressed-unnameable: in this latter case, they verge on psychosis . . . (1976: 70)

Fetishism and psychosis are personal risks posed for the avant-garde. But there are also grave social and political risks involved in signifying practices. The avant-garde text risks co-option or recuperation in functioning as a 'safety valve' or outlet for what may otherwise have become a more disruptive political practice. In reconverting the semiotic back into a new symbolic, its energy is dissipated in the conservation and stabilization of the symbolic. It also risks the opposite extreme, fascism, in which the disruptive semiotic processes are rechannelled into both a (narcissistic) love relation with the charismatic leader, and to a rigidified body organization hierarchized in even tighter form through this identification.

Although exclusively male in Kristeva's terms, the avant-garde is nevertheless the best representative of the repressed, feminine semiotic order, accepting as it does the idea of the split subject, the materiality of language, and the role of sexuality and pleasure in signification. Kristeva seems to regard only men as writers or producers of the avant-garde. When she talks about women's writing, she claims that women tend to write in one of two ways. They may either produce books that are largely compensatory substitutes for a family, that simulate a family structure – novels of autobiography, romance, or family history – they produce stories, images or fantasies in place of an actual family. Or else, women write as hysterical subjects, bound to the body and its rhythms, necessarily unspoken even if represented:

> In women's writing, language seems to be seen from a foreign land; it is seen from the point of view of an asymbolic, spastic body. Virginia Woolf describes suspended states, subtle sen-sations and above all, colours – green, blue – but she does not dissect language as Joyce does. Estranged from language, women are visionaries, dancers who suffer as they speak. (1981b: 166)

Because Kristeva positions men as representatives of a revol-utionary struggle of sexual identity clearly related to feminist struggles, she is able to ignore or discount any of the contributions women make to the establishment of new modes of signification. In her conception, the speaking subject is sexually neutral, a speaker who is both masculine and feminine, participating in both the symbolic and the semiotic. She disembodies femininity from women, and claims that the avant-garde explores femininity without noticing that femininity as expressed in men cannot adequately represent women's femininity.[9] She elevates men, those men who risk their guaranteed positions as subjects in the symbolic, to viable representatives of the feminine. As a result, women are relegated to one of two positions: reduced to maternity, providers of the maternal *chora*, in which case they remain the silent underside of patriarchal functioning. Or they are viewed disjunctively as feminists, in which case their work is necessarily limited, given Kristeva's view of feminist struggles.

For Kristeva, feminism is usually a negative and reactive counter-struggle against sexism. It does not provide the materials needed for developing alternatives. Its function is to say 'no' to this or that view, opposing what exists, without actively contributing something new:

> A feminist practice can only be negative, at odds with what already exists so that we may say 'that is not it!' and 'that's still not it'. In woman, I see something that cannot be represented, something that is not said, something above and beyond nomenclatures and ideologies. (Kristeva, in Marks and Coutrivron, eds: 137)

Because women do not occupy the subject-positions accorded to men in a patriarchal symbolic order, that is, because women are positioned as castrated and men as phallic, women are not *inside* the symbolic in the same way as men. This is why feminism has the function of saying no – the only possible political gesture that may have some effect *from outside*.

Kristeva's mode of textual analysis, the analysis of the interplay of semiotic and symbolic processes, is tied, as she sees it, to modes of sexual differentiation *within* each sex and each text. This differentiation does not divide men and women into distinct categories, nor position them as 'identities'. It is concerned with elements internal to all subjects: 'This musical rhythm bursts out in laughter at the meaningful and demystifies not only all ideology but everything that aspires to be identical with itself' (1976: 65). Ultimately she regards feminism, in opposition to psychoanalysis, as a temporary rather than an interminable analysis, one that, ideally, should aim at its own demise. In her view, feminism has aimed towards equality of opportunity, it has either (over-)valued maternity ('it involves less an idealized archaic mother than the idealization of the *relationship* that binds us to her, one that cannot be localized – an idealization of primary narcissism' (1987: 234) – an anaclitic relation to the maternal) or it ignores the 'real experience' of maternity, resulting in a rejection of maternity outright. For her, feminism should aim at the annihilation of *all* identity, especially sexual identity. Within such a feminism, which Kristeva regards as her own,

> the very dichotomy man/woman as an opposition between two rival entities may be understood as belonging to *meta-physics*. What can 'identity' or even 'sexual identity' mean in a new theoretical and scientific space where the very notion of identity is challenged . . . What I mean is . . . the demassification of the problematic of *difference* . . . (1981a: 34)

Kristeva remains the dutiful daughter in so far as she enacts for herself and reproduces for other women the roles of passivity and subordination dictated to women by patriarchal culture and affirmed by psychoanalysis.

Defiant women

If the dutiful daughter pays homage to the father's Law, even in spite of herself, what place can be granted to the resistances of many women to the patriarchal expectations surrounding their social/psychical roles? If even resistances, such as the masculinity complex, can be read as confirmations of the dominance of the phallus, what hope is there for a transgression or upheaval of this dominance? By what logic are women considered *a priori* castrated, for all history and in all places? Even if it can be acknowledged that women today are put into a castrated position, or must function as if they are castrated, why *must* it be so always? Lacan and Kristeva seem to have no means of historicizing women's (and men's) psycho-social status. How, then, is defiance possible? By what means could a non-phallic yet articulable sexuality be granted to women?

Like Kristeva, Irigaray is clearly well-versed in the complexities of Lacan's position. And, like Kristeva, she takes it as both an object of investigation and as a method by which her investigations proceed. Like Kristeva, her work can be situated in the interstices of dominant discourses (especially philosophical discourses which serve as a 'Master' discourse),[10] sexuality or desire, and relations of power or domination. Irigaray brings together discourses, sexualities, and relations of power, in terms quite different from Kristeva's. Discourses or texts are not restricted to the poetic, literary or the avant-garde. Irigaray is concerned, among other things, with breaching the boundaries between fictional and theoretical texts, asserting one in the face of demands of the other. Sexualities, too, are not seen as blurred and fundamentally bisexual. While Irigaray cannot be seen as an advocate of a pregiven identity or essence, neither is she interested in the issue of the (bisexual) processes of sexual *differentiation*. For her, the question of sexualities must be bound up with the question of *two* sexes, – that is, with the question of sexual specificity. And the concept of power in Irigaray's work is conceived in terms different from Kristeva's.

For Kristeva, power relations are explained in terms of degrees of adherence to symbolic norms. The symbolic is the 'system' against which semiotic subversions are directed. As the unities comprising the state and its various instrumentalities, signifying practices and their norms, and subjectivity integrated under the illusory mastery of the ego, the conception of power she utilizes is a globalized, integrated totality. The oppression of women and the structure of patriarchy is merely one form of a long list of oppressions – class, race, religious – all of which are equally effects of the symbolic structure and are liable to cause ruptures within its operations. The avant-garde ruptures the symbolic to participate in the overthrow of racist, class, and sexual forms of oppression, even if it remains apparently unconcerned with them, and is still produced by (generally) white, western, middle-class men, men whose privilege relies on the oppression of these very groups. These men may shake the patriarchal, bourgeois, imperialist, and racist foundations of the symbolic by striking a blow at the functioning of texts and signifying practices. By contrast, while clearly acknowledging the relevance of class and racial oppressions, Irigaray is directed to the analysis and subversion of *women's* oppression, which for her, provides a perspective from which questions of race and class may be dealt with differently than in phallocentric models. Her conception of power is that of patriarchal material practices and phallocentric discursive procedures, including women's resistances to these male-dominated regimes.

Her aim seems to be the exploration of a new theoretical space and language which may be able to undermine patriarchal and phallocentric domination of the sphere of representations and, more positively, to provide a mode of representation for women as women. If, as she argues, women's bodies are inscribed as a lack or atrophy by dominant representational systems which leave no space for articulating a self-determined femininity, their limits need to be recognized and transgressed. Her interrogation of philosophical and psychoanalytic discourses, seeking their flaws and 'blindspots' (see 1985a: pt.1), her use of these paradigms against themselves is directed towards concrete political goals: the positive reinscription of women's bodies, the positive reconstruction of female morphologies, and thus the creation of perspectives, positions, desires that are inhabitable by women *as* women. This project is simultaneously and undecidably negative, (a reactive feminism of the kind Kristeva most readily identifies as feminist), and constructive (creating positive alternatives, viable methods of knowing, and means of representation for women's autonomy).

In opposition to Kristeva, Irigaray is interested in developing accounts of subjectivity and knowledge that acknowledge the existence of two sexes, two bodies, two forms of desire and two ways of knowing. Instead of a process of sexual differentiation functioning within each subject (obliterating or obscuring any significant differences between subjects), Irigaray directs herself to the question of sexual specificity of subjects. Before elaborating Irigaray's position, it may be worth briefly discussing some of the more immediate connections her work has to Lacan in particular, and to psychoanalysis in general.

Ironically, Lacan's name is never mentioned within the body of *Speculum of the Other Woman*, her most sustained discussion of psychoanalysis. Yet this is clearly a strategic move on Irigaray's part, a mimesis of Lacan's and Freud's relegation of the question of femininity to a side issue in the exploration of the oedipus complex and the name-of-the-father. She attempts to undo psychoanalytic phallocentrism by insinuating the question of sexual specificity into its most central assumptions and propositions. I will first simply note some of the more obvious relations of influence of Lacan's work on Irigaray's; and then briefly mention some of the more serious disagreements between them.

1 Irigaray is strongly influenced by what she regards as the explanatory power of psychoanalysis in relation to the construction and reproduction of patriarchal forms of subjectivity. Moreover, not only does it analyse the human subject, it is also able to make explicit the 'stakes' involved in *all* phallocentric knowledges:

It is not a matter of naively accusing Freud, as if he were a 'bastard'. Freud's discourse represents the symptom of a particular social and cultural economy, which has been maintained

in the West at least since the Greeks.
. . . what Freud demonstrates is quite useful. When he argues –
for example, and according to a still organistic argument – that
women's sex is a 'lack', that castration for her amounts to her
perceiving that she has no sex, he describes rigorously the
consequence of our socio-cultural system. Lacan, using a
linguistic schema, concludes likewise, and repeats the same
process, when he writes that woman is a lack in the discourse,
that she cannot articulate herself . . . *In some sense, this is not
false.* (1977a: 63-4, emphasis added)

Psychoanalysis is symptomatic of an underlying phallocentric
structure governing dominant discourses and cultures as a whole.
In this sense, it has the value of openly saying what usually remains
implicit. Moreover, it is useful in *feminist* terms as a mode of
reading or interpretation, a form of deciphering texts. Irigaray
resists the temptation to psychoanalyse subjects, real or fictional
individuals, in her writings, and instead uses psychoanalysis as a
mode of interpretation of texts, a device for the interrogation of
knowledges. This is not entirely alien to Lacan's own attempts to
destabilize a metaphysics of the *cogito* and its epistemological
underpinnings. He counterposes the psychoanalytic *presumption* of
knowledge (the analyst as the 'supposed subject of knowledge'), a
fraudulent or imaginary lure, to philosophical certainty, demonstrating that certainty is a function of denial and disavowal more
than knowledge (see Lacan 1953). Irigaray too will use psychoanalysis to highlight the aspirations and coercions of knowledge,
including psychoanalysis; knowledge that poses itself as *sexually
neutral*, as indifferent, universal, or disinterested, when in fact it is
the product of men's self-representations.
2 Irigaray utilizes the Freudian distinction between pre-oedipal
and oedipal, or the Lacanian distinction between imaginary and
symbolic as key elements in her own project. Unlike Kristeva, who
takes on these terms as they stand, and as it were applies them to a
linguistic and textual context, Irigaray uses them as critical tools, a
'double-edged knife' to pose the question of a sexual difference
conceived in terms other than those dictated by patriarchy. In other
words, she will attempt to sexualize, to render specific to each sex
the forms that its pre-oedipal and imaginary, or oedipal and
symbolic takes. She asserts that psychoanalysis can only represent
the imaginary and the symbolic from the point of view of the boy; it
has no means available to elaborate what the imaginary and
symbolic may be in the girl's terms. It is for this reason that both
Freud and Lacan must presume a sexual neutral pre-symbolic

being.[11] The little girl must be considered the same as the little boy in order for their symbolic differentiation to be possible. Instead, Irigaray affirms the particularity and the unrepresented forms of pre-oedipal mother-daughter relations, and a feminine imaginary:

> Freud discovers . . . the desire for the same, for the self-identical, the self (as) same, and again of the similar, the alter ego and, to put it in a nutshell, the desire for the . . . auto . . . the homo . . . the male, dominates the representational economy. 'Sexual difference' is a derivation of the problematics of sameness. . . The 'differentiation' into two sexes derives from the a priori assumption of the same, since the little man that the little girl is, must become a man minus certain attributes whose paradigm is morphological – attributes capable of determining, of assuring, the reproduction-specularization of the same. A man minus the possibility of (re)presenting oneself as a man = a normal woman. (1985a: 26–7)

3 Irigaray utilizes Freud's and Lacan's understanding of the unconscious, its economy, logic, and products, as an evocative metaphor of femininity itself, for what is repressed by and intolerable to the social order:

> to say that woman's sexuality is naturally subject to processes of repression, sublimation etc., that's very doubtful. I would rather frame the following question: are women not, partly, the unconscious? That is, is there not in what has been historically constituted as the 'unconscious', some censored, repressed element of the feminine? (1977a: 70)

4   Irigaray harnesses the link that Lacan forges between psychical and linguistic processes. If language is the key to interpreting psychical life, and if the unity/cohesion of the ego, and the parameters and structures of the lived body also rely on signifying practices and symbolic representations, Iragaray's project is a retraversing of the inscription, the 'intextuation', of subjectivity under the primacy of the phallic signifier. Like Lacan, she refuses to talk of women, sexuality, or desire in terms of any Real, nature, or givenness. She forgoes all recourse to anatomy to develop instead an understanding of the morphology, the social/psychical representations, and lived reality, of the female body, which is closely based on Lacan's understanding of the 'imaginary anatomy'. The female body and specificity she seeks is not a pure or given identity, lying underneath a patriarchal overlay. Rather she seeks an active rewriting, this time from women's points of view, of the female

body, and of the possibilities of the female body as a site for the production of knowledge.

In other words, Irigaray *assumes* psychoanalysis as the framework from which she can analyse other knowledges and representations (including those of psychoanalysis itself) examining their elisions and silences – examining them, that is, from the point of view of the repression of femininity. Psychoanalysis becomes a critical and deconstructive tool rather than a truthful or descriptive model.

Her disagreements with psychoanalysis must also be briefly indicated. They include:

a   Where Freud and Lacan posit a sexual difference based on the '*a priori* of the same' – that is, a difference, understood as opposition, binary division, or the presence and absence of a single term, Irigaray attempts to develop a difference understood as Saussurian 'pure difference' – a difference without positive terms. Instead of posing woman as -A in relation to man, defined as A (a logic which inevitably prioritizes the positive term), Irigaray seeks an altogether different space for woman, one not defined in relation to men, but in their own terms – a 'B' rather than a '-A'.

b   Where Freud and Lacan claim universality, neutrality, and indeed a scientific status for psychoanalysis, Irigaray sees it as symptomatic of a historical order of male self-representations, an order that defines itself as 'truth'. She sees psychoanalysis as one of the more clear-cut and incisive examples of male specul(ariz)ation, and thus, as a body of knowledge clearly inscribed with perspectives and interests relevant to men. For example, the psychoanalytic insistence on the primacy of the phallus and the necessity of women's castration makes clear, not a truth about men and women, but the investments masculinity has in disavowing alterity, in denying even the possibility of an otherness outside their own self-definitions.

c   Where Freud and Lacan take social and individual relations as their speculative objects, Irigaray takes psychoanalysis itself as one of her objects of analysis. Like Kristeva, she seems strongly influenced by Derrida's deconstructive strategies. Her work can be seen as a deconstructive reading of Freudian and Lacanian texts.[12]

d   While taking Lacan's understanding of metaphor and metonymy seriously, Irigaray chooses to read him according to his own proclamations, that is, *literally*. Her troping functions as the trope of a trope; her writing position is that of a femininity, as posited by Freud and Lacan, a masquerade, the mimesis of mimicry, the textual *enactment* (not just articulation) of hysteria. Her strategies, in other words, contest psychoanalysis as a whole, subjecting it to its own logic to see what resists its interpretive machinery and what is absorbed by its logic of sameness.

Both Kristeva and Irigaray affirm a polyvocity, plurality, and multiplicity lying dormant within prevailing representational systems – an uncontrolled, excessive textual force or energy. But, in opposition to Kristeva, Irigaray regards this as a space hitherto occupied only by one sex. Her aim is to enable women to claim some place as women, introducing a genuine plurality or alterity into a hitherto mono-sexual model. Her claim is that the masculine can speak of and for the feminine largely because it has emptied itself of any relation to the male body, its specificity, and socio-political existence. This process of evacuating the male body from (an oedipalized) masculinity is the precondition for the establishment of the 'disinterested' neutered space of male specul(ariz)ation. Within this (virtual or imaginary) space, the space of the ego, and its mirror-double, the male can look at itself from outside, take itself as an object while retaining its position as a subject. It gains the illusion of self-distance, the illusion of a space of pure reflection, through the creation of a mirroring surface that duplicates, re-presents, everything *except* itself:

> Are we to assume that a mirror has always been inserted, and speculates every perception and conception of the world *with the exception of itself*. . . Does the subject derive his power from the appropriation of this non-place of the mirror? And from speculation? And as speculation constitutes itself as such in this way, it cannot be analyzed, but falls into oblivion, re-emerging to play its part only when some new effect of symmetry is needed in the system. (1985a: 205–6)

As the title suggests, *Speculum of the Other Woman* (1985a) attempts to traverse the Lacanian mirror of male self-representation which confirms woman in the position of *man's* specular double or alter-ego. His is a mirror, she implies, that can only reflect the masculine subject for whom it functions as a form of self-externalization. Her project, instead, like Alice's (A-Luce), is to pass *through* the looking glass into the 'wonderland' of women's own self-representations 'on the other side'. In place of the 'platitude'/flatness, of the platonic mirror, Irigaray substitutes the speculum, the curved, distorted medium of women's self-observation and self-representation. Her 'mirror', the speculum, surrounds, and is surrounded by, the contours and specificity of the female body. It is not a device of self-distance, but of self-touching, an implicated rather than disinterested self-knowledge. It represents the 'other woman', not woman as man's other, but another woman, altogether different from man's other.

Phallocentrism and sexual difference

Irigarary uses the term, 'phallocentrism' to object not only to the over-valuation of the male sex organ, but to the continuing submersion of women's autonomy in the norms, ideals, and models devised by men. Phallocentrism treats the two sexes as if they are two variations of the one sex. Whenever two sexual symmetries are represented by one, phallocentrism occurs. It occurs when the not necessarily comparable differences between them are reduced to a similarity, which renders them commensurable, and, not surprisingly, positions woman as man's inferior, the 'castrated sex'.

If knowledges and systems of representation are phallocentric, then two discourses, two speaking positions, and perspectives are collapsed into one. As the sexual other to the One sex, woman has only been able to speak or to be heard as an undertone, a murmur, a rupture within discourse; or else she finds her expression in a hysterical fury, where the body 'speaks' a discourse that cannot be verbalized by her.

The patriarchal symbolic order leaves no space or form of representation for women's autonomy. It effaces women's earliest formative relations, particularly through the 'inexorable' repression of the pre-oedipal mother-daughter relation – which leaves women without a pre-history and a positive identificatory model; it places social constraints and systems of meaning on women's behaviour, through intimidation, threats, inscriptions, barriers – materially imposed on women which drive many to a possibly self-destructive hysteria. Irigaray's counter-strategy against women's containment within an image and a logic that renders them mute and hysterical is the revival or reclamation of the hysteric's ability to mime, to displace the Real with its simulacrum. The hysteric mimes, and thus exceeds, the patriarchal requirements of femininity. So too Irigaray mimes, and thus exceeds the strategy of the hysteric; she places herself at the pivot point of the speculum's inversion of the subject's relation to its specular image.

The centre chapter of the book, 'La Mystérique', its point of self-speculation, is half-way through the turning inside-out of phallocentrism. This half-way point, the point at which the mirror, in being held up to itself, folds in on itself to become the curved speculum, is represented by a composite enigmatic feminine figure, the 'mysteric' (1985a: 191). This figure is undecidably the mystic, that female character within theological discourses who exemplifies piety and devotion, and a self-contained pleasure, an inexplicable *jouissance* (as Lacan suggests); the hysteric, who expresses in somatic terms women's relegation to the role of commodities and objects; and at the same time, the mystery, the enigma in the terms in which femininity is conceived in male speculations. The 'mysteric' is the name she gives to a discourse or a movement where masculine consciousness and self-consciousness is no longer master:

> This is the only place in the history of the West in which woman speaks and acts so publicly. What is more, it is for/by woman that man dares to enter the place, to descend to it, condescend to it, even if he gets burned in the attempt. (1985a: 191)

This is Irigaray's response to Lacan's treatment of St Teresa as the object of male speculations on female *jouissance*. Teresa is excessive, but not that excess that man must utilize to find a link with his Maker. If her touch enlightens, illuminates male speculation, it also *burns*:

> And if 'God' has already appeared to me with face unveiled, so my body shines with a light of glory that radiates it. And my eyes have proved sharp enough to look upon that glory without blinking. They would have been seared had they not been that simple eye of the 'soul' that sets fire to what it admires out of its hollow socket. A burning glass is the soul who in her cave joins with the source of light to set everything ablaze that approaches her hearth. Leaving only ashes there, only a hole: fathomless in her incendiary blaze. (ibid.: 197)

The ecstasy, the ex-stasis, the outside-itself attributed to women by male speculation – including psychoanalysis – is in fact the phallic refusal to accept an otherness not modelled on the same. If Lacan eulogizes the *jouissance* of St Teresa, it is because this fantasy of a simultaneously phallic and 'supplementary' *jouissance* 'beyond the phallus' reconfirms the phallus as the fixed reference point, the only given signifier for symbolic and sexual representation. Irigaray instead makes clear that if this *jouissance* is 'beyond the phallus' it is not, for that matter, unsignifiable. This is not a *jouissance* that woman cannot know or say; rather, it is a *jouissance* that Lacan cannot *hear* for he does not know how, or even where, to listen. The valorization of certain modes of representation, the fantasy of an-other subject like the self-same – woman as the incoherent or silent counterpart of man – and the disavowal of his own position as listener makes the male interlocutor unable to hear other than what he wishes to hear:

Woman never speaks the same way. What she emits is flowing, fluctuating. *Blurring*. And she is not listened to, unless proper meaning (meaning of the proper) is lost. Whence the resistances to that voice that overflows the 'subject'. Which the 'subject' then congeals, freezes, in its categories until it paralyzes the voice in its flow.

'And there you have it, Gentlemen, that is why your daughters are dumb.' Even if they chatter, proliferate psychically in works that only signify their aphasia, or the mimetic underside of your desire. And interpreting them where they exhibit only their muteness means subjecting them to a language that exiles them at an ever increasing distance from what perhaps they would have said to you, were already whispering to you. If only your ears were not so formless, so clogged with meaning(s), that they are closed to what does not in some way echo the already heard.
(1985a: 112–13)

Could Narcissus have heard Echo speak *in her own words*? Or is he capable of hearing, as well as seeing, only himself? No longer content to *merely* repeat, Irigaray does, however, mime: like the hysteric, her reading/deconstruction of psychoanalysis is a parody of Lacan's reading of Freud. Or really, a parody of the hysteric's parody of Lacan's reading: a second order *dis*simulation. Yet to understand how Irigaray inverts Lacan (Lacan claimed that he himself was the 'perfect hysteric', see Mitchell and Rose 1982: translator's footnote 6, 160–1; and Clément 1983: 66–7), a more detailed understanding of her relations to Lacan's conception of language will be useful.

Femininity and language

Irigaray does not aim to create a new women's language. Her project, rather, is to utilize already existing systems of meaning or signification, to exceed or overflow the oppositional structures and hierarchizing procedures of phallocentric texts. She stresses their possibilities of ambiguity, their material processes of production and renewal. She affirms the plurality and multiplicity, dormant in dominant discourses, which cover over and rely on the inclusions and exclusions of femininity and its associated attributes. She refuses the 'either/or' logic of dichotomous models by presenting the feminine as a mode of occupying both alternatives, exerting a 'both/and' logic of difference in its place. To speak *as woman* is already to defy the monologism of discursive domination under phallocentrism.

Her assault on patriarchal language consists in showing that those discourses which present themselves as universal and neutral, appropriate to all, are in fact produced and maintained according to male interests. In questioning this neutrality, Irigaray poses the question of sexual enunciation: of who speaks, for whom, and with what interests. Men – philosophers, psychoanalysts, scientists, writers – have spoken for women for too long. Women remain the objects of speculation, the source of metaphors and images necessary for the production of discourse, but disavowed in its pronouncements, while they are denied access to positions as producing subjects: 'A language that presents itself as universal, and which is in fact maintained by men only, is this not what maintains the alienation and exploitation of women in and by society' (Irigaray 1977b: 67). The domination by one sex of the right to speak is in part an effect of its capacity to achieve a distance from its object of analysis. The masculine is able to speak of and for women because it has emptied itself of any relation to the male body. The male body as such must be renounced when the boy gives up his oedipal and pre-oedipal pleasures in exchange for the hierarchization accomplished by the phallus. The mirror-image reflected to the pre-oedipal, imaginary subject is regarded as sexually neutral, or 'masculine'. But its neutrality or indifference to the child's sex is not a plausible hypothesis, given the *meaning* the child's body already has for the mother and father. The establishment of the ego through its visual representation in the mirror-image forms the preconditions for the alienation required for language, in the first instance, and for knowledge and truth in the second. The evacuation of the male body is the condition required to create a space of reflection, of specul(ariz)ation from which it can look at itself from the outside. This distance is the space necessary for *metalanguage* or metadiscourse, the space of hierarchized reflection. Metalanguage distinguishes between language as object and language as the means of analysing this object. This discursive separation into logical levels is an attempt to unify and order terms, positioning them into their 'proper', unambiguous places, subsumed under a knowing, masterful gaze. While capable of reflecting on language as object, metalanguage is not capable of self-reflection, it cannot observe itself, without creating a higher order meta-metalanguage.

Irigaray refuses to concede the 'logic' of this ordering, and the imposition of these boundaries and borders. Where such borders exist, they are a form of solidification of the fluid polyvocity and ambiguity constitutive of all language. The distinction between these levels has evolved, in part, as an attempt to resolve the problem posed to truth by the existence of paradoxes. If we take the classical liar's paradox, 'I am lying', it is true only if it is false, and false only if it is true. In an attempt to resolve and make sense of such paradoxical assertions, philosophers of language (such as Bertrand Russell) will divide the statement into two distinct levels. The paradox is generated because the statement is undecidably part of object- and meta-language. 'I am lying' is a statement both referring to an 'I' (at the object-level) and about the processes of making a statement (at the meta-level). By distinguishing the object- from the meta-language the paradox can be neutralized: 'I am lying – except in uttering this statement.' This distinction has evolved as an attempt to justify the languages of science and truth from the language of their objects of investigation. This rigid confinement of terms, phrases, sentences, propositions, etc. is an attempt to curtail the possibility, outlined by Saussure, of any linguistic relation of 'pure difference.' This an attempt to constrict and narrow meaning, to organize singular, hierarchical principles to master the wayward reliance of language on a constitutive ambiguity. This move is *isomorphic* with oedipalized male sexuality, and is alien to femininity defined as the 'other' of the masculine:

> a feminine language would undo the unique meaning, the proper meaning of words, of nouns: which still regulates all discourse. In order for there to be a proper meaning, there must indeed be a unity somewhere. But if feminine language cannot be brought back to any unity, it cannot be simply described or defined: there is no feminine meta-language. The masculine can partly look at itself, speculate about itself, represent itself and describe itself for what it is, whilst the feminine can try to speak to itself through a new language, but cannot describe itself from outside or in formal terms, except by identifying itself with the masculine, and thus by losing itself. (Irigaray 1977b: 65)

A language that considers itself readily translatable, capable of being formalized in the terminology of logic, in the form of axioms, deductions, conclusions, theorems, and aims to limit the play of multiple meanings so that only one clear, precise meaning exists is analogous to oedipalized male sexuality (which puts in place of the pleasures of the whole body/language system, the primacy of one organ/meaning). In effacing the play of materiality and corporeality, of signification, such a language is 'reduced' and 'purified'. It is a servile language reduced to the manipulative control of the knowing subject. Language becomes the expression of pre-existing ideas and rational thought, a language without play or pleasure. While Lacan is not guilty of eliminating pleasure from discourse and even though he specifically claims 'there is no metalanguage' (1970) nevertheless his disclaimer is directed elsewhere.[13] He remains committed to a position that, while implicated in what it says, denies its sexually coded enunciative position. His discourse is nevertheless a discourse about other discourses, a theorization of the language and language-like behaviour of others.

To acknowledge the *independent* otherness of feminine pleasure and sexuality beyond the service of orgasm and production involves giving up the coercive control and self-definition the masculine and the meta-theoretical provide for themselves. In claiming that there are other forms of language and modes of articulating pleasure, Irigaray makes clear the violent appropriation by masculine representational and libidinal systems of a field that is heterogeneous and capable of rich plurality. A language isomorphic with an autonomous non-reductive femininity and pleasure would have to overcome this prevailing self-understanding of masculinity.

> That *'elsewhere' of feminine pleasure can be found only at the price of crossing back through the mirror that subtends all speculation* . . . the issue is not one of elaborating a new theory of which woman would be the *subject* of the *object*, but of jamming the theoretical machinery itself, of suspending its pretension to the production of a truth and of a meaning that are excessively univocal. Which presupposes that women do not aspire simply to be men's equals in knowledge . . . but rather repeating/interpreting the way in which within discourse the feminine finds itself defined as lack, deficiency, as imitation and negative image of the subject, they should signify that with respect to this topic, a *disruptive excess* is possible on the feminine side. (Irigaray 1985b: 77–8)

While Irigaray does not speculate on what a feminine language should be, she does imply what it cannot be: it cannot be based on phallocentrism – singular meanings, hierarchical organization, polar oppositions, the division into subject-predicate form, a commitment to the intertranslatability of concepts. These values represent the privileged self-distance of masculinity and its denial of the material residue impervious to rational control; they are correlative with the elevation of male sexuality at the expense of femininity:

> Nothing is ever to be *posited* that is not also reversed and caught up again in the *supplementarity of this reversal* . . . we need to proceed in such a way that linear reading is no longer possible: that is, the retrospective impact of the end of each word,

utterance, or sentence upon its beginning must be taken into consideration in order to undo the power of its teleological effect, including its deferred action. That would hold good also for the opposition between structures of horizontality and verticality that are at work in language. (Irigaray 1985b: 79–80)

Her concentration on those phallocentric discourses which comprise the history of philosophy is a consequence of her methodology. She will focus on the reading of key texts, including those of Freud and Lacan, with the aim of showing their elisions, repressions, paradoxes, and unspoken assumptions. These assumptions, these blind-spots within patriarchal knowledges, are invariably associated with the ways in which masculinity, femininity, or male and female, are conceived. Discourses refuse to acknowledge that their own partiality, their own perspectivity, their own interests and values, implicitly rely upon conceptions of women and femininity in order to maintain their 'objectivity', 'scientificity', or 'truth' – that is, their veiled masculinity.

If this is the case, then Irigaray's project of developing a space in and from which women may speak for themselves, makes explicit the hitherto ignored sexualization of discursive positions – the degrees to which texts and representations do or do not adhere to the symbolic norms regulating them. In order to make the trajectory more overt, I will turn to her rearticulation of the mother-daughter relation and her reinscription of women's eroticism.

The genealogy of women

One of the key, if unspoken, questions throughout Irigaray's work on psychoanalysis is: why is the mother considered phallic? Why does the child regard her as phallic? and why does she herself take on this position?

Irigaray claims that within the Freudian schema of the familial, oedipal triangle, the child is always represented on the model of the son; and the mother is only understood in some relation to the phallus. This implies that, in our culture, the child, boy or girl, does not have an adequate representation of the *two* sexes. It is confronted with the male sex, and, given the woman's submersion in maternity, with a mother. There is no representation of the female sex. It thus makes perfect sense that the boy would consider his mother phallic. But the girl?

It is indispensable that the child, girl or boy, have a representation of the *two* sexes . . . But in the traditional conception of the family, in fact, he or she doesn't have this. Because if the mother is uniquely *mother*, the child has no image of woman, and thus of sexual difference. (1979: 40)

The mother/daughter relation is the 'dark continent of the dark continent, the most obscure area of our social order'. To 'enlighten' its blackness would pose a threat to the social order which has taken so much trouble to cover it over. It covers over the debt culture owes to maternity but cannot accept. The son, for example, cannot accept the debt of life, body, nourishment, and social existence he owes to the mother. A whole history of philosophy seems intent on rationalizing this debt away by providing men with a series of images of self-creation culminating in the idea of God as the paternal 'mother', creator of the universe in place of women/mothers. Man's self-reflecting Other, God, functions to obliterate the positive fecundity and creativity of women. Born of woman, man devises religion, theory, and culture as an attempt to disavow this foundational, unspeakable debt.

The burial of women under the phallocentric reduction to maternity is crippling for both mother and daughter. For the mother, it implies the constriction of her possibilities of self-definition and autonomy, her subjection to the Law of the Father, her subsumption under the name of her husband, and her giving up her identity as a woman. While she remains the condition of subjectivity and culture, she herself remains mute, unrepresented, and confined to a given role, a 'mute substratum'. This constriction implies, furthermore, that she is left with few possibilities of personal development and expression. The mother is thus able to consider herself phallic, if she does, because her only socially valued role *as a woman* is bound up with maternity and with her role as the object of desire.

She is the mother who has *nothing but* food/love to give – food/love that risks choking or smothering the child, force-feeding it with herself, gaining her identity through it. This love, so painfully articulated in 'And One Doesn't Stir Without the Other' (Irigaray 1981a) describes a suffocation the child will sooner or later attempt to escape:

> You have made something to eat. You bring me something to eat. But you give yourself too much, as if you wanted to fill me all up with what you bring me. You put yourself into my mouth and I suffocate. Put less of yourself in me and let me look at you. I'd like to see you while you are feeding me. Not to lose my/your sight when I open my mouth to you. And that you should still remain close to me while I am drinking you. But continue to be

181

on the outside as well. Keep yourself and keep me just as outside, too. Do not swallow yourself up, do not swallow me down in that which flows from you to me. I'd like it so much if we could be there, both of us. So that one does not disappear into the other, or the other into the one. (1981a: 11)

This constricted, suffocating motherhood is not the result of the mothers phallic *lack*, but an excess that can find no other social avenue or validated outlet. This excess, or its reverse – the refusal to be absorbed, to give enough, which keeps the child clamouring for more (love, food, attention) – is not inevitable, but an effect of women's eclipse in maternity. Maternity under patriarchy curtails the mother's possibilities of expression; it also 'exiles' the daughter from her origins and her potential development as a woman. She has no *woman* with whom to identify. She is introduced to the sociocultural cycle of reproduction when she takes the mother's place, replacing her, symbolically 'murdering' her.

Her oedipus complex deprives her of direct access to the maternal body, and a positive evaluation of her sexuality and identity. It erases her potential as an active lover, situating her in a narcissistic, passive position as the love object of an active, phallic male lover. Her earliest – homosexual – attachment must be given up so that she is able to enter the circuits of sexual exchange, her pre-history is erased and her relation to the primal love object, to a body similar to her own, is lost.

Freud's account of the mother-daughter relation is not a false picture (except in so far as it is rendered eternal and unchangeable) for it describes what patriarchy requires of women. In opposition to Freud, Irigaray suggests that this model is neither logically nor culturally necessary. In particular, psychoanalysis does not allow a space for restructuring or reconceptualizing female relations, or re-inventing a body-to-body and woman-to-woman relation with the mother. For Irigaray, this possibility can be concretized only by a multi-directional quest – the search for a history that has been rendered invisible by the refusal to accord women a name and place of their own; as well as the construction of a future which involves the painful process of giving up the mother as haven, refuge or shelter in return for seeing her as a woman.

This may involve something of a provisional loss for women, for maternity is one of the few sites where women – daughters – are sheltered from the demands of sexual, political, and economic exchange. Yet this sacrifice of a maternal shelter also implies the possibility of a rejuvenation, a rediscovery of the identity shared by mother and daughter which may give to both a certain strength to resist these circuits of exchange. The mother may give the daughter not just food, but words to nourish her; this gift will be reciprocated by the daughter's new found ability to speak *to*, rather than *at* her mother.

It requires a new kind of language in which both the mother's and daughter's identities as women can be articulated. It also implies restructuring of desire itself, so that the maternal body – the 'lost object' initiating the metonymic chain of substitutions (including language) – is not relinquished or lost, both a fusion with and a differentiation from the mother. It defies the patriarchal demand for a separation of mother from child, which introduces the symbolic order and socio-sexual exchange. This possibility is lyrically evoked in the concluding chapter of *This Sex Which is Not One*, translated as 'When Our Two Lips Speak Together', which supersedes the suffocating paralysis of 'And One Doesn't Stir Without the Other'. It announces a new relation between mother and daughter in which the demands for division, separation and singularity are rejected and replaced with a positive relation between the two women:

> We are luminous. Neither 'one' nor 'two'. I've never known how to count. Up to you. In their calculations, we make two. Really, two? . . . An odd sort of two. And yet not one. Especially not one. Let's leave *one* to them: their oneness, with its prerogatives, its domination, its solipsism: like the sun's. And the strange way they divide up their couples. With the other as the image of the one. Only an image. So any move toward the other means turning back to the attraction of one's own mirage. A (scarcely) living mirror, she/it is frozen, mute. Dedicated to reproducing – the sameness in we have remained for centuries, as the other. (1985b: 207)

Irigaray speaks indistinguishably as both mother and daughter; not an 'I' addressing a distinct 'you', but an I/you: a 'we'. This 'we' does not subsume one identity in the other. It is a fusion of identities without residue or loss. It is both speech and pleasure, sameness and difference, textuality and sexuality, the evocation of a space women are able to occupy as women without being silenced or mediated by masculinity. It is an exchange without debt, loss, or guilt, a space the feminine may reclaim for itself.

Seducer or seduced?

Lacan's flirtatious courtship of women, whether hysterics, analysts, or feminists, has not always succeeded in sexual conquest. Not all those women who have worked on or with psychoanalysis have 'come across' with the answers he seeks. Not all are interested in his seductive ploys, his prancing with the women in order to know them better, to seduce them, to act the ladies' man. In *Feminism and Psychoanalysis. The Daughter's Seduction* (1982a) Jane Gallop describes Lacan's solicitous questioning of woman's desire as an ambivalently phallocentric and a surprisingly anti-phallic gesture. He is both the Father embodying Law, and the delinquent or better, the pervert, who evades the Law, in seeking a pleasure outside its scope:

> Feminists have been hard on the ladies' man, presuming that his intentions are strictly dishonourable. They're right. But should not feminism be working to undo the reign of honour, and all those virile virtues? In as much as feminists are hard on anyone, they betray an inappropriate (which is to say, all too appropriate and proper) phallicization.
> [But] . . . he is no mere father figure out to purvey the truth of his authority; he also comes out seeking his pleasure in a relation that the phallocentric universe does not circumscribe. To designate Lacan at his most stimulating and forceful is to call him something more than just phallocentric. He is also phallo-eccentric. Or, in more pointed language, he is a prick. (Gallop 1982b: 35–6)

If, as Gallop suggests, Lacan is both phallus and prick, both authority and its excess, both phallocentric and beyond the phallus, it is not surprising that his work has generated controversy and disagreement among feminists. Kristeva and Irigaray may be taken as representative of the kinds of differences and debates occupying feminists since reading or hearing his lectures.

While critical of details of his position, Kristeva, Mitchell, and others ultimately fall victim to his seductive display. Each actively affirms, not the excessive, self-deconstructive, *jouissant* Lacan, Lacan the 'floozie' as Gallop calls him (42), but Lacan the Law-giver. Each claims that the Father's Law or the oedipal interdict is one of the necessary conditions for the existence of the social, in whatever form it may take. Each affirms that the child must be definitively separated from its immediate, maternal dependencies, which threaten it with suffocation or annihilation and the loss of an independent position or place in the social. And each affirms that, because of his purely cultural or significatory role in paternity, the father (or the Father's Name) is ideally placed to perform this operation. The institution of the Father's Law, while objectionable in some of its forms, is nevertheless regarded as the necessary condition of stable discursive and social relations. In short, their adherences to psychoanalysis are framed (in various ways) in terms of the universality or cultural necessity of some oedipal-like structure.

In other words, the 'Kristevan' position, as it could be called, maintains an ambivalence towards the figure of the mother. The maternal relation represents nature, immediacy, pleasure, identification, blurring, or fusion of identities, and ultimately, entrapment, if it persists as the child's most direct and overwhelming relation. The mother is the potential devourer of the child's subjectivity and enunciative position, the crucial factor in psychosis, the source of all that, as culturally and personally threatening, has been expelled from conscious recognition. Again, while there may be disagreements about the form that the symbolic Father or Law-giver takes, the 'dutiful daughters' of psychoanalysis affirm that it must be someone *other* than the mother who introduces the law to the child, severing it from its crippling identifications and enabling it to take up a position outside her desire.

Ironically, then, those women seduced by Lacan, swayed by his arguments and by his manner, are not seduced by what Gallop has described as the prick; on the contrary, it is as Law-giver, Father, indeed as the subject-supposed-to-know that he is desired. If Lacan woos the women, it is only dutiful daughters, daughters true to the Father, embodiments of the Law, who answer his call. And *these* women who are obedient to the Law cannot tell him about what he wants to know – about women's desire, about *Was will das Weib*? It is as alien to a 'lawful' femininity as to a phallic masculinity. It is that *jouissance* in excess of the Law, the *jouissance* of the 'prick', not the phallus that he seeks to know (and master?)

But if Lacan takes on the role of symbolic Father for these women, what is his position for those other feminists who defy his claims? If Lacan remains phallus for the Kristevans, is he the prick, the penis beyond the phallus, for those wayward women I will designate by Irigaray's name (including Cixous, Kofman, and, with some hesitation, Gallop)? Even if they remain to some extent outside the framework of Lacan theory, is it the *jouissance* of his position that nevertheless attracts Irigaray, Cixous *et al.*? In other words, does Lacan manage, in a rather convoluted, and aggressive passion, to seduce these feminists as well?

This is a relevant question to ask of these feminists only if the ambiguous nature of seduction is understood. Seduction differs from rape in so far as the woman's desire functions as a kind of activity. In the seduction, in other words, it is unclear who is seducing whom. The question that must be posed, then, is: does Lacan seduce the 'Irigarayans' (in spite of their protests)? Or is it that he is seduced by them?

Irigaray herself describes her relations to psychoanalysis, and the history of philosophy in flirtatious terms. Her seduction, like Lacan's, is strategic: a 'nuptial' strategy:

> Thus it was necessary to destroy, but . . . with nuptial tools. The tool is not a feminine attribute. But woman may re-utilize its marks on her, in her. To put it another way: the option left to me was to *have a fling with the philosophers*, which is easier said than done. . . (1985b: 150)

It is a strategy for utilizing, u-tool-izing a 'machinery' hostile to one's interests so that it works against itself. Hers, in short, is the seductive strategy of the hysteric. Seduction is the strategy of the mistress, not the wife. Refusing to be the wife of philosophers (a self-annihilation, as Irigaray indicates, ibid.: 152), to tidy up after their own self-reflective 'truths', in her role as seducer, Irigaray does not take on the role of surrogate, either wife or mother. Instead, her role-model is that of the arch-mimic, the hysteric.

Dora is the most articulate of all Freud's studies of hysterics. Dora expresses and resists the Father's Law. She is made the object of a sexual exchange between Herr K., who will exchange 'his' 'object', Frau K., with Dora's father in return for a sexualized access to Dora. Dora is put into an impossible position: she is unable to remove herself from this unspoken contractual exchange the men have established; she is unable to say no to Herr K.'s advances with any authority (when she reports that he tried to kiss her to her parents, they do not believe her); and she is unwilling to say yes. What strategy does she develop? How is there a way out for her? She brilliantly manages to have the last laugh on all those who betrayed or used her. Above all, she uses the pre-eminently feminine strategy of seduction. She never actually says no to Herr K. She accepts his gifts, his letters, his attention, she cares for his children, she is 'interested' in him. She does not prevent him from his passions. Instead, she uses a well-worn feminine strategy: seduction. She actively takes on her passive position. She then refuses what Herr K. has presumed she has 'promised'. Or, in Gallop's terminology, she is a *prick-teaser*, the sexual strategy designed to give women at least something of their desires, without having to pay 'the full price'. She eggs Herr K. on, more or less encouraging him, only to say no at the last moment. And even then, her 'no' takes the form of corporeal spasms – a retching and choking when Herr K. kisses her. She uses the *veneer*, the charms and attributes of femininity, not to uphold the law but to gain some pleasure, even if this be at the expense of the man's dignity or self-image. In other words, like the women Cixous invokes at the beginning of her paper 'Castration or Decapitation' (1981), Irigaray knows that the best strategy for challenging the phallic authority of the penis is *laughter*, disinvestment of interest, *in*difference presented as interest or commitment.

Is the 'Irigarayan' strategy prick-teasing? Is it by flirtatious flattery that she can have her fling, and enjoy it too? If she seduces, is she not, in turn, also seduced? Or is her position that of *miming* seduction, the hysterical inversion of its goals? Prick-teasing, or rather, prick-deflating, a refusal to over-value the phallus through desire?

How is one to decide about Lacan's relations to feminism? Is he an arch-phallocrat, the latest in a long line of misogynist thinkers? or is he the prick who dares to speak its name, to reveal the self-deception behind the masculine aspiration to phallic status? Does his work affirm or undermine phallocentrism? Or does it do *both*?

Conclusion

I have attempted to provide an overview of Lacan's analysis of the two crucial 'moments' in the social genesis of subjectivity – the mirror phase and the formation of the ego; and the name-of-the-father and entry into the symbolic order. Constructed out of these two infantile 'events' is the structure of adult sexuality, desire, and the unconscious. Throughout this discussion, I have asserted the issue of sexual difference and specificity, suggesting that even at the mirror phase the two sexes are treated, and function differently (even if a child of either sex may not yet have a comparative understanding of his or her position). Sexual difference becomes codified into the presence or absence of a single feature – the male sexual organ – as a condition of the paternal metaphor and the edicts issued by the symbolic father. From the time a child of either sex has resolved the paternal interdict forbidding incest, he or she is positioned as a social, sexualized, split subject. Each sex is then able to take up the pre-designated positions of masculinity or femininity in accordance with patriarchal requirements.

However, if each sex *can* occupy its place within the symbolic, this is not to say that each necessarily *does* occupy it. The appeal of Lacan's position resides in his cynical attitude to the avowals of consciousness, the acknowledgement of a self-interested ego, and the pretensions to self-knowledge and certainty, the assurances of those 'in' power – those who think they *have* the phallus. Lurking beneath the demands for recognition uttered by the *cogito* (this is Hegel's 'solution' to the problem of the solipsism of the *cogito*[1]), by the subject (to the other), and by the masculine subject (to an unknowable femininity) is a *disavowed*, repressed or unspoken *desire*. Desire is a movement, a trajectory that asymptotically approaches its object but never attains it. Desire, as unconscious, belies and subverts the subject's conscious demands; it attests to the irruptive power of the 'other scene', the archaic unconscious discourse within all rational discourses, the open-endedness of all human goals, ideals, aspirations, and objects. If Lacan has explained how patriarchal culture transmits and reproduces itself, he also elaborates in what ways it exceeds itself, oversteps its own boundaries, posing a real risk to culture (which is why culture requires repression and hence, an unconscious). If, in other words, he has explained how the law-like functioning of language constitutes the subject as such, he also makes clear the always open, ambiguous, and uncontrollable nature of language, its supra- and trans-subjective status. He shows that language is inherently open to new meanings, reinterpretations, recontextualizations that are capable, by deferred action, of giving it meaning other than that intended.

This means, among other things, that the lack constitutive of the subject – biological lack, lack of identity, lack of object, lack of organ, lack of language – functions both as a serious limitation to subjectivity, and as the condition of retroaction by which all events and meaning are capable of re-interpretation *ad infinitum*. The subject's lack of a stable, finalized identity, its lack of a hold on the semiosis constituting language, and its lack of (a chain of) objects provide the conditions of the possible *resistance* to the expectations of the symbolic. Where certainty is rendered problematic, the exploration of different possibilities becomes imperative. Lacan's work, this is to say, contains the elements necessary for its own deconstruction.[2]

If, that is, Lacan is guilty of a certain logocentrism, as Derrida claims, and a certain phallocentrism, as Irigaray argues (1985a, 1985b: ch.1), this does not mean that feminists must abandon his work altogether. On the contrary, it may be *because* of his logocentric and phallocentric commitments that his work is so useful in the projects of many feminists. What I am suggesting here is that the problems as much as any solutions raised by a text may justify a careful reading and use of that text. The phallo(logo)centric orientation of his work may indeed explain why psychoanalysis in its Freudian and Lacanian forms has been able to act as a paradigm of other discourses and knowledges. It renders explicit and articulates presumptions that function in all socially valorized or dominant knowledges, but remain unspoken by them. Psychoanalysis acts, thus, as both investigative object of feminist researches, and as critical, and strategically valuable, tool. Furthermore, this may help explain why, up to the present time at least, even those feminists who remain critical of psychoanalysis must develop their objections from within its frame. Objections and critiques levelled from outside its terms – which have usually taken the form of arguments about its 'non-scientific' (i.e. non-verifiable

and non-falsifiable) status, its implausibility as a mode of explanation, or its historical inappropriateness for the present (granted its
relevance to *fin de siècle* Vienna) – seem to have little success in
convincing feminists that other accounts are preferable.

Some kind of deconstruction is necessary if critiques are to be
developed from a position internal to psychoanalysis, and if one
wishes to preserve at least some elements of it while not adhering to
its overall framework or all its central presuppositions. Deconstruction involves a very careful, patient reading of the text, inhabiting it
from a point of view sympathetic to the text's concerns and its logic;
and at the same time, reading it from the point of view of what is
left out, foreclosed, or unarticulated by it but is necessary for its
functioning. If deconstruction is a mode of reading a text from both
inside and outside its terms, i.e., from its margins, then such a
reading must remain ambivalently an act of love and respect, and of
self-assertion and critical distancing:

> The movements of deconstruction do not destroy structures
> from the outside. They are not possible and effective, nor can
> they take accurate aim, except by inhabiting those structures.
> Inhabiting them *in a certain way*, because one always inhabits,
> and all the more so when one does not suspect it. Operating
> necessarily from the inside, borrowing all from the old structure
> . . . the enterprise of deconstruction always in a certain way falls
> prey to its own work. (Derrida 1976: 24)

To preserve what is of insight or strategic use in his work, while
maintaining a critical distance from what is problematic would be
the aim of a deconstructive reading of Lacan. At the same time,
such a reading would need to show, not how separable and
delimitable the problems and insights are, but rather, how the
insights are necessarily dependent on what is problematic. In other
words, such a reading would need to show how psychoanalysis both
participates in and departs from phallo(logo)centrism in ways that
are not clearly distinguished. Feminist critiques need to occupy its
internal 'intellectual space' but always from a perspective outside its
parameters.

What I am suggesting is the cultivation of a critical *ambivalence*,
a simultaneous love and distance, a paradoxical inhabiting yet
living outside of its precepts. Freud defined ambivalence as a
wavering or 'vicissitude' of libidinal affect between affectionate and
hostile currents, between, that is, love and hate: 'The history of the
origins and relations of love makes us understand how it is that love
so frequently manifests itself as 'ambivalent' – that is, as accom-
panied by impulses of hate against the same object' (Freud 1914b:

139). If Lacan is correct in his equation of transference love with the supposition of a subject-who-knows; and if he is correct in his claim that the transformation of love into one of its opposites, hate, is the stripping of the supposed subject-of-knowledge of his epistemic status ('When I say that they hate me, what I mean is that they de-suppose me of knowledge', Mitchell and Rose 1982: 139) then ambivalence seems the only appropriate intellectual attitude femi-nists can take to his work.

This ambivalence, in Lacanian terms, implies the synchronous (and illusory) supposition and de-supposition of knowledge. Such an ambivalence is *not* psychotic. It is not a *disavowal* or foreclosure of his position (its simultaneous affirmation and denial) because it is a fluctuation of *affect* not of attitude or belief. The feminist does not so much believe and not believe in his work; rather, she feels simultaneously drawn towards and yet also kept at a distance. She supposes 'him' of knowledge in order to use his work to explain the (psychical) operations of patriarchy, to explain what is expected of men and women within patriarchal, bourgeois, imperialist culture. Yet she de-supposes him of knowledge about femininity, female sexuality, and female specificity. If he describes how patriarchy constructs subjects in its (phallic) image, he fails to describe the resistance, the struggles, the coercion invested in both accepting or refusing this image. He *knows* (in so far as this is possible) what the Law requires; but he is ignorant of how and where to seek its transgressions, its subversions. If he helps us to understand how the structure of familial specular identifications and linguistic regula-tion produce men and women as social beings, he does not, indeed, cannot know *what woman wants*.

To utilize Lacan's insights without being ensnared by them: this seems the task for those feminists interested in analysing and theorizing subjectivity. A cultivated ambivalence may help to sustain the arduous and pleasurable task of reading Lacan; and the more tedious but productive task of criticizing and moving beyond his position, creating from its remainders a new kind of account of subjectivity that grants women autonomous positions as subjects and objects of knowledge.

A feminism interested in the questions of subjectivity, knowledge, and desire can afford to ignore Lacan's work at its own peril. His work is among the most wide-ranging, philosophically sustained, incisive, and self-critical accounts of subjectivity thus developed within our intellectual history. For this reason, his work seems difficult to reject in favour of another, superior, more explanatory, or strategically useful position. Yet feminists can accept his views and perspectives only at great cost – that of feminist commitments – for his position is clearly antagonistic to, not agnostic about,[3] any feminism committed to an equality of the two sexes, and an autonomous position for each.

Feminists cannot afford to accept or reject his work. This ambivalence is not, however, a failure to 'make up one's mind'. Rather, from the present vantage point, it can be seen as a tactical position enabling feminists to use his work where it serves their interests without being committed to its more troublesome presumptions.

Lacan sees himself, like the hysteric, bound up with the question of love. Clément describes love as his '*idée fixe*', in discussing 'his passion for love' as that 'which he never stopped trying to elucidate' (1983: 188). He titles one of his infamous lectures on Woman in *Encore*, 'A Love Letter', a letter sent presumably to women: 'So what was I writing you? – the only thing one can do with a measure of seriousness – a love letter' (Mitchell and Rose 1982: 154). Ambivalence, then, can be seen as a kind of transitional point: it is the refusal to reciprocate the love Lacan offers for *his* own pleasure and not woman's (ibid.: 147). Hate may be a mode of continuing a love relation, but also, as a provisional stage, it is a form of disinvestment or decathexis associated with mourning and giving up the object. In other words, it may be a transitional stage in between love and *indifference*. Lacan asserts that the phallus is *never* a matter of indifference for women:

> Ever since Rabelais we have known that the phallus, her man as she calls it, is not a matter of indifference to her. Only, and this is the whole issue, she has various ways of taking it on, this phallus, and of keeping it for herself. (ibid.: 145)

But what if is she *is* indifferent? This indifference itself may be the mark of her (sexual) difference, the trace of her location elsewhere. From her *in*difference to, and thus her distance from, the phallus, and from psychoanalysis itself, her autonomy as a desiring subject may be theorized.

Notes

Introduction

1 cf 'the universal narcissism of men, their self-love, has up to the present suffered three severe blows . . . The destruction of this narcissistic illusion is associated in our minds with the name and work of Copernicus in the sixteenth century . . . When this discovery achieved general recognition, the self-love of mankind suffered its first blow, the *cosmological* one' (Freud 1917b: 139–40, see also 284–5).

2 Catherine Clément (1983) describes him in the following terms: 'He is French to the very tip of his tongue, down to his erudite and antiquated way of citing a text in Latin, Greek or any other language – and without translation' (29).

1 Psychoanalysis and scandal

1 In his article, 'What is an Author?' (in Bouchard, ed., 1977), Foucault claims that Freud together with Marx are authors whose status is quite different from others. Psychoanalysis and Marxism are not sciences like any other, where later observations and hypotheses replace or refute earlier ones, leading to a progressive concept of scientific development. As 'initiators of discursive practices', they establish the very possibilities of certain kinds of knowledge, including even those propositions critical of their work:

> they not only made possible a certain number of analogies that could be adopted by future texts, but, as importantly, they also made possible a certain number of differences. They cleared the space for the introduction of elements other than their own, which, nevertheless, remain within the field of discourse they initiated. In saying that Freud founded psycho-analysis we do not simply mean that the concept of libido or technique of dream

193

analysis reappear in the writings of Karl Abraham or Melanie Klein, but that he made possible a certain number of differences with respect to his books, concepts, and hypotheses, which all arise out of psychoanalytic discourse.

. . . the initiation of a discursive practice is heterogeneous to its ulterior transformations. To extend psychoanalytic practice, as initiated by Freud, is not to presume a formal generality that was not claimed at the outset; it is to explore a number of possible applications. To limit it is to isolate in the original texts a small set of propositions or statements of inaugurative value that mark other Freudian concepts or theories as derivative. Finally, there are no 'false' statements in the works of these initiators: those statements considered inessential or 'pre-historic' . . . are simply neglected in favour of the more pertinent aspects of the work. The initiation of a discursive practice, unlike the founding of a science, overshadows and is necessarily detached from its later developments and transformations. (132–4)

2   On the development of his different therapeutic procedures, Freud's own (somewhat romanticized) views are presented in 'An Outline of Psychoanalysis' (1938a); see also E. Jones (1961) for more of an outsider's perspective.

3   Freud talks about the 'dream-book' or 'decoding' conceptions of dream-interpretation; those techniques are based on the one-to-one correlation of a dream-image and its symbolic meaning. While Freud himself relies on these methods, especially in the analysis of fictional characters or of individuals with whom he is unfamiliar, this method remains basically antagonistic to the techniques of free association. The latter forbid any unmediated or one-to-one correlation between image and meaning. See Freud 1900: 238.

4   Jane Gallop discusses the controversy surrounding the non-appearance of the announced but unpublished translation of this paper in *The International Journal of Psychoanalysis* in 1937. Its proposed title was to be 'The Looking Glass Phase'. See Gallop 1985: 75.

5   The lecture notes of these weekly seminars are published – *The Four Fundamental Concepts of Psycho-analysis* (1977b) is the first seminar to be translated into English.

6   Gallop articulates very clearly and convincingly where Mitchell fails to convey the radical subversion posed by Lacan's understanding of the unconscious. Gallop attributes this to her because of her neglect of language, particularly semiological conceptions of language. This is developed in both her 1976 and 1983 texts. See also B. Johnson 'The Critical Difference' (1978).

7   Mitchell's position, admittedly now well over a decade old, is nevertheless affirmed in her more recent introduction to Lacan in *Feminine Sexuality* (1982). It still seems to suffer the same or similar problems to those raised by *Psychoanalysis and Feminism* (1974). To summarize these objections in the briefest way, Mitchell, along with many contemporary Marxist-feminists, argues that Freud describes the (psychological) features of patriarchal ideology, and Marx, bourgeois ideology. Patriarchy and Capitalism. Twin systems of oppression of women and class. Mitchell's problem is that there is no way of integrating these two disparate, perhaps even incommensurable, theories. In positing a 'dual system' account of our culture Mitchell faces the problem of all dualisms: the question of their interactions and relations.

She is also accused of universalizing the category of subject, as well as patriarchal ideology. These seem universal cultural categories, in her account, governed by cross-cultural and transhistorical laws: the law of the father, the prohibition of incest, and the signification of the phallus (and thus, women's castration) are all, for her, universal *a priori* cultural conditions. This presumption of a pre-given structural grid, inherently privileging masculinity at the expense of femininity cannot be accepted in anything but a descriptive or historical sense by feminists, for it dooms as *logically impossible* the struggles of women to achieve autonomy from men (Mitchell 1974: 391, 409). Mitchell remains entirely uncritical of the psychoanalytic tools she uses to develop her account of the construction of femininity. She regards Freudian theory as compatible with feminist principles, without any need of modification, or critical distance. In her eagerness to validate psychoanalysis in feminist terms, against her 'adversaries', Greer, Freidan, Millett, *et al.*, she affirms a wholesale acceptance of all of Freudian theory. This remains problematic in so far as Freud's work, without interpretation and reworking, is contradictory and inconsistent (although often in a most productive way!); and because there are indeed features of it that require feminist scrutiny and criticism in terms of its presumptions about male and female subjectivity. For further details, see E. Gross 1984: 69-88.

8   For a most convincing discussion of the problems associated with the separation of sex from gender, as Chodorow, Dinnerstein, Stoller, and probably the majority of feminists today presume, see M. Gatens, 'A Critique of the Sex/Gender Distinction', *Intervention* No. 17 ('Beyond Marxism'), 1983.

2 The ego and the imaginary

1   See Lacan's scathing pronouncements in 'Some Reflections on the Ego' (1953), and his remarks in *Écrits. A Selection* (1977a). For example, 'it appears incontestable that the conception of psycho-analysis in the United States has inclined towards the adaptation of the individual to the social environment, towards the quest for behaviour patterns, and towards all the objectification implied in the notion of "human relations". And the indigenous term, "human engineering" strongly implies a privileged position of exclusion in relation to the human object' (1977a: 38; see also, 321).

2   Lacan makes it clear that analysis does not deal with the 'total' or 'real' person; it is not a form of counselling or friendly advice: 'Are we in the same sphere as in everyday life, when we meet our fellow man and render psychological judgements about him? Are we in the same sphere when we say that such-and-such has a strong personality? Certainly not . . . We must admit this direct judgement of a person is of little importance in the analytic experience. It is not the *real* relationship that constitutes the proper field of analysis' (Lacan and Granoff 1956: 270).

3   Particularly in 'On Narcissism' (1914a) and in 'Contributions to the Psychology of Love' (1911a), to be further discussed in chapter 5.

4   For Freud, the ego is not a photograph of the body, but a map of the degrees of erotogenicity on its surface, an image of its significance. It may thus be suggested that, if the body and its erotogenic zones differ, according to sex, so too must the ego. Freud also regards the 'map' as a kind of reflection of the 'cortical homunculus', which Lacan will cash out in neurological terms with his suggestion of an 'intra-organic mirror' (see Lacan 1953).

5   Irigaray's conception of bodily morphology, for example, is both a development and deconstruction of Lacan's notion of the body's representational status, and Freud's proposition about the ego as projection of the body's surface. See Irigaray's text, *This Sex Which is Not One* 1985b: ch. 1.

6   See 'The *mirror stage* is a drama whose internal thrust is pre-cipitated from insufficiency to anticipation. . .' (Lacan 1977a: 4).

7   Caillois's paper provides a brilliant analysis of psychæsthenia, a disturbance in the relations between 'personality and space'. In the phenomenon of mimicry,

> It is with represented space that the drama becomes specific since the living creature, the organism, is no longer the origin of the coordinates, but one point among others; it is dispossessed of its privilege and literally *no longer knows where to place itself . . .*

the feeling of personality considered as the organism's feeling of distinction from its surroundings, of the connections between consciousness and a particular point in space, cannot fail under these conditions to be seriously undermined. . .

For example, the invariable response of schizophrenics to the question: where are you? *I know where I am, but I do not feel as though I'm at the spot where I find myself.* To these dispossessed souls, space seems to be a devouring force. Space pursues them, encircles them, digests them in a gigantic phagocytosis. It ends by replacing them. Then the body separates itself from thought, the individual breaks the boundaries of his skin and occupies the other side of his senses. He tries to look at *himself from* any point whatever in space. He feels himself becoming space, *dark space where things cannot be put.* He is similar, not similar to something, but just *similar.* . . (Caillois 1984: 29–30)

8   In this book, I will represent Lacan's conception of the Real by always using the capital 'R' to differentiate his technical term from the more everyday uses of the term. His translators usually translate the term in lower case.

9   See Köhler's account of the chimpanzee Rana's interest in her mirror-image: 'We gave the chimpanzees a hand-mirror for the first time, they looked into it and at once became intensely interested. Each one wanted to have a look, and take the wonderful object out of the other's hand . . . Eventually Rana captured the hand-glass and escaped with it to a remote corner of the room. She gazed long and intently at the mirror, looked up then down, put it to her face, and licked it once, stared at it again and suddenly her free hand rose and grasped – as though at a body behind the mirror. But as she grasped emptiness she dropped the mirror sideways, to her astonishment. Then she lifted it again, stared fixedly at the other ape, and again was misled into grasping into empty space. She became impatient and struck out violently behind the mirror, finding this, too, in vain, she 'lay in wait', after the manner of chimpanzees when they watch. . .' (Köhler 1951: 317–18).

10   In 'The Child's Relation to Others', Merleau-Ponty uses the work of Wallon, Stern, Schilder, and others to attempt his description of the phenomenology of our perceptions of space: 'As has often been said, the body is at first "buccal" in nature. Stern has even spoken of a "buccal space" at the beginning of the child's life, meaning by this that the limit of the world for the child is the space that can be contained in, or explored by his mouth . . . Not the mouth but the whole respiratory apparatus gives the child a kind of experience of space. . . . After that, other regions of the body

intervene and come into prominence. . .' (1964: 122).
11   The symbolic father is carefully distinguished from the real (i.e. imaginary) father in Lacan: 'The symbolic father is to be distinguished from the imaginary father (often surprisingly distant from the real father) to whom is related the whole dialectic of aggressivity and identification. In all its strictness, the symbolic father is to be conceived as 'transcendent', as an irreducible given of the signifier. The symbolic father – he who is capable of saying 'I am who I am' can only be imperfectly incarnate in the real father. He is nowhere . . . the real father takes over from the symbolic father. That is why the real father has a decisive function in castration, which is always deeply marked by his intervention or thrown off balance by his absence' (Lacan, quoted in Wilden 1981: 271).
12   See J. Mehlman's *A Structural Study of Autobiography* (1974a) for further elaboration on this impossibility.

3   Sexuality and the symbolic order

1   According to Paul Guillaume in *Imitation in Children* (1971), at around the eighth month, the child experiences an intensified shyness and anxiety when the mother goes away or when someone else returns unexpectedly in her place.
2   See Jean Laplanche, *Life and Death in Psychoanalysis* (1976), especially chapter 2, for his elaboration of the interrelations between these two models.
3   See Gallop (1982a; 1985), Burnheimer and Kahane, Masson, and Malcolm for the details of this dispute.
4   The section called 'Self-Consciousness' is relevant to Lacan's account, and the sub-section, on 'Lordship and Bondage' is particularly significant to Lacan's account of desire.
5   See Freud, *The Ego and the Id* (1923: 34), where he claims that through the acquisition of the superego, the boy is heir to all that is 'rightfully' the father's: '*You ought to be like this* (like your father).' It also comprises the prohibition: 'You may *not* do all the things that he does; some things are his prerogative.'
6   In, for example, the case of Little Hans, Freud describes the oedipus complex as a preordained developmental unfolding, able to be predicted in advance: 'Long before he was in the world, I went on, I had known that a little Hans would come into the world who would be so fond of his mother that he would be bound to be afraid of his father because of it' (1909b: 42).
7   In his analysis of 'The Purloined Letter'; another version is reproduced in Wilden.

8   In the latter case the Es is the barred subject 'S', *moi* is the ego
who enters analysis with the demand for cure, and the *autre* is the
analyst as imaginary double or counterpart to whom the analysand
addresses his/her demand. The *Autre* is the position the analyst
must come to occupy if the subject's (unconscious) desire is to be
found through or beneath the demand. This line of desire comes
from the Other to the Es, which can now be considered the *'je'* or 'I'
of discourse, the discourse of the unconscious. In working through
the analysand's demand by its frustration, the analyst opens up the
question of desire.
9   Lacan makes the peculiar relation between the scopic drive, the
('outside') field of the Other and the scopic object clear in the
following anecdote: 'One day, I was on a small boat, with a few
people from a family of fishermen in a small port . . . [A]s we were
waiting for the moment to pull in the nets, an individual known as
Petit-Jean . . . pointed out to me something floating on the surface
of the waves. It was a small can, a sardine can. It floated there in the
sun, a witness to the canning industry . . . It glittered in the sun.
And Petit-Jean said to me – *You see that can? Do you see it? Well,
it doesn't see you*' (1977b: 95).

4   Language and the unconscious

1   See Michel Tort, 'The Freudian Concept of Representative',
Economy and Society, 1974: 3, 18–40, for an excellent discussion of
the translation problems posed by this peculiarly doubled term.
2   Thirty years later, Freud again returns to the question of finding
an appropriate model to describe the complex functions of psychical agencies in the paper, 'A Note Upon a Mystic Writing Pad'
(1925c). Here he argues that one and the same system, represented
by the writing pad, should be able to represent the two functions of
perception and memory. This writing pad, made with waxed paper,
plastic, and cardboard has the capacity to receive fresh impression
by being able to erase what is written on it; as well as the ability to
retain permanent records of past transcriptions indelibly inscribed
in the cardboard underneath the waxed paper. It is no longer a
neural system but, as Derrida suggests, a system of writing. See also
Derrida, 'Freud and the Scene of Writing' (1978).
3   Psychoanalysis has, for this reason, been a major source of
inspiration in structural and post-structural literary theory and
interpretation, particularly among the French, who have clearly
been influenced by Lacan's reading of Freud. See, for example,
Derrida (1978; 1982) and a number of American critics influenced
by deconstruction – Hartman, de Man, Miller, Spivak, etc. It is

significant that, in opposition to the hermeneutic insistence on interpreting text as a *totality*, each will analyse texts in terms of their heterogeneity, their dispersal of meaning. Cf. Lacan's remarks about hermeneutics (1977b: 7–8).

4　Freud claimed that the dream must be regarded as a rebus, a picture puzzle in which each element must be interpreted individually to reveal the proposition it contains. The techniques of the dream, like the cryptic cross-word puzzle, use systematic rules – reversals, verbal jumbles, absurdities – in order to tangle, complicate, and disguise the relevant words or phrases. I am grateful to Moira Gatens for pointing out this analogy.

5　Lacan mentions the rhetorical devices (1977a: 169): 'Periphrasis, hyperbaton, ellipsis, suspension, anticipation, retraction, negation, digression, irony . . . catachresis, litotes, antonomasia, hypotyposis . . .'

6　Saussure implies that language has no positive 'objects' or elements which combine, like building blocks, to form a language. Instead, neither signifier nor signified pre-exist signification. The entire structure of language is necessary for any sign, signifier, or signified to exist as such.

7　See Jakobson's discussion of the processes of selection and combination at the level of phonemes/graphemes, and semantemes to produce words, and sentences, etc., in Jakobson and Halle 1956: chapter 2; and Benveniste 1971: 101–2.

8　Saussure defines the two relations between signs as syntagmatic and paradigmatic. Syntagmatic relations are those between terms actually present in a given context (Jakobson's category of combination or metonymy); paradigmatic relations are those between terms, some of which are not present in a given context, but are associatively connected to a particular term (Jakobson's category of selection/metaphor).

9　Aphasia results in the breakdown of linguistic functions, including word-loss, word-blindness, the inability to initiate conversation, the inability to define words, the inability to decompose and recompose sounds and other severe forms of language disorder.

10　These are Saussure's defining features of the linguistic sign.

11　Jean Laplanche, in his paper written with Leclaire (1972) transcribes and expands Lacan's formulations according to the principles governing fractions. Thus, for Lacan's metaphoric formula,

$$\frac{S}{S} \cdot \frac{S}{S} \rightarrow S^1 . \ ^1/_5$$

Laplanche (157) transcribes the right-hand side as

$$\frac{\frac{S^1}{s}}{\frac{S}{S}}$$

according to the formula:

$$\frac{A}{B} \cdot \frac{C}{D} = \frac{\frac{A}{D}}{\frac{B}{C}}$$

Laplanche argues that this four-layered formula provides a graphic representation of the relation between primary and secondary processes. The numerator, S^1/s, refers to secondary processes and the preconscious/conscious level of discourse, while the denominator, S/S, refers to the primary processes and the unconscious discourse.

Not surprisingly, Lacan firmly disagrees with Laplanche's literalism. He claims that the metaphoric formula is not a fraction, for this implies that the bar is merely the fractional line and not an unbreachable barrier. In any case, he claims: 'Such a formula is quite definitely unsatisfactory . . . because one ought to know that there can be no relations between the signifier and itself, the peculiarity of the signifier being the fact that it is unable to signify itself, without producing some error in logic' (1977b: 249).

12   Lacan develops the myth of the lamella to describe the drive's role in structuring the split subject. He asks us to imagine a flat amoeba, which Clément describes as 'a wafer' (1983: 96), inserting itself into the rim-like orifices of erotogenic zones. The circulation of this lamella in and around the child's body inscribes the path of what will become the sites and sources of the sexual drives. The lamella is 'the organ of libido' (1977b: 200): 'The Hommelette was what Freud called libido' (Clément 1983: 97).

5   Sexual relations

1   To avoid charges of naturalism, or the assumption of a natural harmony between the sexes, Lacan refuses to describe female sexuality as complementary to male sexuality; instead he describes is as 'supplementary', excessive, or 'beyond' the phallus (see Lacan, 'God and the Jouissance of The Woman', Mitchell and Rose 1982: 144). Derrida also uses the notion of the supplement to confound or

unhinge the (phallogocentric) binary opposition between lack and excess (Derrida, *Dissemination*, 1981). Yet if we assume that a supplementarity describes the relation between female and male sexuality, even if Lacan sees female pleasure as a reserve largely untapped by the phallus, nevertheless, it is still described in terms of the phallus – in this case, by its degree of distance from phallic sexuality. The phallus remains the fixed point of reference for all sexualities, as far as psychoanalysis is concerned.

2   As Nancy Jay, in her paper, 'Gender and Dichotomy' (1981) points out, relations of difference, described in logical symbols as a relation between A and B, are reduced to an oppositional form in phallocentric discourses, which takes the form of relations between A and not-A. The presence and absence of a single term defines the oppositional pair; while relations of difference, by contrast, are based on the presence of different attributes for the terms in the pair.

3   'Little Harry' is one of A. Lorand's cases. See 'Fetishism in *Statu Nascendi*', *The International Journal of Psychoanalysis*, 1930 (2): 419–27.

4   The phallus signifies the act of signification itself, seeing that it is the signifier which both constitutes lack, and functions to fill the lack, just as the sign does in the absence of the thing. The sanscrit noun, *lakshana* (Lacan, 'The Function and Field of Speech and Language', 1977a: 104 and fn. 108) is both the mark, token, sign, or rather, signifier, and the 'sign or organ of virility' (Wilden 1981: 151).

5   Along with Nancy Jay (1981), Anthony Wilden will posit a difference between difference and distinction. Difference is a term capable of defining *analog* or continuous relations between terms, while distinction or (binary) opposition refers to *digital* relations between discontinuous terms. Distinctions rely on an empty space, a lack, dividing its two terms, which philosophers have described as the 'excluded middle'. Difference, by contrast, implies no necessary gap or boundary separating one term from another. See Wilden 1972: chapter 7, 'Analog and Digital Communication: On Negation, Signification and Meaning'.

6   Wilden refers to Malinowski's analysis, in *Argonauts of the Western Pacific*, of the ritualized circulation of 'gifts' in relations of exchange in Kula society. This serves as an illustration of the circulation of an order that can only be seen as the exchange of the signifier, not a trade governed by economic or biological imperatives. The objects exchanged are not just particularly useful; often they cannot be used – bracelets which can't be worn or used as ornaments, shells which have no use value: 'the circuit of exchange

consists in two vast circles of channels along which "bits" of one type are constantly substituted for "bits" of the other type. Thousands of partners are provided with dyadic links through the exchange, but the dyads are a function of the circuit as a whole, not of any individual connections . . . This highly complex network of relations is governed by strict communicational rules as regards the flow of the "Symbolic object" (bracelets move from left hand to right hand and from north-west to south-west and never in the other direction) but the "value" of the object "owed" is a matter of unarticulated reciprocity not of convention' (Wilden 1972: 256).

7　In 'On Narcissism. An Introduction' (1914a), Freud outlines the four 'versions' of narcissistic love classified together as adult narcissism: 'A person may love: (1) According to the narcissistic type: (a) what he himself is (i.e. himself); (b) what he himself was; (c) what he himself would like to be (d)someone who was once part of himself. . .' (90). In loving the child, the narcissistic woman satisfies all four variations simultaneously: she can love herself as mother and nurturer of the child; the child is what she herself once was, and represents a chance for the mother to vicariously relive her lost opportunities through the child; and the child was once literally a part of the mother's body.

6　Lacan and feminism

1　There are two distinct senses to the psychoanalytic term, 'sexual', which are often confused. On the one hand, it refers to questions about libido, energy, drive, impulse; and on the other, to questions about sexual identity, subjective positions, the construction of masculine and feminine attributes. Both of these must be kept in mind in the following section.

2　Foucault argues that ours is the age that could be defined by the insistence of the question, 'Who am I?' and the answer, 'My sexuality defines who I am'. See his introduction to *The History of Sexuality. An Introduction* (1978).

3　Freud seems to explain away whatever resistance there is in the behaviour of the two female homosexuals he treats, Dora, and the young woman in his case study of female homosexuality (1920b) by ascribing their libidinal attachments to paternal figures, instead of recognizing the underlying attachment to their mothers.

4　These are the three dimensions within which Kristeva's project is developed. See Kristeva 1976.

5　The earlier texts include *The Revolution in Poetic Language* (1984a), *Desire in Language* (1980), *Séméiotiké. Recherches pour un Sémanalyse* (1969); while among the later texts are *Powers of Horror* (1982a), *Tales of Love* (1987), 'Unes femmes', and 'Ne dis rien. A propos de l' "interdit de la représentation" ', *Tel Quel*, 91, Spring, 1982.

6 For example, her concept of the semiotic collapses together Lacan's Real and imaginary orders; she even develops the hybrid category of the 'imaginary symbolic'. Yet her notion of the semiotic remains very close to Lacan's, except for its more immediately significatory context in her work.

7 In *The Revolution in Poetic Language* (1984a), Kristeva more or less uses Lacan's account of symbolic development as the outline of her interrogation of textuality.

8 See *Powers of Horror*. The projection of a subject into this, the most threatening of all bodily boundaries, must be disavowed or covered up by the projection of an omnipotent subject, the phallic mother.

9 For a convincing challenge to the by-now common feminist separation of sex from gender, and the relegation of sex to a purely biological status, and gender to a purely environmental status, see M. Gatens 1983.

10 Irigaray takes on philosophical discourses, discourses which serve as the Master knowledges of other discourses, as her critical object: 'it is precisely philosophical discourse that we have to challenge, and *disrupt*, inasmuch as it constitutes the discourse on discourse' (Irigaray 1985b: 74).

11 Lacan and, particularly, Freud seem to take no account of the formative role of the *specificity of the body*, its concrete 'shape' of orifices, sexual zones, erotogenic sources, in the construction of the ego and in the development of sexuality and the unconscious. Freud acknowledges the fact that the ego is the projection of the body-surface (see chapter 2) yet he seems to ignore that topographical differences between body-surfaces may have effects on the ego thereby projected. See M. Campioni, 'Psychoanalysis and Marxist-Feminism' (1976).

12 For the link between Irigaray and Derrida, see Gross 1986a.

13 He rallies against communicational models of language, those which see the model of sender-message-receiver primary to language: 'My own conception of the message is . . . the linguistic message. Many people talk nowadays about messages everywhere, inside the organism a hormone is a message, a beam of light to obtain teleguidance to a plane or from a satellite is a message and so on; but the message in language is absolutely different. The message, our message, in all cases comes from the Other, by which I understand, "from the place of the Other" ' (Lacan 1970: 186).

Conclusion

1 The Cartesian *cogito* is, at best, certain of its mind or its thinking. Its logical extension is the solipsistic subject, the subject who is sure of its own existence but unsure of the existence of others. Hegel's solution to the 'reef of solipsism' (as Sartre described it) is ingenious: the *cogito*, the thinking being, in order to be a self-consciousness, requires the recognition of an other *as its internal* condition. There can be no self-consciousness without the other both confirming and robbing the subject of its immediate certainty. See his section on 'Lordship and Bondage', *The Phenomenology of Spirit* (Hegel 1979).

2 This is in many ways close to Derrida's own analyses of Lacan in 'Freud and the Scene of Writing' (Derrida 1978), which, while critical of his 'phonocentrism', his privileging of the voice over writing, is also remarkably close to Lacan's affirmation of the materiality of signification.

3 Cf. Ragland-Sullivan's description of Lacan's 'agnosticism' on the question of phallocentric commitments. She argues, in a manner I do not find entirely convincing: 'I find no a priori Lacanian support for phallocentrism – any more than for Lacanian-supported feminism. Lacan discovered the phallic signifier, its effects and the resulting substitutive Desire. These intrinsically neutral elements give rise to ideologies of the masculine and the feminine . . .' (1986: 298).

Bibliography

Adams, P. (1978) 'Representation and Sexuality', *m/f*, 1.
Adams, P. and Minson, J. (1978) 'The "Subject" of Feminism', *m/f*, 2.
Allison, D. (ed.) (1985) *The New Nietzsche*, Boston: MIT Press.
Althusser, L. (1971a) 'Ideology and Ideological State Apparatuses', in *Lenin and Philosophy and Other Essays*, London: New Left Books.
Althusser, L. (1971b) 'Freud and Lacan', in *Lenin and Philosophy and Other Essays*, London: New Left Books.
Barthes, R. (1967) *Writing Degree Zero*, New York: Hill and Wang.
Barthes, R. (1973) *Mythologies,* London: Paladin.
Benveniste, E. (1971) *Problems in General Linguistics*, Miami: University of Miami Press.
Benvenuto, B. and Kennedy, R. (1986) *The Works of Jacques Lacan. An Introduction*, London: Free Association Books.
Bersani, L. (1977) *Baudelaire and Freud*, Berkeley: The University of California Press.
Bersani, L. (1986) *The Freudian Body. Psychoanalysis and Art,* New York: Columbia University Press.
Bühler, C., Hexler, H. and Tudor-Hart, B. (1927) *Sociological and Psychological Studies on the First Year of Life*, Jena.
Bernheimer, C. and Kahane C. (eds) (1985) *In Dora's Case. Freud–Hysteria–Feminism*, New York: Columbia University Press.
Caillois, R. (1984) 'Mimicry and Legendary Psychaesthenia', *October*, 31, Winter, 17–32.
Campioni, M. (1976) 'Psychoanalysis and Marxist-Feminism', *Working Papers in Sex, Science and Culture*, 2.
Campioni, M. and Gross, E. (1978) 'Little Hans: The Production of Oedipus', in *Language, Sexuality and Subversion*, eds, P. Foss and M. Morris, Sydney: Feral.
Chodorow, N. (1978) *The Reproduction of Mothering: Psychoanalysis and the Sociology of Gender*, Berkeley: University of California Press.
Cixous, H. (1976) 'The Laugh of the Medusa', *Signs*, 7 (1).
Cixous, H. (1981) 'Castration or Decapitation?', *Signs*, 7(1).
Clément, C. (1983) *The Lives and Legends of Jacques Lacan*, New York: Columbia University Press.
Conley, V. (1977) 'Missexual Mistery', *Diacritics*, Summer.

Conley, V. (1984) *Hélène Cixous, Writing the Feminine*, Lincoln: University of Nebraska Press.
Coward, R. (1976) 'Lacan and Signification', *Edinburgh Review*, 1.
Davis, R. C. (ed.) (1983) *Lacan and Narration. The Psychoanalytic Difference in Narrative Theory*. Baltimore: The Johns Hopkins University Press.
Derrida, J. (1976) *Of Grammatology*, trans. G. C. Spivak, Baltimore: The Johns Hopkins University Press.
Derrida, J. (1978) 'Freud and the Scene of Writing', in *Writing and Difference*, London: Routledge & Kegan Paul.
Derrida, J. (1981) *Dissemination*, trans. B. Johnson, Chicago: University of Chicago Press.
Derrida, J. (1982) 'White Mythologies', in *Margins of Philosophy*, Chicago: University of Chicago Press.
Felman, S. (1975) 'Woman and Madness: The Critical Phallacy', *Diacritics*, Winter.
Felman, S. (1980) 'The Originality of Jacques Lacan', *Poetics Today*, 2.
Forrester, J. (1980) *Language and the Origins of Psychoanalysis*, New York: Columbia University Press.
Foucault, M. (1977) 'What is an Author?' in *Language, Counter-Memory, Practice*, ed. D. Bouchard, Oxford: Basil Blackwell.
Foucault, M. (1978) *The History of Sexuality, An Introduction*, 1, New York: Pantheon.
Freud, S. (1888) 'Hysteria', *The Standard Edition of the Complete Psychological Works of Sigmund Freud* (SE), London: The Hogarth Press, vol. 1.
Freud, S. (1892–9) 'Extracts from the Fliess Papers' SE 1.
Freud, S. (1894) 'The Neuropsychoses of Defence', SE 3.
Freud, S. (1895) 'The Project for a Scientific Psychology', SE 1.
Freud, S. (1896a) 'Heredity and the Ætiology of the Neuroses', SE 3.
Freud, S. (1896b) 'The Ætiology of Hysteria', SE 3.
Freud, S. (1899) 'Screen Memories', SE 3.
Freud, S. (1900) *The Interpretation of Dreams*, SE 4/5S.
Freud, S. (1905) *The Three Essays on the Theory of Sexuality*, SE 7.
Freud, S. (1908a) 'Hysterical Phantasies and their Relation to Bisexuality', SE 9.
Freud, S. (1908b) 'Character and Anal Eroticism', SE 9.
Freud, S. (1909a) 'Family Romances', SE 9.
Freud, S. (1909b) 'Analysis of a Phobia in a Five-Year-Old Boy' (Little Hans), SE 10.
Freud, S. (1910a) 'Five Lectures on Psychoanalysis', SE 11.
Freud, S. (1910b) 'Leonardo de Vinci', SE 11.
Freud, S. (1910c) 'A Special Type of Object Choice Made by Men', SE 11.
Freud, S. (1911a) 'Contributions to the Psychology of Love', SE 11.
Freud, S. (1911b) 'Formulations of Two Principles of Mental Functioning', SE 12.
Freud, S. (1912a) 'On the Tendency to Debasement in the Sphere of Love', SE 11.

Freud, S. (1912b) 'A Note on the Unconscious in Psycho-analysis', SE, 12.
Freud, S. (1912–13) *Totem and Taboo*, SE 13.
Freud, S. (1914a) 'On Narcissism. An Introduction', SE 14.
Freud, S. (1914b) 'Instincts and Their Vicissitudes', SE 14.
Freud, S. (1914c) 'The Unconscious', SE 14.
Freud, S. (1915a) 'Mourning and Melancholia', SE 14.
Freud, S. (1915b) 'Repression', SE 14.
Freud, S. (1916a) 'The Paths to the Formation of Symptoms', SE 16.
Freud, S. (1916b) 'The Libido Theory and Narcissism', SE 16.
Freud, S. (1917a) 'On the Transformation of Instinct as Exemplified in Anal Eroticism', SE 17.
Freud, S. (1917b) 'A Difficulty on the Path of Psycho-Analysis', SE 17.
Freud, S. (1917c) 'Mourning and Melancholia', SE 17.
Freud, S. (1918) 'The Taboo of Virginity', SE 11.
Freud, S. (1919a) 'A Child is Being Beaten: A Contribution to the Study of the Origin of Sexual Perversions', SE 17.
Freud, S. (1919b) *Beyond the Pleasure Principle*, SE 18.
Freud, S. (1920) 'The Psychogenesis of a Case of Homosexuality in a Woman', SE 18.
Freud, S. (1921) 'Group Psychology and the Analysis of the Ego', SE 18.
Freud, S. (1923) *The Ego and the Id*, SE 19.
Freud, S. (1924a) 'The Dissolution of the Oedipus Complex', SE 19.
Freud, S. (1924b) 'The Economic Problem of Masochism', SE 19.
Freud, S. (1925a) 'Some Psychical Consequences of the Anatomical Distinction Between the Sexes', SE 19.
Freud, S. (1925b) 'Negation', SE 19.
Freud, S. (1925c) 'A Note Upon the "Mystic Writing Pad"', SE 19.
Freud, S. (1927a) 'Fetishism', SE 19.
Freud, S. (1927b) *Civilisation and Its Discontents*, SE 21.
Freud, S. (1931) 'Female Sexuality', SE 21.
Freud, S. (1933) 'Femininity', SE 22.
Freud, S. (1937) 'Analysis Terminable and Interminable', SE 23.
Freud, S. (1938a) 'An Outline of Psychoanalysis', SE 23.
Freud, S. (1938b) 'The Splitting of the Ego in the Process of Defence', SE 23.
Freud, S. (1974) *The Cocaine Papers*, New York: Stonehill.
Freud, S. and Breuer, J. (1893–5) *Studies on Hysteria*, SE 2.
Gallop, J. (1982a) *Feminism and Psychoanalysis. The Daughter's Seduction*, London: Macmillan.
Gallop, J. (1982b) 'Nurse Freud: Class Struggle in the Family', *Hecate*, 3(1).
Gallop, J. (1982c) 'Writing and Sexual Difference. The Difference Within', in *Writing and Sexual Difference*, ed. E. Abel, Chicago: University of Chicago Press.
Gallop, J. (1985) *Reading Lacan*, Ithaca: Cornell University Press.
Gatens, M. (1983) 'A Critique of the Sex/Gender Distinction',

Intervention (Beyond Marxism?), 17.
Gross, E. (1976) 'Lacan, the Symbolic, the Imaginary and the Real',
Working Papers in Sex, Science and Culture, 2.
Gross, E. (1982) 'Women and Writing: The Work of Julia Kristeva in
Perspective', *Refactory Girl*, 23.
Gross, E. (1984) 'Love Letters in the Sand. Jacques Lacan and *Feminine
Sexuality*', *Critical Philosophy*, 2.
Gross, E. (1986a) 'Derrida, Irigaray and Deconstruction', *Intervention*,
20 ('Leftwright').
Gross, E. (1986b) 'Irigaray and Sexual Difference. A Review-Essay',
Australian Feminist Studies, 2.
Gross, E. (1986c) 'Irigaray and the Divine', *Local Consumption
Occasional Papers*, 9, Sydney.
Gross, E. (1987) 'Language and the Limits of the Body. Kristeva and
Abjection', in *Futur*Fall. Excursions Into Postmodernity*, eds, E.
Gross, T. Threadgold, D. Kelly, *et al.*, Sydney: Power Institute
Publications, Sydney.
Guillaume, P. (1971) *Imitation in Children*, Chicago: University of
Chicago Press.
Heath, S. (1978) 'Difference', *Screen*, 19(3).
Hegel, G. W. F. (1979) *The Phenomenology of Spirit*, trans. A. V.
Miller, Oxford: Clarendon Press.
Hollier, D. (1984) 'Mimesis and Castration', *October*, 31.
Irigaray, L. (1977a) 'Women's Exile', *Ideology and Consciousness*, 1.
Irigaray, L. (1977b) *Ce sexe qui n'en est pas un*, Paris: Minuit.
Irigaray, L. (1979) 'Etablir un généalogie des femmes', *Maintenant*, 12,
May.
Irigaray, L. (1981a) *Le Corps-à-corps avec la mére*, Montreal: La Pleine
lune.
Irigaray, L. (1981b) 'And One Doesn't Stir Without the Other', *Signs*,
7(1) Autumn.
Irigaray, L. (1983) 'For Centuries We've Been Living in the Mother-Son
Relation . . .', *Hecate*, 9(1/2).
Irigaray, L. (1984) *L'Ethique de la difference sexuelle*, Paris: Minuit.
Irigaray, L. (1985a) *Speculum of the Other Woman*, Ithaca: Cornell
University Press.
Irigaray, L. (1985b) *This Sex Which Is Not One*, Ithaca: Cornell
University Press.
Irigaray, L. (1985c) 'Is the Subject of Science Sexed?', *Cultural Critique*,
1(1), Fall.
Irigaray, L. (1986a) 'Divine Women', *Local Consumption Occasional
Papers*, 8, Sydney.
Irigaray, L. (1986b) 'The Fecundity of the Caress', in *Face-to-Face with
Levinas*, ed. R. A. Cohen, New York: State University of New York.
Jacobus, M. (1986) *Reading Woman*, Ithaca: Cornell University Press.
Jakobson, R. and Halle, M. (1956) *The Fundamentals of Language*, The
Hague: Mouton and Co.
Jay, N. (1981) 'Gender and Dichotomy', *Feminist Studies*, 7(1), Spring.

Bibliography

Jardine, A. (1985) *Gynesis: Configurations of Woman and Modernity*, Ithaca: Cornell University Press.

Johnson, B. (1978) 'The Critical Difference', *Diacritics*, Summer.

Jones, E. (1961) *The Life and Works of Sigmund Freud*, New York: Basic Books.

Kofman, S. (1985) *The Enigma of Woman*, Ithaca: Cornell University Press.

Köhler, W. (1951) *The Mentality of Apes*, London: Routledge & Kegan Paul.

Kristeva, J. (1969) *Séméiotiké. Recherches pour une Sémanalyse*, Paris: Seuil.

Kristeva, J. (1972) 'The Semiotic Activity'. *Screen*, 14(1,2).

Kristeva, J. (1974a) 'Phonetics, Phonology and Impulsional Basis', *Diacritics*, Fall.

Kristeva, J. (1974b) 'The Subject in Signifying Practice', *Semiotext(e)*, 1(2).

Kristeva, J. (1974c) 'Four Types of Signifying Practice', *Semiotext(e)*, 1(1).

Kristeva, J. (1976) 'Signifying Practice and Mode of Production', *Edinburgh Review*, 1.

Kristeva, J. (1977) 'L'Héréthique de l'amour' *Tel Quel*, 74.

Kristeva, J. (1980) *Desire in Language*, Oxford: Basil Blackwell.

Kristeva, J. (1981a) 'Women's Time', *Signs*, 7(1).

Kristeva, J. (1981b) 'Interview – 1974', *m/f*, 5/6.

Kristeva, J. (1981c) 'The Maternal Body', *m/f*, 5/6.

Kristeva, J. (1982a) *Powers of Horror. An Essay on Abjection*, New York: Columbia University Press.

Kristeva, J. (1982b) 'Ne dis rien. A propos de l' "interdit de la représentation" ', *Tel Quel*, 91.

Kristeva, J. (1982c) 'Psychoanalysis and the Polis', *Critical Inquiry*, 9(1).

Kristeva, J. (1983a) *Histoires d'amour*, Paris: Editions Denoël.

Kristeva, J. (1983b) 'The Father, Love and Banishment', in *Literature and Psychoanalysis*, eds, E. Kurzweil and W. Phillips, New York: Columbia University Press.

Kristeva, J. (1984a) *The Revolution in Poetic Language*, New York: Columbia University Press.

Kristeva, J. (1984b) 'My Memory's Hyperbole', in *The Female Autograph*, ed., D. C. Stanton, New York Literary Forum, 261–76.

Kristeva, J. (1984c) 'In conversation with Rosalind Coward', *I. C. A. Documents*: (Desire), 1.

Kristeva, J. (1987) *Tales of Love*, New York: Columbia University Press.

Lacan, J. (1953) 'Some Reflections on the Ego', *International Journal of Psychoanalysis*, 34.

Lacan, J. (1966) *Écrits*, 1 and 2, Paris: Editions du Seuil.

Lacan, J. (1970) 'Of Structure as an Inmixing of Otherness Prerequisite to Any Subject Whatever', in *The Languages of Criticism and Sciences of Man. The Structuralist Controversy*, eds, R. Mackesay and E. Donato, New York: Doubleday Anchor.

Lacan, J. (1972) 'Seminar on "The Purloined Letter"', *Yale French Studies*, 48.
Lacan, J. (1977a) *Écrits. A Selection*, London: Tavistock.
Lacan, J. (1977b) *The Four Fundamental Concepts of Psycho-analysis*, London: The Hogarth Press.
Lacan, J. (1977c) 'Desire and the Interpretation of Desire in *Hamlet*', *Yale French Studies*, 55 and 56.
Lacan, J. (1980a) 'A Lacanian Psychosis: Interview by Lacan', in *Returning to Freud*, ed., S. Schneiderman, New York: Yale University Press.
Lacan, J. (1980b) 'Seminars, Paris 10th and 12th June', *Papers of the Freudian School of Melbourne*.
Lacan, J. (1981a) 'The Oedipus Complex', *Semiotext(e)*, 10.
Lacan, J. (1981b) 'Ste Anne. . .'. *Semiotext(e)*, 10.
Lacan, J. and Granoff, W. (1956) 'Fetishism: the Symbolic, the Imaginary, and the Real', in M. Balint (ed.), *Perversions, Psychodynamics and Therapy*, London: Tavistock.
Laplanche, J. (1976) *Life and Death in Psychoanalysis*, Baltimore: The Johns Hopkins University Press.
Laplanche, J. and Leclaire, S. (1972) 'The Unconscious. A Psychoanalytic Study', *Yale French Studies*, 48.
Laplanche, J. and Pontalis, J. B. (1968) 'Fantasy and the Origins of Sexuality', *International Journal of Psychoanalysis*, 49.
Laplanche, J. and Pontalis, J. B. (1973) *The Language of Psychoanalysis*, London: Hogarth Press.
Leclaire, S. (1964) 'The Economic Standpoint – Recent Views', *International Journal of Psychoanalysis*, 45.
Lemaire, A. (1977) *Jacques Lacan*, London: Routledge & Kegan Paul.
Levi-Strauss, C. (1961) *Structural Anthropology*, New York: Basic Books.
Levi-Strauss, C. (1969) *The Elementary Structures of Kinship*, Boston: Beacon Press.
Lingis, A. (1978) 'Savages', *Semiotext(e)*, 8.
Lingis, A. (1982) *Excesses, Eros and Culture*, New York: State University of New York.
Lingis, A. (1985) *Libido, Six Existentialist Thinkers*, New York: State University of New York.
Lorand, A. (1930) 'Fetishism in *Statu Nascendi*', *International Journal of Psychoanalysis*, 2.
Lyotard, J. F. (1978) 'One of the Things at Stake in Women's Struggles', *Sub-Stance*, 20.
Macey, D. (1978) 'Review of Jacques Lacan', *Ideology and Consciousness*, 4.
Macey, D. (1983) 'Fragments of an Analysis. Lacan in Context', *Radical Philosophy*, 35.
Malcolm, J. (1983) *In the Freud Archive*, London: Jonathan Cape.
Mannoni, M. (1970) *The Child, His Illness and The Others*, London: Tavistock.

Bibliography

Mannoni, O. (1971) *Freud, The Theory of the Unconscious*, London: New Left Books.

Marks, E. and Courtivron, J. (1980) *New French Feminisms*, Amherst: University of Massachusetts Press.

Masson, J. (1984) *The Assault on Truth. Freud's Suppression of the Seduction Theory*, New York: Farrar, Straus & Giroux.

Masson, J. (1985) *The Complete Letters of Sigmund Freud to Wilhelm Fliess*, Cambridge: Harvard University Press.

Mehlman, J. (1972) 'The Floating Signifier', *Yale French Studies*, 48.

Mehlman, J. (1974a) *A Structural Study of Autobiography*, Ithaca: Cornell University Press.

Mehlman, J. (1974b) 'How to Read Freud on Jokes: The Critic as *Schadchen*', *New Literary History*, 6(21).

Mehlman, J. (1975) 'Poe-Pourri: Lacan's Purloined Letter', *Semiotext(e)*, 1(3).

Merleau-Ponty, M. (1964) *The Primary of Perception*, Evanston: Northwestern University Press.

Merleau-Ponty, M. (1984) *The Visible and the Invisible*, Evanston: Northwestern University Press.

Mitchell, J. (1974) *Psychoanalysis and Feminism*, London: Allen Lane.

Mitchell, J. and Rose, J. (1982) *Feminine Sexuality. Jacques Lacan and the école freudienne*, London: Macmillan.

Montrelay, M. (1978) 'Inquiry into Femininity', *m/f*, 1.

Muller, J. P. and Richardson, W. J. (1982) *Lacan and Language. A Reader's Guide to Écrits*, New York: International Universities Press.

Plaza, M. (1978) ' "Phallomorphic Power" and the Psychology of "Woman" ', *Ideology and Consciousness*, 4.

Pontalis, J.-B. (1981) *Frontiers in Psychoanalysis. Between The Dream and Psychic Pain*, London: The Hogarth Press.

Ragland-Sullivan, E. (1982) 'Jacques Lacan. Feminism and the Problem of Gender Identity', *Sub-Stance*, 36.

Ragland-Sullivan, E. (1986) *Jacques Lacan and the Philosophy of Psychoanalysis*, Urbana: University of Illinois Press.

Roazen, P. (1976) *Freud and his Followers*, London: Allen Lane.

Roustang, F. (1982) *Dire Mastery. Discipleship from Freud to Lacan*, Baltimore: The Johns Hopkins University Press.

Safouan, M. (1981) 'Is the Oedipus Complex Universal?' *m/f*, 5 and 6.

Safouan, M. (1983) *Pleasure and Being, Hedonism from a Psychoanalytic Point of View*, London: Macmillan.

Sartre, J. P. (1974) *Being and Nothingness*, Harmondsworth: Penguin.

Saussure, F. de (1974) *Course in General Linguistics*, London: Fontana.

Schneiderman, S. (ed.) (1980) *Returning to Freud*, New Haven: Yale University Press.

Schneiderman, S. (1983) *Jacques Lacan. The Death of An Intellectual Hero*, Cambridge: Harvard University Press.

Schilder, P. (1978) *The Image and Appearance of the Human Body*, Oxford: Basil Blackwell.

Smith, J. H. and Kerrigan, W. (eds) (1983) *Interpreting Lacan*, New Haven: Yale University Press.

Spitz, R. A. (1965) *The First Year of Life. A Psychoanalytic Study of Normal and Deviant Development of Object Relations*, New York: International Universities Press.

Stanton, M. (1983) *Outside the Dream, Lacan and French Styles of Psychoanalysis*, London: Routledge & Kegan Paul.

Thom, M. (1976) 'The Unconscious Structured Like a Language', *Economy and Society*, 5.

Tort, M. (1974) 'The Freudian Concept of Representative', *Economy and Society*, 3.

Turkle, S. (1978) *Psychoanalytic Politics. Freud's French Revolution*, New York: Basic Books.

Turner, B. S. (1984) *The Body and Society. Explorations in Social Theory*, Oxford: Basil Blackwell.

Weber, S. (1977) 'The Divaricator: Remarks on Freud's *Witz*', *Glyph*, 1.

Weber, S. (1982) *The Legend of Freud*, Minneapolis: University of Minnesota Press.

Wilden, A. (1972) *System and Structure. Essays in Communication and Exchange*, London: Tavistock.

Wilden, A. (1981) *Speech and Language in Psychoanalysis*, Baltimore: The Johns Hopkins University Press.

Index